Andreas Könsgen

Design and Simulation of Spectrum Management Methods
for Wireless Local Area Networks

T0188843

VIEWEG+TEUBNER RESEARCH

Advanced Studies Mobile Research Center Bremen

Herausgeber | Editors:

Prof. Dr. Otthein Herzog
Prof. Dr. Carmelita Görg
Prof. Dr.-Ing. Bernd Scholz-Reiter

Das Mobile Research Center Bremen (MRC) erforscht, entwickelt und erprobt in enger Zusammenarbeit mit der Wirtschaft mobile Informatik-, Informations- und Kommunikationstechnologien. Als Forschungs- und Transferinstitut des Landes Bremen vernetzt und koordiniert das MRC hochschulübergreifend eine Vielzahl von Arbeitsgruppen, die sich mit der Entwicklung und Anwendung mobiler Lösungen beschäftigen. Die Reihe „Advanced Studies" präsentiert ausgewählte hervorragende Arbeitsergebnisse aus der Forschungstätigkeit der Mitglieder des MRC.

In close collaboration with the industry, the Mobile Research Center Bremen (MRC) investigates, develops and tests mobile computing, information and communication technologies. This research association from the state of Bremen links together and coordinates a multiplicity of research teams from different universities and institutions, which are concerned with the development and application of mobile solutions. The series "Advanced Studies" presents a selection of outstanding results of MRC's research projects.

Andreas Könsgen

Design and Simulation of Spectrum Management Methods for Wireless Local Area Networks

VIEWEG+TEUBNER RESEARCH

Bibliographic information published by the Deutsche Nationalbibliothek
The Deutsche Nationalbibliothek lists this publication in the Deutsche Nationalbibliografie;
detailed bibliographic data are available in the Internet at http://dnb.d-nb.de.

Dissertation Universität Bremen, 2009

Mobile Research Center

Gedruckt mit freundlicher Unterstützung des
MRC Mobile Research Center der Universität Bremen

Printed with friendly support of
MRC Mobile Research Center, Universität Bremen

1st Edition 2010

Editorial Office: Ute Wrasmann | Anita Wilke

Vieweg+Teubner Verlag is a brand of Springer Fachmedien.
Springer Fachmedien is part of Springer Science+Business Media.
www.viewegteubner.de

Cover design: KünkelLopka Medienentwicklung, Heidelberg
Printing company: STRAUSS GMBH, Mörlenbach
Printed on acid-free paper

ISBN 978-3-8348-1244-5

Für meine Eltern ● *For my parents*

අයිරාට ● *For Ira*

Preface

Wireless communication has become an integral part of daily life which results in an increasing number of wireless LAN devices deployed both in business, educational and residential environments and thus in increasing mutual interference between these devices. In addition, the requirements for the transmission platforms are increasing: voice-over-IP or video telephony rely on quality-of-service guarantees which have to be maintained even in case of concurrent access of multiple users.

This work discusses possible solutions for the above-mentioned problems based on research work which I did in two projects funded by the German Research Foundation (Deutsche Forschungsgemeinschaft, DFG): In CoCoNet, automated spectrum management between neighbouring networks to reduce mutual interference was investigated while in XLayer, the focus was the resource allocation of a wireless LAN base station which serves a number of mobile terminals with data flows.

I thank Prof. Carmelita Görg for giving the opportunity to perform this research work under her supervision, and to Prof. Bernhard Walke, Stefan Mangold and Guido Hiertz, Aachen University of Technology, for the cooperation in the Co-CoNet research project and for providing the WARP2 simulator which was used as a working basis in this analysis. Further thanks to Prof. Karl-Dirk Kammeyer, University of Bremen, who co-supervised the XLayer project and was also a reviewer of this work. Furthermore, I thank Ronald Böhnke and Andreas Timm-Giel for the cooperation in the XLayer project.

I also thank the development community of Linux and various software tools, in particular the TEX/LATEX typesetting system, which were used to run the simulations and edit the manuscript.

Finally, I wish to say thank you to my wife Irangani for her endless patience and mental support during the years that I worked on this research project.

Andreas Könsgen

Abstract

Wireless local area networks (WLANs) according to the IEEE 802.11 standards have rapidly emerged in recent years. Increasing demands for quality of service require an efficient usage of spectrum resources. Optimising the working principles of WLANs is possible in different ways. The interference between neighbouring networks can be reduced by methods defined in the 802.11h standard: Dynamic Frequency Selection (DFS) can change the frequency channel during an ongoing connection, whereas Transmit Power Control (TPC) reduces the transmission power to a minimum which is required to transmit with a given data rate. For the data traffic inside a network, further optimisations are possible by centralised allocation of airtime by the access point so that each user is served at an optimum time; this is defined in 802.11e. Improvements can also be achieved by enhancing the radio transmission by multiple-antenna systems (MIMO), which is considered in 802.11n.

However, the standards only describe the signalling, for example to initiate a measurement or the assignment of airtime to a certain station. The decision methods to access radio channel resources such as allocating transmit power or airtime are not treated in the standard.

These decision methods for the spectrum management are the topic of this work. The theoretical basics for the design of spectrum management methods are discussed. Based on this, different spectrum assignment methods for decentralised and centralised networks are developed. In case of centralised channel access, a cross-layer approach between the media access layer and the physical layer is introduced which allows the assignment of channel resources both considering the quality-of-service requirements of the applications and the conditions of the MIMO radio channel.

For the investigation of networks compliant to the IEEE 802.11 standard, a simulator called WARP2 is used which is extended by the spectrum management functions mentioned above.

The effects of the different spectrum management algorithms on the interference and the quality-of-service parameters of the throughput and latency are evaluated. It is shown that by spectrum management these parameters can be significantly improved; the best results are achieved if the different spectrum management methods are combined. An increase of the throughput also reduces the latency due to smaller queueing delays and less channel congestion. In case of centralised access control, it is possible to match QoS requirements of time-critical data flows according to the user requirements. Non-time-critical flows are served in a best-effort manner; the QoS for these flows is significantly enhanced by providing parallelised transmission based on OFDMA or SDMA in combination with cross-layer communication between the MAC and the PHY layer.

Contents

List of Tables

List of Figures

List of Abbreviations

ACK	Acknowledge	**DS**	Distribution System
AP	Access Point	**DSSS**	Direct Sequence Spread Spectrum
ARQ	Automatic Repeat reQuest		
BER	Bit Error Rate	**EDCA**	Enhanced Distributed Channel Access
BSS	Basic Service Set		
CCA	Clear Channel Assessment	**ESS**	Extended Service Set
CCDF	Complementary Cumulative Distribution Function	**FCS**	Frame Check Sequence
		FEC	Forward Error Correction
		FDM	Frequency Division Multiplex
CFP	Contention Free Period	**GHz**	Gigahertz
CNCL	Communication Networks Class Library	**GSM**	Global System for Mobile Communication
CPU	Central Processing Unit	**HCCA**	HCF Controlled Channel Access
CRC	Cyclic Redundancy Check		
CSMA/CA	Carrier Sense Multiple Access with Collision Avoidance	**HCF**	Hybrid Coordination Function
		HLA	High Level Architecture
CTS	Clear To Send	**IBSS**	Independent Basic Service Set
DARPA	Defense Advance Researach Project Agency	**IEEE**	Institute of Electrical and Electronics Enigneers
dB	Decibels	**IFS**	Interframe Spacing
dBm	Decibels related to 1 mW	**IP**	Internet Protocl
DBPSK	Differential Binary Phase Shift Keying	**ISO**	International Organization for Standardization
		kHz	Kilohertz
DCF	Distributed Coordination Function	**LAN**	Local Area Network
DFS	Dynamic Frequency Selection	**LLC**	Logical Link Control
DIFS	Distributed Coordination Function Interframe Spacing	**ms**	Milliseconds
		μs	Microseconds
DQPSK	Differential Quaternary Phase Shift Keying	**Mbit/s**	Megabit per Second
		MAC	Media Access Control

MHz	Megahertz	**RA**	Receiver Address
MIMO	Multiple Input Multiple Output	**RF**	Radio Frequency
MLME	MAC Layer Management Entity	**RTI**	Real Time Infrastructure
OFDM	Orthogonal Frequency Division Multiplex	**RTS**	Request To Send
		RR	Round Robin
OFDMA	Orthogonal Frequency Division Multiple Access	**RX**	Receiver
		SA	Sender Address
OSI	Open Systems Interconnection	**SAP**	Service Access Point
PCF	Point Coordination Function	**SDMA**	Space Division Multiple Access
PDF	Probability Distribution Function	**SDU**	Service Data Unit
PDU	Protocol Data Unit	**SIFS**	Short Interframe Spacing
PHY	Physical	**SME**	Station Management Entity
PIFS	Point Coordination Function Interframe Spacing	**STA**	Station
PLCP	Physical Layer Convergence Protocol	**TA**	Transmitter Address
		TCP	Transport Control Protocol
PLME	Physical Layer Management Entity	**TDMA**	Time Division Multiple Access
PMD	Physical Media Dependent	**TPC**	Transmit Power Control
PPDU	Physical layer Protocol Data Unit	**TX**	Transmitter
		WLAN	Wireless Local Area Network
QAM	Quadrature Amplitude Modulation	**WPAN**	Wireless Personal Area Network
QoS	Quality of Service	**WM**	Wireless Media

List of Symbols

Symbol	Area	See Page	Meaning
α	SpecMan	115	weighting factor for genetic algorithm
β	MAC	74	used in calculation of WLAN capacity
γ	PHY	62	attenuation factor
Δf	PHY	17	frequency spacing between OFDM sub-carriers
θ	PHY	144	waterfilling level
λ	PHY	144	eigenvalue of channel matrix
μ	SpecMan	92	mean value
ψ	PHY	147	weighting factor for OFDMA/SDMA algorithm
σ	MAC	64	length of a backoff time slot
σ	SpecMan	169	standard deviation
τ	MAC	65	probability that a station transmits within a particular time slot
ρ	SpecMan	115	vigilance for DFS algorithm
A_{recv}	PHY	62	surface of the sphere across which the power of a station is distributed
avgTxLen(i)	XLayer	141	average transmission length for flow i
$a(i)$	SpecMan	112	fuzzy AND input value
$b(i, k)$	MAC	67	stationary distribution for the backoff counter
$b(j)$	SpecMan	112	fuzzy AND input value
C	PHY	144	transmission capacity
C_i	XLayer	141	weighting factor for flow i
C/I	PHY	105	carrier to interference
$c(i, j)$	SpecMan	112	fuzzy AND output value
D	MAC	64	minimum contention window size
d	SpecMan	114	Euclidean distance
$E[D]$	MAC	71	expected value of user payload
$\mathbf{H}$	PHY	47	channel matrix

Symbol	Area	See Page	Meaning
$\mathbf{H}^{\mathrm{T}}$	PHY	47	transposed channel matrix
$\mathbf{I}$	PHY	47	identity matrix
i	MAC	65	backoff stage counter
K	PHY	147	number of users in MIMO system
k	MAC	66	backoff counter
k	SpecMan	118	Boltzmann constant
k	PHY	147	user index in MIMO system
L	PHY	147	number of OFDM subcarriers
l	PHY	144	subcarrier index in OFDM transmission
M	PHY	147	number of transmit antennas
m	PHY	147	transmit antenna index
$m(x)$	SpecMan	111	fuzzy membership function
maxDel(i)	XLayer	141	maximum delay for user i
maxDdel(i)	XLayer	141	maximum delay for user related to transmission time i
N	PHY	147	number of receive antennas
n	MAC	71	number of stations
n	MAC	64	slot number within a backoff period
n	MAC	72	number of items available for choice
PktAge	XLayer	141	packet age
P_{R}	PHY	62	received power
P_{T}	PHY	62	transmit power
p_{1256}	MAC	81	successful transmission probability in a 6-station scenario
p_{34}	MAC	82	successful transmission prob. in a 6-station scenario
$p\{i, k\vert l, m\}$	MAC	67	transition probability from backoff slot i and backoff stage k to backoff slot l and backoff stage m
p_{s}	MAC	70	conditional probability for a successful transmission
p_{c}	MAC	77	collision probability
p	SpecMan	115	probability for prototype selection
$\mathbf{Q}$	PHY	150	covariance matrix
r	PHY	61	carrier-sense range
r	PHY	62	minimum of M and N

Symbol	Area	See Page	Meaning
S	SpecMan	64	fuzzy associative memory matrix
T_B	MAC	73	average time spent in backoff
T_s	MAC	71	time which elapses for a successful 802.11 transmission
T_c	MAC	71	time which elapses for a collision
T_{early}	XLayer	141	timer for cross-layer scheduler
T_{late}	XLayer	141	timer for cross-layer scheduler
t_{ACK}	MAC	64	time to send an ACK packet
$t_{backoff}$	MAC	64	backoff time
t_{DATA}	MAC	64	time to send user data
t_{DIFS}	MAC	64	DIFS time
t_{SIFS}	MAC	64	SIFS time
W	MAC	64	contention window size
W	PHY	144	radio channel bandwidth
W_i	MAC	67	contention window size in backoff stage i
W_{min}	MAC	64	minimum contention window size

1 Introduction

Wireless communication technologies play an increasingly important role in recent years. The GSM telephone network has experienced a rapid deployment within 15 years: starting with the first GSM call in 1991, there are more than 3.5 billion subscribers as of the 4th quarter 2008 [122]. Furthermore, triggered by the rapid deployment for small portable computers like laptops and PDAs, or home applications such as video streaming between a file server and the TV, there is now also a growing demand for wireless data network access. The development of Wireless Local Area Networks (WLANs) started in the middle of the 1990s [120]. The first solutions were proprietary, such as RadioLAN WIN or Lucent WaveLAN computer plug-in cards, i. e. there was no common standard available for the radio interface which ensured that WLAN devices could communicate with devices from other manufacturers. This lack of interoperability prevented WLANs from being sold in large numbers.

Two approaches to overcome this problem by standardisation were taken: One standard called Hiperlan was published by the ETSI (European Telecommunication Standards Institute) in 1997. However, this standard never left the experimental status, there was no hardware available on the market. At about the same time, in the USA, the IEEE (Institute of Electrical and Electronics Engineers) published the standard 802.11. This approach was more successful, the first hardware appeared on the market, but still did not become very popular. This changed in 1999 when the 802.11b extension appeared which provides data rates up to 11 Mbit/s. In the following years, the data rates were further enhanced up to 54 Mbit/s in the standards 802.11a and 802.11g. WLAN hardware which is currently available in the market complies to at least one of these three standards. In parallel, the ETSI has enhanced the Hiperlan standard to Hiperlan/2; however, hardware implementations of this standard never became available on the market.

The rapidly increasing number of wireless devices results in a higher spatial density of such devices; hence it becomes more likely that devices belonging to one particular wireless network overlap with their radio coverage with the devices belonging to another neighboring network. In particular, this applies to IEEE 802.11g since there are only three non-overlapping frequency channels available. The low amount of spectral resources shared by a high number of users can result in mutual interference. Since it is likely that the total number of wireless devices will further increase in the future, it will become more likely that this kind of interfer-

ence will occur. Besides that, the frequency bands which are used by 802.11b or
802.11a have to be shared with other wireless communication platforms: On the
2.4 GHz band, there are for example Bluetooth and HomeRF devices. In addition,
the 2.4 GHz band is a so-called ISM band (Industrial, Scientific and Medical), so
that there are various sources of interference by devices whose aim is not communication, such as microwave ovens or medical therapy devices. On the 5 GHz
band, the spectrum has to be shared with radar systems and other applications. A
part of the band at 5.8 GHz is also used for ISM applications.

The problem of interfering wireless networks results in demands for automatic
methods (i. e. without user intervention) to reduce the mutual interference, also
called spectrum management methods. The Defense Advanced Research Project
Agency (DARPA) in the USA launched a project concerning this topic with the
name DARPA XG [22]. The approach of this project is general: a device shall be
able to modify any parameter concerning its transmission characteristics, such as
the transmission frequency and power, RF bandwidth, modulation schemes, airtime utilisation etc.

In the initial IEEE 802.11 standard, spectrum management is not considered.
Hence the IEEE has introduced another extension to the WLAN standards called
802.11h. In this extension, spectrum management is provided in two ways:

- A network experiencing an interfered frequency channel should automatically attempt to find a less interfered channel (Dynamic Frequency Selection, DFS).

- The power which a sending station uses to transmit the data should not be
  higher than required to transfer the data with a sufficiently low error rate to
  the receiver (Transmit Power Control, TPC).

The 802.11h extension introduces DFS and TPC into the wireless LAN and
describes the additional signalling which is required to control the spectrum management. However, the standard only describes the signalling; it does not consider
the algorithms which are needed to decide which frequency channel or transmit
power should be used at a given time.

A main goal of this work is the investigation of such spectrum management algorithms. Besides the development of these algorithms this also requires a quantitative analysis by simulation, i. e. running the algorithms in representative scenarios under predefined conditions, evaluating the performance and identifying the
most suitable algorithms.

The DFS and TPC algorithms are useful in case of spectrum sharing between
a number of wireless networks in order to support fairness between each other by

minimising the individual spectrum usage. Due to the reduced interference, there is less channel occupation from neighbouring networks, so more frequent transmissions are possible which enhance the quality-of-service parameters throughput as well as the delay. The optimum allocation of the radio channel is, however, also possible inside a single network. The idea in this case is to allocate resources in order to provide quality-of-service (QoS) to the data flows from the access point to the stations. This policy is implemented by a two-stage cross-layer scheduler in the access point located in the media access (MAC) and the physical (PHY) layer. The MAC layer stage of the scheduler has knowledge about the application requirements and about the states of the queues which keep the packets for each data flow. In each turn of the scheduling process, the MAC stage selects packets from these queues for transmission. An importance metric for each data flow is assigned which is then handed over to the PHY stage. The latter is based on a multi-user MIMO transmission; it dynamically allocates channel resources to the packets according to the determined importance metrics by means of OFDMA or SDMA algorithms. Due to the channel conditions, it might happen that not all data flows which were selected by the MAC scheduler can be transmitted by the PHY scheduler. In the cross-layer approach, the MAC layer is notified which packets actually can be transmitted so that it can take the packets from their respective queues and send them to the transmission.

In this work, a discrete-event simulator called WARP2 (Wireless Access Radio Protocol 2) is used for the simulation of wireless networks which implements the 802.11 protocol stack. For the investigations about spectrum management and cross-layer scheduling, the simulator is extended so that the WLAN enhancement methods which are proposed in this work can be evaluated by numerical results.

This document is structured in the following way: Chapter 2 gives an overview of the IEEE 802.11 standard and its most relevant extensions. An overview on related work on the topic of spectrum management is given in chapter 3. This chapter also discusses theoretical aspects about the effect of spectrum management on the behaviour of wireless LANs. In chapter 4, spectrum management algorithms are discussed: Dynamic Frequency Selection changes the frequency during an ongoing communication to avoid congested channels; Transmit Power Control adapts the transmission power of the stations to reduce interference, and Link Adaptation changes the physical bit rate of the transmissions according to the channel conditions. In chapter 5 another approach for controlling wireless stations is presented, which in contrast to the approaches given in chapter 4 does not aim to coordinate the channel access of neighbouring networks, but optimises the assignment of channel resources to the stations inside a network which is centrally controlled by an access point. The structure of the WARP2 simulator which was used for the investigations in this work is described in chapter 6; details are given how the HLA communication and the spectrum management extensions are integrated into the simulator. Chapter 7 presents the results for the different methods which are elaborated in this work. The performance of spectrum management based on changing the frequency, transmit power and physical rate adaptation is investigated, also in comparison with analytical results. Finally, the efficiency of the cross-layer based centralised access is analysed. Conclusions are drawn in chapter 8 where also an outlook for future work is given.

2 The IEEE 802.11 Standard Series

In communication systems, it is crucial that the interface which controls the information exchange between networked nodes is standardised between different manufacturers. The most important institutions for standardisation in this area are the European Telecommunication Standardisation Institute (ETSI), the IEEE (Institute of Electrical and Electronics Engineers) and the ITU (International Telecommunications Union) with the subdivision ITU-T focused on wired communication systems and ITU-R for radio communication systems. The ETSI introduced, for example, the GSM standard for wireless telephones (Global System for Mobile Communication) and initiated the mobile broadband communication standard UMTS (Universal Mobile Telecommunication System). In the field of local area networks, the ETSI specified Hiperlan (High Performance LAN) providing data rates up to 2 Mbit/s and Hiperlan/2 (an enhanced version with data rates up to 54 Mbit/s). The IEEE introduced the 802 series of standards which define various kinds of communication networks. This standardisation series is maintained by a number of working groups which deal with different types of communication networks. Some examples are:

- 802.3: LAN/MAN CSMA/CD Access Method and Physical Layer Specifications [54]. This standard resulted out of the introduction of Ethernet which was a proprietary product in the beginning and has become one of the most widely deployed architectures for wired networks.

- 802.11: LAN/MAN Wireless LANs [50]. This working group is discussed in more detail below.

- 802.15: Wireless Personal Area Networks. This standard specifies low-range networks which focus on a low power consumption and a low complexity, allowing it to be implemented in small-volume, low-cost hardware. There is a sub-standard 802.15.1 which specifies the PHY and the MAC layer for personal devices such as the connection between a mobile phone and a wireless headset [52]. This platform is marketed since some years under the name *Bluetooth* [9]. On the the other hand, the sub-standard 802.15.4 [53] covers the PHY and MAC layer for measuring and control functions like wireless medical sensor equipment and remote control for home devices (TV, lights, heating, etc.) which was introduced under the name *Zigbee* [133].

- 802.16 Broadband Wireless Access. This standard is known as WiMAX (Wireless Microwave Access). This group develops Wireless Metropolitan Area Networks (WMANs) which were in the beginning designed for the wireless interconnection of buildings and stationary wireless access, for example as a replacement for DSL Internet connections. Features of these networks are high data rates and Quality-of-Service support. Two sets of transmission frequency bands are defined between 2 and 11 GHz and between 10 and 66 GHz [97]. In further development steps, the standard was extended for mobility support and handover between radio cells.

- 802.20 Mobile Broadband Wireless Access [55]. In this group, a protocol architecture is developed which is optimised for mobile wireless access. Frequency bands below 3.5 GHz will be used, the peak data rate is above 1 Mbit/s. The mobility support works up to speeds of 250 km/h and thus is also suitable for vehicular wireless access. It competes with the 802.16d standard which is designed for broadband mobility access as well.

- 802.21 Media Independent Handoff [56]. This group deals with the wireless roaming of mobile devices which support a number of 802 and non-802 wireless interfaces. Due to the mobility, the coverage of different wireless networks in the environment changes so that a handoff between these networks must be supported.

The problem of interoperability between devices from different manufacturers also applies for wireless local area networks: When the first devices appeared on the market, only proprietary solutions were available so that a wireless node could only be connected to another node of the same manufacturer. For this reason, the IEEE introduced the 802.11 standard in 1999 which specifies the architecture of a wireless local area network. Basically, the physical and the logical link control layer are defined. In later years, the 802.11 standard was extended by several task groups, for example to increase the physical bit rate or to improve authentication and encryption between nodes. Table 2.1 gives an overview on the enhancements of the 802.11 standard.

Some of these working groups have finalised their standard extension, others are in the development phase. At the time this work is published, the extensions which are finalised are a to j; they meanwhile have been merged into the standard IEEE 802.11-2007 [51] and are no longer listed as separate extensions. The remaining extensions are drafts and still under development.

The titles of the standard extensions a, b and g can be misleading regarding the available transmission rates which are provided in each of the extensions. In

Task Group	Topic
a	High Speed Physical Layer in the 5 GHz Band
b	High Speed Physical Layer Extension in the 2.4 GHz Band
d	Specification for operation in additional regulatory domains
e	MAC Enhancements for QoS
F	IEEE Trial-Use Recommended Practice for Multi-Vendor Access Point Interoperability via an Inter-Access Point Protocol Across Distribution Systems Supporting IEEE 802.11 Operation
g	Further Higher Data Rate Extension in the 2.4 GHz
h	Spectrum and Transmit Power Management Extensions in the 5 GHz band in Europe
i	Medium Access Control (MAC) Security Enhancements
j	4.9 – 5 GHz operation in Japan
k	Radio Resource Measurements
m	Standard Maintenance
n	High Throughput (among other things, by MIMO transmission)
p	Wireless Access in Vehicular Environments
r	Fast Roaming
s	ESS (Extended Service Set, see sec. 2.2) Mesh Networking
T	Wireless Performance
u	Interworking with External Networks
v	Wireless Network Management of Wireless LANs
w	Protected Management Frames
y	3650-3700 MHz operation in the USA
z	Extensions to Direct Link Setup
aa	Video Transport Streams

Table 2.1: IEEE 802.11 task groups

802.11b, up to 11 Mbit/s are available, whereas in 802.11a and g, up to 54 Mbit/s are provided. Details on the extensions a, b and g are discussed in section 2.3.1. The h, e and n extensions are the basis for the research work presented in this work; they are presented in detail in later sections.

2.1 The ISO/OSI Reference Model

When discussing networks, it is important to define a model which describes the different functions of the network in an abstract way which is independent of a particular standard or implementation, such as the physical transmission, error recovery, routing, flow control and so on. Such a model has been specified by the ISO (International Standardisation Organisation) and it is called the ISO/OSI Reference Model (OSI: Open Systems Interconnection) [125, 91]. This model is illustrated in figure 2.1.

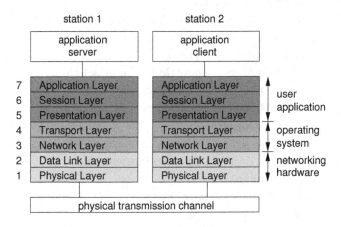

Figure 2.1: OSI reference model

The figure shows two stations which transmit data over the physical channel. The data to be transmitted is generated by some user application. A generated data packet, for example a frame of a video transmission captured by a camera, is passed to the protocol stack whose upper three layers – application, presentation, session – are usually located inside the application software itself. The network-oriented transport and network layers are implemented by the operating system, whereas the data link and physical layer are maintained by the networking hardware.

While the packet travels down the protocol stack, each layer *encapsulates* the packet which it received from the upper layer by adding a header or trailer with control information which is needed by the particular protocol, as shown in fig. 2.1. For example, the presentation layer might add information about the format of a video stream; the network layer includes information about the destination address

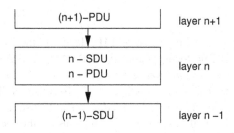

Figure 2.2: Interface between the protocol layers

of the packet. After the encapsulation process, the packet is handed over to the lower layer. At the lowest layer, which is the PHY layer, the packet is transmitted over the channel. In this state of the packet, where it is encapsulated by all protocol headers, the header of the lowest layer is at the beginning of the packet. At the receiver side, in each layer, the packet is decapsulated which means the header corresponding to this layer is removed from the packet and the control information contained in the respective header is evaluated. After the application layer has processed the packet, the data is submitted to the part of the application which interprets the data, for example showing an image on the screen.

Figure 2.3: Encapsulation of a packet by protocol layers

In a formal description, each layer provides services (the so-called primitives) to the upper layer and uses services from the lower layer which is illustrated in figure 2.2. The data which layer n submits to layer $n - 1$ is called a *Service Data Unit* (SDU). After the layer n has processed the data and added its header, the resulting packet is called a *Protocol Data Unit* (PDU). This PDU is submitted to the layer $n - 1$, which again considers the packet as an SDU an so forth. The lower layer provides services to the upper layer through a *Service Access Point* (SAP).

In the following paragraphs, details about the functions of the different layers in the OSI model are given in a formal description, each layer provides services (the so-called primitives) to the upper layer and uses services from the lower layer.

Physical Layer

The physical layer (often abbreviated as PHY layer) is the lowest layer in the model. In the IEEE 802 protocol specifications, the layer is divided into two sublayers: the *Physical Layer Convergence Protocol* includes the functions which are independent of the particular transmission media, for example the formatting of the PHY protocol header. The *Physical Media Dependent* sublayer (PMD) specifies the the physical signals which are used to transmit the individual data bits from the sender to the receiver. The PMD is dependent on the type of transmission media, i.e. coaxial cable, twisted-pair cable, terrestrial radio, satellite radio, laser links and so on. The PMD layer specifies the modulation schemes, spectrum spreading schemes and the type of forward error correction.

Data Link Layer

The data link layer (often termed as DLL layer) realizes the transmission of packets between two or more stations which are directly physically linked. The layer has two major functions, the channel access and the recovery of lost packets. Because of this fact, in the IEEE 802 protocol stack, it is grouped into two sublayers called Medium Access Control (MAC) and Logical Link Control (LLC). The MAC layer controls the channel access, i.e. at what time a station is allowed to send and how collisions should be treated. The term collision means that two or more stations sharing the same physical media and being inside each other's range transmit signals simultaneously. In this case, none of the signals can be correctly received and thus the sent data is lost. The LLC layer provides error detection and recovery, i.e. identifying lost packets and resending them.

Network Layer

Inside a communication network, the peer stations which run a communication are in most cases not physically connected. In this case, the support of additional stations is required which forward packets between the communication peers. These forwarding stations are called routers. The sending peer station transmits the packet to the router which is physically connected to it. The router forwards the packet to a neighbouring router to which a physical connection is available. This process is continued until the packet has reached the receiving peer station. The routing path, which means the sequence of routers along which a packet travels is determined by a routing algorithm which relies on the information provided by the network layer protocol. The most well known example for a network layer protocol is the Internet Protocol (IP) [42].

Transport Layer

The task of the transport layer is providing a reliable connection which guarantees that all packets that were sent by a station arrive correctly at the receiver. When a data flow is routed between sender and receiver, it is likely to be affected by errors: packets can be lost due to broken links between neighboring hops or due to overload of a link (the so-called congestion); they can be duplicated due to malfunctioning routers. Finally, the order of the packets at the receiver can be changed due to the fact that each single packet can take another route. Hence, if at the sender packet A is sent before packet B, it can happen that packet B travels along a faster route than packet A and thus will arrive at the receiver before A. The receiver then has to put the packets into the correct order again. These functions of recovering lost packets, removing duplicates and reordering packets are performed on the transport layer. Another function of the transport layer is flow control: The throughput capacity of the communication link is limited; if the load is too high, congestion and thus data loss will result. On the other hand, due to performance reasons, the flow control should not underutilise the available link capacity. In the IP based protocol stack, there are two major transport protocols: the Transfer Control Protocol (TCP) [42] provides error correction and flow control as described above, whereas the User Datagram Protocol (UDP) is an unreliable protocol without flow control. It is considered as a transport layer protocol, however it does not provide the features given above.

Session Layer

The protocol layers discussed up to now were related to the network itself. The remaining three layers are related to the application. The lowest of these layers is the Session Layer which is responsible for basic functions which are needed in all applications, such as opening or closing a connection (on the application level) or resuming a connection which has been interrupted. An example for a session layer protocol is the Session Initiation Protocol (SIP) which can for example be used to set up an IP based telephone call (Voice over IP, VoIP).

Presentation Layer

When exchanging data, it must be made sure that the sender and the receiver interpret the data in the same way. For example, some CPUs store integer numbers with the least significant byte fist, others do it with the most significant byte first. Another example is the format of text files, where end-of-line is encoded differently dependent on different operating systems. For the transmission in the network inside the network, there are three options in which format the data can be transmitted.

- The receiver knows the data format used by the sender and converts arriving packets into its own format.

- The sender knows the data format of the receiver and converts the data into the receiver format before transmitting.

- The sender and the receiver use a special format dedicated for the network transmission which differs from the sender's and receiver's internal format. A conversion takes place both in the sender and the receiver.

Application Layer

The application layer provides the functions which are specific for the particular application whose data is transferred. Examples are:

- user authentication,

- e-mails: specifying sender and receiver address, deleting mails stored on the server,

- file transfers: request for up- or download, specification of the file name to be transferred,

- name service: specifying the name of a station for which the IP number should be determined.

2.2 IEEE 802.11 Architecture

In the 802.11 standard, a node which is equipped with a wireless LAN interface is called a *station* (STA). A number of stations which join the same radio cell and exchange information are called *Basic Service Set* (BSS). The stations inside the BSS can operate in one of two modes: In the *infrastructure mode*, there is exactly one special station inside each BSS which is called *Access Point* (AP). The AP connects the STAs inside its radio coverage to the *Distribution System* (DS). The DS is a backbone network which connects a number of APs and which can provide access to external networks such as the Internet through a router. In practice, access points usually only provide a wired link for the backbone connection. The standard, however, does not specify the physical properties of the backbone link, so the wireless medium can be used as well.

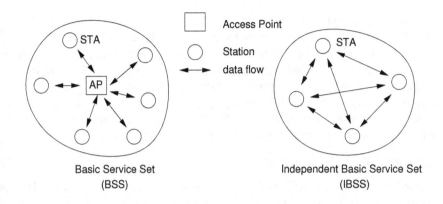

Figure 2.4: Infrastructure (BSS) and ad-hoc network (IBSS)

All BSSes which are connected to the same DS are called *Extended Service Set* (ESS), cf. fig. 2.5. The 802.11 protocol allows for STAs to move between APs of the same ESS without interrupting ongoing connections; this feature is called *roaming*.

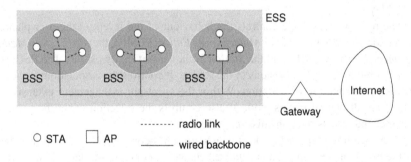

Figure 2.5: Infrastructure networks forming an ESS

The different modes of operation are depicted in fig. 2.4. In the infrastructure mode, there is no direct communication between the stations; data is only sent between a STA and the AP and vice versa. If a STA wants to send data to another STA inside the same BSS, this data is sent via the AP.

Once a station wishes to use a particular AP for communication, it has to register with this AP which is called *association*. After this step has been successfully executed, in the next step termed *authentication* the STA has to identify itself at the AP. When both steps are complete the data transmission can be started.

Besides the infrastructure mode which requires fixed installations like the APs and the DS, the 802.11 standard defines the *ad-hoc mode* where the STAs inside a radio cell which is in this case termed Independent BSS (IBSS) can exchange data directly between each other without any additional facilities. The ad-hoc mode is for example useful in case that no WLAN infrastructure is available, e.g. for meetings between a number of users or in emergency scenarios.

2.3 IEEE 802.11 Protocol Stack

The overall structure of the IEEE 802.11a protocol stack is shown in figure 2.6. The protocol stack is divided into a user plane and a management plane. The task of the user plane is the processing of the user data. It includes the PHY layer and the MAC layer; the specification of the higher protocol layers is outside the scope of the 802.11 standard series. The PHY layer is divided into two sublayers which are not specified in the OSI reference model: the Physical Layer Convergence Protocol (PLCP) is an abstraction layer between the MAC layer and the Physical Media Dependent Layer (PMD) which is specific for the particular transmission method being used. An important task of the PLCP is the Clear Channel Assessment which informs higher layers if the channel is busy while hiding details specific to the PMD layer.

The management plane controls the behaviour of the layers in the user plane. It includes the *Physical Layer Management Entity* (PLME), the *MAC Layer Management Entity* (MLME) and the *Station Management Entity* (SME). The SME is responsible for general decisions of the station. It controls the association, authentication and roaming of a station. Within the spectrum management extensions which are discussed in this work, it also controls the selection of the frequency channel and selects the transmission power.

There are three types of packets which are sent between STAs. The user plane of the protocol stack maintains data packets which contain user data; they are received from the higher protocol layers of the STA by the MAC layer of the WLAN interface. Management packets are generated inside the WLAN protocol stack inside the management plane, in particular by the MLME. They are then sent for transmission to the MAC layer inside the user plane like user data packets. A third type of packets, the control packets, are provided by the user plane to control the transmission of both data and management packets. These three different packet types are discussed in detail later. The PLME does not generate management packets; it exchanges control information with other stations through the PHY headers of the exchanged packets.

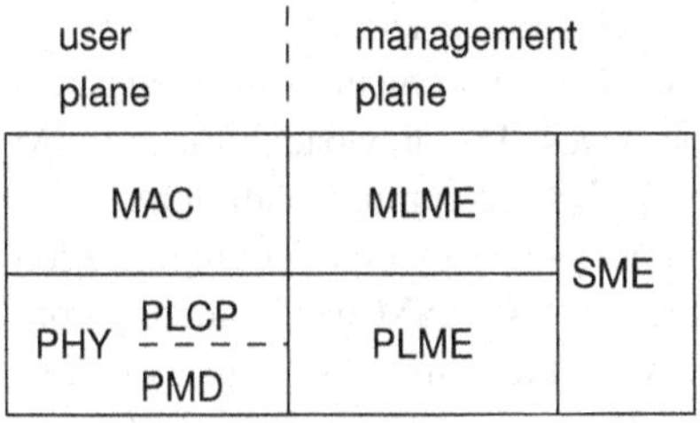

user plane	management plane	
MAC	MLME	SME
PHY PLCP – – – PMD	PLME	

MAC: media access control
PHY: physical layer
MLME: MAC layer management entity
PLME: PHY layer management entity
SME: station management entity
PLCP: PHY layer convergence protocol
PMD: physical media dependent layer

Figure 2.6: IEEE 802.11 protocol stack

The MLME resp. PLME provide means to control the behaviour of the MAC resp. PHY layer. This change of the behaviour can be an internal action where no signalling over the radio channel with the corresponding station is required. An example for this would be changing the bit rate at which transmitted packets are sent. In this case, the SME would decide to switch the bit rate and send a request to the PLME which then would execute all required steps to perform the desired action. On the other hand, a management action can require signalling over the radio channel, for example when the STA wants to associate with an AP. In this case, the MLME gets a request from the SME to initiate the association. The MLME then generates a management packet called Association Request which is sent to the MAC layer. From there, it is forwarded across the PHY layer and the radio channel to the Access Point's MLME. The AP's MLME identifies the packet as an Association Request and forwards this request to the SME. If the AP's SME decides to accept the Association Request, it sends a message to the MLME that the request to associate is accepted. The AP's MLME generates the corresponding Association Response management packet and sends it back to the STA.

2.3.1 IEEE 802.11 PHY Layer

The physical layer of IEEE 802.11 has been extended several times during the on-going development of the standard. The original 802.11 standard was introduced in 1999. The basic idea of the standard is to use unlicensed frequency bands for the transmission. This allows manufacturers to sell WLAN devices without the requirement of obtaining licenses and paying fees for the frequency usage. These so-called ISM bands which are distributed over the whole radio frequency spectrum allow devices whose application is in the industrial, scientific or medical field to radiate RF within prescribed limits which would be a problem in reserved bands such as those used for TV or cellular phone services. The drawback of using ISM bands for communication purposes is, however, that the communication might be affected by interference of neighbouring ISM devices or by other communication systems using the ISM band. For 802.11, the 2.4 GHz ISM band ranging from 2.400 to 2.4825 GHz is used. In order to increase the resilience against interference, the radio signal is spread with the FHSS (Frequency Hopping Spread Spectrum) or the Direct Sequence Spread Spectrum (DSSS) as the spreading scheme. The FHSS scheme was, however, only used in early 802.11 hardware. Based on frequency channels with an RF bandwidth of 22 MHz, two PHY modes with 1 and 2 Mbit/s are defined both for the FHSS and DSSS transmission. In case of DSSS, the signal is modulated by BPSK (Binary Phase Shift Keying) for 1 Mbit/s and QPSK (Quaternary Phase Shift Keying) for 2 Mbit/s.

The transmit power is limited to 100 mW, which is important to reduce interference to neighbouring networks or non-802.11 applications. In addition, the standard also specifies the transmission of signals by infrared light, which was, however, never implemented in practice.

In the same year when the 802.11 standard was published, the extension 802.11b [46] was finalised which enhances the transmission scheme so that with the same RF bandwidth of the frequency channels as in 802.11, now in addition the faster bit rates 5.5 and 11 Mbit/s can be transported based on DSSS. For modulation, QPSK (Quaternary Phase Shift Keying) is used as in legacy 802.11. The higher user data rates are achieved by reducing the spreading factor, which means the ratio between the bit rate of the spread signal which is transmitted and the unspread user data signal. In addition, 802.11a was proposed which utilises the 5.2 GHz frequency band. Instead of spreading, the transmission scheme used here is OFDM (Orthogonal Frequency Division Multiplex) which is explained in detail in the next section. The channel bandwidth is the same as in 802.11 and 802.11b, however now data rates up to 54 Mbit/s can be transmitted which is achieved by higher-order modulation schemes. Besides BPSK and QPSK which are used for lower bit rates, 16QAM (Quadrature Amplitude Modulation with 16 states) and 64QAM are provided as well.

In the 802.11g standard published in 2003 [47], OFDM was also introduced into the 2.4 GHz, again keeping the same RF channel bandwidth as it is used in the other 802.11 standards.

The following paragraphs specify the details of the 802.11a PHY layer. First the OFDM transmission and the different modulations schemes for the OFDM subcarriers are described; after that, the structure of the 802.11a PHY header is explained. Most of the details also apply for 802.11g which basically differs from 802.11a by the frequency bands which are used for transmission.

2.3.1.1 OFDM Transmission

The principle of OFDM is the transmission of a data signal over a number of orthogonal narrow-band subcarriers instead of one single wide-band carrier. The frequencies of two consecutive subcarriers have a constant frequency spacing Δf. In the time domain, an OFDM transmission can be described mathematically as

$$s(t) = \sum_{l=0}^{L-1} x_l e^{j2\pi lt/T} \tag{2.1}$$

where x_l is the data symbol to be transmitted on subcarrier l, L is the number of subcarriers and T is the reciprocal of the subcarrier spacing: $T = 1/\Delta f$. Two subcarriers l_1, l_2 are orthogonal inside the time interval T because of

$$\frac{1}{T} \int_0^T \left(e^{j2\pi l_1 t/T} \right)^* \left(e^{j2\pi l_2 t/T} \right) \mathrm{d}t = \frac{1}{T} \int_0^T \left(e^{j2\pi (l_1 - l_2)t/T} \right)$$
$$= 1 \text{ for } l_1 = l_2, \text{ 0 else,} \tag{2.2}$$

where $(\cdot)^*$ means the conjugate complex of the expression and T is one symbol duration. The result of the equation is a constant value which means there is no interference between the subcarriers.

Figure 2.7 shows the frequency spectrum $S(f)$ of an OFDM signal with 5 subcarriers which are located with a spacing of Δf. The signal components overlap in the way that at the maximum of one carrier, the others have their zero crossing. Due to this property, the first Nyquist criterion is fulfilled which is a prerequisite for orthogonality.

The partitioning of a data signal into subcarriers allows the parallel transmission of a high number of data bits with a low symbol rate, whereas a single-carrier transmission would require a serial transmission with a high symbol rate. The low symbol rate results in a high symbol duration so that guard intervals between consecutive symbols can be included without significantly reducing the available user bit rate. Guard intervals are important to avoid inter-symbol interference (ISI): Because of multipath propagation, the signal arrives at the receiver split into several components which propagate along paths of different lengths and thus experience different delays. This effect increases the duration of the symbol and therefore results in an overlapping of the symbols so that a received symbol occupies a longer

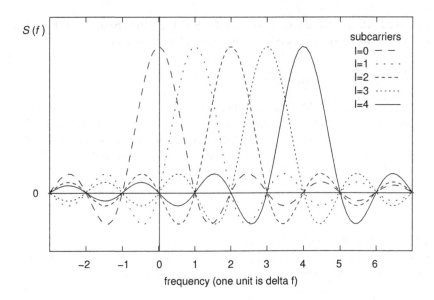

Figure 2.7: Frequency spectrum $S(f)$ of an OFDM signal with 5 subcarriers numbered from $l = 0$ to 4. Δf is the frequency spacing between two consecutive subcarriers.

time interval than the corresponding transmitted symbol. The guard intervals prevent overlapping as long as the delay difference between the received signal components with the shortest resp. longest path is not higher than the length of the guard interval.

Furthermore, the usage of narrow-band subcarriers simplifies the process of the channel equalisation. The channel has a time-variant transfer function $G(t, f)$ and the corresponding impulse response $g(t, \tau)$ in the time domain which has to be estimated by the transmission system. Equalisers in the sender or the receiver have to provide a compensation to the channel transfer function. The received signal $r(t)$ is a result of the transmission of a signal $s(t)$ over a channel with the impulse response $g(t)$ and the noise $n(t)$, described as

$$r(t) = \int_{-\infty}^{\infty} g(t, \tau) s(t - \tau) \, d\tau + n(\tau) . \tag{2.3}$$

The effect described by eqn. 2.3 is a convolution between $g(t)$ and $s(t)$. If $c(t)$ is frequency-selective, complex equalisers may be required to recover the original signal $s(t)$ at the receiver [23]. In case of OFDM, the subcarrier bandwidth is sufficiently low so that the subcarriers can be assumed as not frequency-selective and thus can be described by a single complex coefficient. However, the bandwidth of a subcarrier should not be selected too low, otherwise the symbols get too long so that the channel characteristics can no longer be considered time-invariant during one symbol duration.

The partitioning of the channel bandwidth into subcarriers provides resilience against frequency-selective channels: If the channel transfer function has a minimum at a particular frequency, only a few subcarriers are affected while the transmission on the other subcarriers can be continued.

OFDM can be easily implemented: at the transmitter, an Inverse Fast Fourier Transform (IFFT) is used to generate the time-domain signal out of the data bit sequence to be transmitted illustrated in eqn. 2.1; at the receiver, the reverse operation Fast Fourier Transform (FFT) is performed.

As previously mentioned, in IEEE 802.11a, each of the OFDM subcarriers is modulated with one of the modulation schemes: BPSK, QPSK, 16QAM or 64QAM. This means that in a single step, one subcarrier can transport a certain number of bits which is dependent on the number of possible symbols of the particular modulation scheme. Since the transport of c bits inside one modulation symbol of a subcarrier requires 2^c states, each of the modulation schemes can transmit the following number of bits per symbol and subcarrier:

modulation scheme	number of symbols per OFDM subcarrier	number of bits per OFDM symbol
BPSK	2	1
QPSK	4	2
16QAM	16	4
64QAM	64	6

Table 2.2: Modulation schemes used for the OFDM subcarriers

In the 802.11a standard, the duration of each modulation symbol is independent of the selected modulation scheme. All subcarriers are modulated with the same scheme, which means that a change of the modulation scheme is always applied in the same way for all subcarriers. All individual symbols of each subcarrier at a particular point of time together form an OFDM symbol.

Given the fact that the same modulation is used for all subcarriers in 802.11a, within one OFDM symbol duration $c \cdot L$ bits can be transmitted when L subcarriers are used.

In an 802.11a transmission, 52 subcarriers are used with a frequency spacing of 312.5 kHz (20 MHz divided by 64). 48 subcarriers transport data, the 4 remaining ones are so-called *pilots* which are used to synchronise the receiver to the OFDM symbol clock.

For the transmission of a PHY PDU, the data is first scrambled to provide an equal distribution of 0- and 1-bits. After the scrambling step, a forward error correction (FEC) is introduced to provide resilience against bit errors. This FEC is based on convolutional coding. The quotient of the number of data bits d and the resulting number of code bits c is called *coding rate*. In the 802.11a standard, the coding rates $\frac{1}{2}$, $\frac{2}{3}$ and $\frac{3}{4}$ are used. The different PHY modes which are available in the 802.11a standard result from combinations between different combinations of modulation schemes for the subcarriers and coding rates. Table 2.3 gives an overview of the PHY modes available in the 802.11a standard.

PHY mode Mbit/s	subcarrier modulation	coding rate	code bits per subcarrier symbol	code bits per OFDM symbol	data bits per OFDM symbol
6	BPSK	1/2	1	48	24
9	BPSK	3/4	1	48	36
12	QPSK	1/2	2	96	48
18	QPSK	3/4	2	96	72
24	16QAM	1/2	4	192	96
36	16QAM	3/4	4	192	144
48	64QAM	2/3	6	288	192
54	64QAM	3/4	6	288	216

Table 2.3: PHY modes used for IEEE 802.11a/g

Due to the transmission using OFDM symbols, the number of bits which are transmitted in a packet are always an integer multiple of the OFDM symbol size (specified as bits per OFDM symbol in the table above). If the number of bits which have to be transmitted is not an integer multiple of the symbol size, the remaining bits have to be filled with so-called tail bits.

2.3.1.2 Structure of the 802.11a PHY PDU

The PLCP adds data to the PHY SDU which is delivered from the MAC layer. The resulting PHY PDU (PPDU) is then sent to the scrambler and the convolutional encoder as described above. The PLCP data provides the signalling which is required to control the functions of the PHY layer.

The meanings of the fields are:

- PLCP preamble – supports the receiver to synchronise to the OFDM symbol clock and to the beginning of a received frame. The preamble is always transmitted using the slowest available PHY mode, i. e. 6 Mbit/s.

- SIGNAL – contains the control information required by the PHY layer. This field is, in the same way as the preamble, always transmitted using the slowest PHY mode. The SIGNAL field represents most parts of the PLCP header, except for a subfield called SERVICE which is included into the DATA field.

- DATA – contains the SERVICE subfield of the header, the user data (PHY SDU) as well as tail and pad bits. This field is transmitted in one of the available PHY modes listed in table 2.3. The SERVICE subfield of the header is included into the DATA field because in this way it can be transmitted at a higher PHY mode than the rest of the header to achieve a speedup.

The SIGNAL field contains the following subfields:

- RATE – specifies the data rate used in the PSDU field,

- Reserved – unused,

- LENGTH – number of bytes in the PSDU to be transmitted,

- Parity – even parity over the RATE, Reserved and LENGTH field.

- Tail – the SIGNAL field is transmitted as one OFDM symbol at the lowest PHY mode with an OFDM symbol size of 24 bits. The fields RATE, Reserved, LENGTH and Parity require 18 bits, so the remaining 6 bits are filled in with tail bits.

The DATA field includes the following subfields:

- SERVICE – The first 6 bits of this field are needed to synchronise the descrambler in the receiver. The remaining bits are reserved.

- PSDU – this field contains the data supplied by the MAC layer.

- Tail Bits – needed due to the convolutional encoding by which the data is processed before transmitting it.

- Pad bits – needed to fill up the bits up to an integer multiple of the OFDM symbol size.

2.3.1.3 Clear Channel Assessment

Besides the formatting of the data to be transmitted over the radio channel, another task of the PHY layer is to indicate to the MAC layer if the wireless media (WM) is busy or free. This mechanism is termed as *Clear Channel Assessment* (CCA). Any change of the medium state is reported to the MAC layer by the service primitive PHY_CCA.indicate. The CCA reports the WM as busy if one of the two following conditions is fulfilled:

- The signal on the WM has been identified as a valid OFDM signal by detecting the preamble. In this case, the WM is considered as busy if the signal level is at least the minimum sensitivity for the slowest PHY mode (6 Mbit/s), which is $-82\,\mathrm{dBm}$ according to the standard. The threshold is the same regardless of the actual PHY mode of the received signal.

- The signal on the WM is not an OFDM signal, i.e. no preamble has been detected. In this case, the WM is considered as busy if the signal level is at least 20 dB above the minimum sensitivity mentioned above, which yields $-62\,\mathrm{dBm}$.

2.3.2 IEEE 802.11 MAC Layer

The task of the MAC layer is the control of the access to the radio channel. The MAC layer makes sure that a station only transmits if the channel is free. In addition, a station does not immediately start the transmission once it gets data from the higher protocol layers; instead it delays the transmission for a certain amount of time in order to give other stations a chance to transmit as well. If two or more stations share the same channel, a basic problem is the resolution or avoidance of collisions. A collision occurs if two or more stations send data at the same time. This can happen due to two reasons:

- Limited range. Figure 2.8 shows three stations, where the receiving station B is inside the coverage of both the transmitting stations A and C; however, the stations A and C are not inside mutual coverage. This means that stations A and C cannot hear if the respective other station is transmitting. It considers the channel as free and hence starts a transmission. If transmissions of A and C overlap in time, then from the view of station B there is a collision. This phenomenon is also referred to as the *hidden station problem.*

- Finite channel busy detection time. A collision can also occur if two transmitting stations are inside mutual coverage. The time for the radio signal to propagate from one station to the other is determined by the light speed $c \approx 3 \cdot 10^8$ m/s and the receiving station's hardware needs some amount of time to detect that the channel has become busy. This means that a station inside the coverage of the transmitting station still considers the channel as free until the above-mentioned time interval has elapsed, it can decide to start a transmission during this time interval which then results in a collision. Fig. 2.9 shows two stations A and B which are located in the distance d. A radio signal sent by station A propagates to station B within the time $t = d/c$. Some further time t_{det} is needed to detect the signal by the hardware of station B. Hence the total time which is critical for a collision is

$$t_{\text{crit}} = d/c + t_{\text{det}}. \tag{2.4}$$

A collision can occur if station B decides to transmit during t_{crit}.

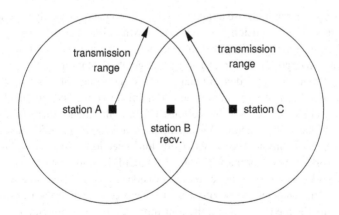

Figure 2.8: Hidden station problem

To handle the problem of properly assigning the channel and reducing or avoiding collisions, there are several possible approaches:

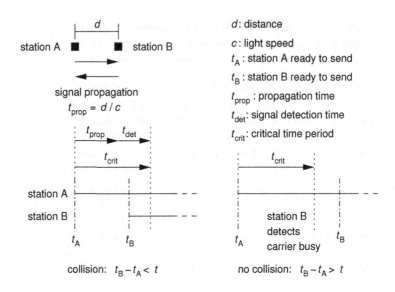

Figure 2.9: Illustration of problem with finite signal propagation speed

- Contention methods use a random delay after a packet is ready to send. This method is not collision-free, but it is shown below that for repeated transmissions, the probability that the packet is transmitted successfully at some time converges against one. The advantage of contention methods is that no central station is needed; all stations have the same policies to access the channel. Furthermore, there is no communication overhead to negotiate the channel usage between the stations. On the other hand, there is time loss due to the random delay. One example for this method is CSMA/CD (Carrier Sense Multiple Access with Collision Detection) which is used in wired networks defined by the IEEE 802.3 standard. It is not suitable for wireless networks because it assumes that a collision can be detected: In a wired network, the channel can be observed by the receiver while the transmitter is sending. If the received and the transmitted signals are not equal, this indicates a collision. An example for a contention-based channel access scheme in wireless networks is CSMA/CA (CSMA with Collision Avoidance) which is defined in the 802.11 standard and discussed in detail below. In the 802.11 context, since there is no central station, this method of operation is called *Distributed Coordination Function* (DCF).

- Assignment methods use a central station which in turn queries (*polls*) all stations on the channel if they have something to send. This method is collision free; the disadvantages are the communication overhead for the polling and the time which is being lost to poll stations which are not ready to send. An example for an assignment method is an option which is defined in the 802.11 standard called *Point Coordination Function* (PCF) which can be used as an alternative to DCF. The PCF can only be used in infrastructure mode when an access point is available. The access point controls the channel and assigns airtime to each station by polling. However, PCF has never been implemented in existing WLAN hardware.

- Allocation methods use a central station like assignment methods. The central station regularly sends a special packet with a table which specifies the allocation of the channel to particular stations at given time slots. The station sends the data when its time slot starts. Allocation methods are collision free like assignment methods. An example is the GSM telephone network where each mobile station is assigned a fixed time slot by the base station, both for the downlink and the uplink.

For the channel allocation and collision resolution, the 802.11 standard defines the channel access method *Carrier Sense Multiple Access with Collision Avoidance* (CSMA/CA). This scheme includes two steps: during the *Carrier Sense*, the channel is observed to check if it is free for a transmission or busy due to transmissions of another station. In case of a busy channel, all transmission activity is stopped until the channel becomes free again. The second step is the *Collision Avoidance* which is entered once the channel becomes free. The basic idea is that a station does not send a packet once it is ready to be sent, but after a random delay. To show the effect of the collision resolution, two stations are considered which at the same time get a packet which is ready to be sent. It is assumed that both stations, after they received a packet to be sent from the higher protocol layers, select a random time t within a so-called *contention window*, which is a time interval $t_{min} < t < t_{max}$. After this random time has elapsed, they send the packet. This waiting process is also called *backoff*. For reasons of simplicity, it is assumed that the packet length t_{pkt} is the same for both stations. The time that a collision blocks the channel is dependent on the policy when A and B may start their transmissions. Figure 2.10 illustrates this effect. If the stations may start the transmission at any time, which is shown in the upper part of the figure and labelled as unslotted access, the length of the collision time interval t_{crit} is $2t_{pkt}$. If the start of the transmission is constrained to discrete points of time, shown in the lower

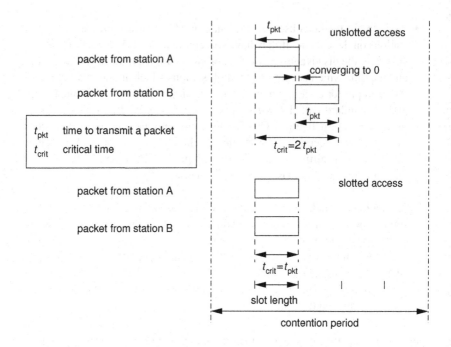

Figure 2.10: Unslotted and slotted channel access

part of the figure labelled slotted access, the length of a collision is t_{crit} which is equal to t_{pkt}, i. e. the airtime lost due to the collision is reduced by a factor of 2.

Besides the length of the collision period, the collision probability also changes when slotting is introduced. A contention window with the time $t = n \cdot t_{\mathrm{pkt}}$ is considered as shown in Fig. 2.10. If the stations may transmit at any time, a collision occurs if they is any overlapping between two packets, which can occur within a critical time $t_{\mathrm{crit}} = 2t_{\mathrm{pkt}}$ as discussed before; thus the collision probability is then $p = t_{\mathrm{crit}}/t = 2/n$. In case of slotting, both stations have to select the same time slot. If one station has selected any slot, the probability that the other station selects the same one is $1/n$. Hence the slotting reduces the collision probability by a factor of two.

Further details about the calculation of collision probabilities in wireless LANs are given in chapter 3.

If the collision probability p is known, the probability P_1 for a successful transmission after one transmission attempt is then

$$P_1 = 1 - p. \tag{2.5}$$

After a collision has occurred, the stations retry sending their packets; for the above example with two stations, the probability that the transmission is successful after the second try is

$$P_2 = p \cdot (1 - p). \tag{2.6}$$

The probability for a successful transmission at exactly the n-th try is

$$P_n = p^{n-1} \cdot (1 - p). \tag{2.7}$$

The probability for a successful transmission at the latest after n tries is

$$P_{1...n} = (1 - p) \sum_{i=0}^{n-1} p^i. \tag{2.8}$$

The sum is a geometric sequence for which the following relation applies:

$$\sum_{i=0}^{n} p^i = \frac{p^{n-1} - 1}{p - 1}. \tag{2.9}$$

For an infinite number of tries, the limit for $n \to \infty$ is calculated:

$$\lim_{n \to \infty} \frac{p^{n-1} - 1}{p - 1} = \frac{1}{1 - p}. \tag{2.10}$$

As p is a probability with $0 < p < 1$, the term p^{n-1} converges against 0 for $n \to \infty$.

It can be seen that P converges against 1 for increasing n, which means the higher the number of retransmissions, the higher is the probability that the packet was successfully transmitted. This is the way how a collision is resolved by the introduction of a random time interval for the packet transmission.

The slotting mechanism discussed in this section is used in the CSMA/CA algorithm to optimise the performance. For reasons of simplicity, it was assumed in the previous example that the length of a time slot is equal to the packet length. This policy was used in Pure resp. Slotted Aloha which were the first and most simple channel access schemes for wireless networks [115]. In the 802.11 CSMA/CA, the length of a packet is larger that the slot time, however the desired effect of slotting, i. e. reducing the collision probability, is still kept. The slotting is not needed during the entire length of a packet, but only to keep the channel silent while one or more stations are unable to detect a change of the channel state. This is the case during the time period when the transmitting station needs to switch from receiving to transmitting mode and vice versa, plus the time which the receiving station needs to detect the signal, which means reporting the channel as busy by the CCA. In the 802.11 standard, the value δ for the slot length is set to 9 µs.

2.3.2.1 Contention Window Size Control

The contention window length inside which the random time for the backoff is selected is not constant. For the first trial to transmit a packet, a time interval with the starting length $t_{min} = n_{min}\delta$ is used, where n_{min} is the number of time slots. The length of the congestion window is always an integer multiple of the slot length δ. Whenever the transmission of the packet fails, which means if no acknowledgement is received, the length of the time interval is doubled in relation to the length which was used in the previous trial. The doubling of the length is introduced based on the assumption that a packet loss occurs due to a collision. In order to reduce the collision probability, the backoff time period is increased for each transmission retry up to a limit $t_{max} = n_{max}\delta$. If the packet has been retransmitted so often that t_{max} has been reached, the contention window length is kept constant at t_{max} for further retries. To avoid an infinite number of retries, a retry counter is introduced. If this counter exceeds a predefined maximum number of retries, the transmission of the packet is stopped and the packet is discarded. This avoids that the system is infinitely locked by transmitting a particular packet.

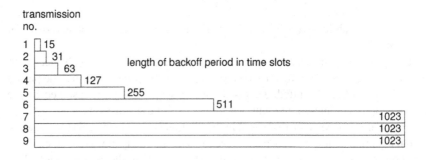

Figure 2.11: IEEE 802.11 backoff timings

The values for the limits t_{min}, t_{max} and for the maximum number of retries are not given in the standard, they can be specified by the WLAN hardware vendor.

2.3.2.2 Interframe Spacing

In the previous section, the contention window for the random backoff was discussed. In the 802.11 standard, besides the random component, an additional amount of time is also defined called *interframe spacing* (IFS) whose length depends on the priority of the packets. The priority, as well as the usage of the random backoff, is determined by the packet type and by the operation mode DCF or PCF. The 802.11 standard defines three sorts of packets:

- Data packets containing the user data to be transmitted.

- Management packets controlling the connection of a station to an access point or, in ad-hoc mode, to another station. The functions supported by management packets are authenticating, associating and dis-associating from APs and the control of the power management. In the 802.11h extension, they are also used to maintain the Dynamic Frequency Selection and the Transmit Power Control mechanisms.

- Control packets are used to control the transmission of individual data or management packets. These packets can be acknowledgements which are sent by the receiving station after a data or management packet has been successfully received. Furthermore, the 802.11 standard supports an optional handshake mechanism called RTS/CTS which also uses control packets.

In 802.11, three different types of IFS are defined. They are listed according to ascending time period:

- SIFS – Short IFS: used for control frames. The length of an SIFS has been defined considering the time delay which occurs between the arrival of a signal at a station and the detection of that signal by the station's hardware due to the finite processing speed of the hardware.

- PIFS – PCF IFS: used for polling frames in the point coordination function. The length of a PIFS is the length of a SIFS plus one slottime.

- DIFS – DCF IFS: used for data and management frames in the distributed coordination function. The length of a DIFS is the length of a SIFS plus 2 slottimes.

If a station is willing to send, the IFS starts once the channel has become free. The different IFS lengths allow a priorisation of the packets. The SIFS is shortest, thus a station planning to send a control packet is always the next station which gets channel access. The PIFS is longer than a SIFS, but shorter that a DIFS, so a station which wishes to control the channel in PCF waits until other stations sent their control packets and then gets the chance to control the channel before the lowest-priority DCF access is granted. Since contention only occurs for DCF, only the DIFS is followed by a backoff period.

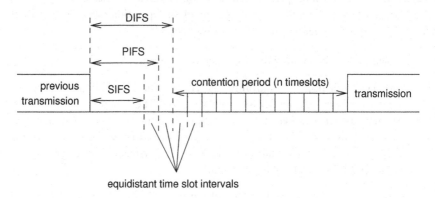

equidistant time slot intervals

Figure 2.12: Timing for IEEE 802.11

2.3.2.3 Timing sequence of a 802.11 DCF packet transmission

In the previous sections, the individual elements of the transmission have been discussed. Now an overview of the timing of the entire transmission sequence in DCF mode is given.

- The MAC layer of the station receives a packet to be transmitted from higher layers.

- The station checks if the WM is free. If it is busy, it waits until it becomes free, otherwise it immediately continues with the next step.

- Once the WM becomes or is free, the station waits until the DIFS period has expired.

- The random number for the random backoff is drawn. The station waits until the random backoff time interval has expired.

- The packet is sent.

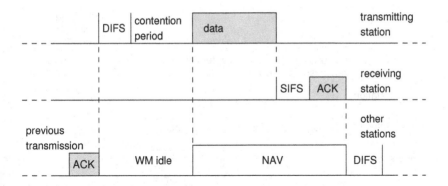

Figure 2.13: Structure of the 802.11 IFS/backoff period

- The receiving station sets the SIFS timer and waits until it has expired.

- The receiving station sends the ACK packet to the sending station.

- Any other station, as denoted in the bottom line of the figure, sets the *Network Allocation Vector* for the time the channel is expected to be busy. In case of the example, this is the duration of the data packet, the following SIFS and the length of the acknowledgement packet.

Figure 2.14 shows the case that the WM becomes busy during the backoff period. In this case, after the WM has become free again, the station waits again for the DIFS period. After that, it waits for the remaining backoff time which is calculated as follows: let n be the number of timeslots which were determined by the random generator before starting the backoff period and m the number of timeslots which elapsed until the channel becomes busy again, then the station has to wait for the remaining $n - m$ time slots after the channel has become free again. If the WM becomes busy during the DIFS period, the DIFS is repeated in full length when the WM becomes free again.

The standard also considers another special case which can occur if the channel load is low so there are long breaks between consecutive packets. A backoff process is started immediately after the channel gets free even if there is no packet ready to be sent. On arrival of the next packet from the higher layers, the backoff is then already over so that it can be transmitted just after completing the DIFS.

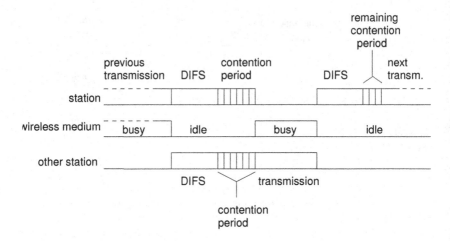

Figure 2.14: Suspending the backoff when the wireless medium becomes busy

2.3.3 RTS/CTS Extension

As pointed out in the beginning of this section, a major cause for collisions is the hidden station problem. The 802.11 standard specifies an option for the DCF which reduces the problem by using a handshake before the actual data transmission starts. The principle is explained using the example given in fig. 2.15. Station A is ready to send a packet to station B. Instead of sending the packet immediately to station B, it sends a Ready To Send (RTS) packet to B first. This RTS packet is a control packet which requests for the reservation of airtime on the WM. When the packet arrives at station B, it responds with a CTS (Clear To Send). The CTS packet contains time information which specifies how long the channel is reserved for station A. During this time, no other station may use the WM. The RTS and CTS packets are also heard by the stations C to E which set their Network Allocation Vector. This is a mechanism which tags the channel as busy for the time given in the RTS or CTS packet so that the station is silent for the reserved time period. Now, A can send the actual data packet which is then acknowledged by B in the normal way. Collisions due to the hidden station problem can be avoided in this way. In the example given in fig. 2.15, station A is a hidden station with respect to station E, because E cannot hear the transmissions of A. This means, if A and E had data to send to B, collisions might occur. Due to the introduction of RTS/CTS, E is notified by the CTS packet of B about the upcoming transmission from A.

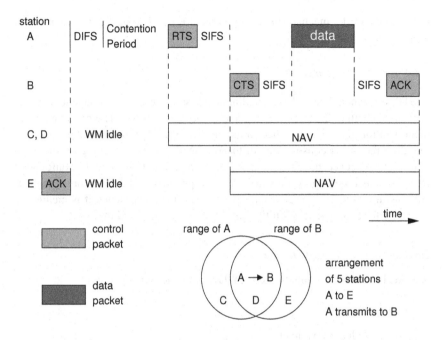

Figure 2.15: Timing Chart for RTS/CTS

Fig. 2.15 shows the timing diagram. Before sending the RTS packet, station A waits for a DIFS and then for a random backoff period. Each of the further packets (the CTS, the data packet and the ACK) are then sent after SIFS intervals.

It can be seen that collisions cannot be avoided entirely using RTS/CTS, since there can be a collision while the RTS packet is sent. However, the RTS packet is a short control packet, so in case of a collision, less airtime is lost than in the case that a long data packet is transmitted. Hence RTS/CTS is in particular useful for applications where long packets are sent, such as file transfers or video telephony. It is not useful for applications where the data packets are short, for example a Telnet session where the user data payload is small. In a telnet session, the user logs in on a remote computer to execute commands. Each keystroke generates one data packet which contains besides the TCP and IP header only one byte of user data (the key being hit). Using RTS/CTS in this situation would not reduce the collision probability, but just increase the communication overhead. For this reason, the wireless LAN hardware usually provides an option called *RTS Thresh-*

old. The RTS/CTS mechanism is only applied if the data packet is larger than a user-specified minimum size.

2.3.4 Power Management

The 802.11 standard describes signalling which supports power management which is available both in the infrastructure and in the ad-hoc mode. The power management mentioned here is specified in the original 802.11 standard and is a method to reduce the power consumption of the WLAN device by switching off the radio unit when no packets have to be transmitted or received. It must not be confounded with the transmission power control which is specified in 802.11h. For the considerations in this work, power management is not included, hence it is mentioned here only for completeness. Further information can be found in [50].

2.3.5 Format of the MAC Frame

A MAC PDU which is sent to the PHY layer includes three parts:

- MAC header

- variable length payload

- Frame Check Sequence (FCS) containing a 32-bit CRC

2	2	6	6	6	2	6	0–2312	2	bytes
FC	Du	addr1	addr2	addr3	SC	addr4	data	CRC	

Figure 2.16: Generic MAC packet

The MAC header includes the following fields (see fig. 2.16):

- Frame Control (FC): this field contains a number of subfields which are explained separately below.

- Duration (Du): specifies the length of the frame. The interpretation of this field depends on the type of frame to be transmitted, i. e. data, control or management frame.

- Address 1 to 3: These are 3 fields to specify MAC addresses. The interpretation of the fields depends on if the packet is sent in the uplink or in the downlink, and if it is sent in infrastructure or ad-hoc mode.

- Sequence Control: This field contains the sequence number and, if the current packet is fragmented, the number of the fragment.

- Address 4: This field is needed for some particular packet types.

As it was shown above, the MAC frame can contain up to 4 addresses. The interpretation of the address fields depends on the type of frame to be sent. The information contained in an address field can be as follows:

- BSSID. In infrastructure mode, this is the MAC address of the AP which controls the BSS. In ad-hoc mode, this is a random number.

- Destination Address (DA): the address of the station to which the packet finally should be sent.

- Source Address (SA): the address of the station which generated the packet.

- Receiver Address (RA): the address of the station which is the next hop to receive the packet. Depending on the situation, this address can be different from the DA: if STA1 sends a packet to another STA2 via an AP, then the DA is that of STA2 while the RA is that of the access point.

- Transmitter Address (TA): the address of the station which is the previous hop to send the packet. Depending on the situation, this address can be different from the SA: if STA2 receives a packet from STA1 via an AP, then the SA is that of STA1 while the TA is that of the access point.

2.4 IEEE 802.11h Spectrum Management Extensions

The IEEE 802.11h standard defines two extensions which support the spectrum management for WLANs: *Dynamic Frequency Selection* (DFS) and *Transmit Power Control* (TPC) [48]. The signalling needed to maintain these extensions is provided by additional management packet subtypes. The structure of a management packet is depicted in figure 2.17. The user data section of a frame with a generic MAC header contains an *action field*. This action field includes:

- category: the type of action to be taken. For spectrum management, this value is 1.

- action: type of spectrum management action (Dynamic Frequency Selection or Transmit Power Control)

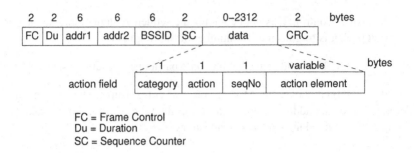

Figure 2.17: General structure of a spectrum management frame

- action element: a field which contains individual information for the different spectrum management actions.

The standard only describes the signalling to control the measurements based on which the frequency or the transmit power is selected and the signalling to control the change of the frequency and the power. The methods according to which the frequency channel or the transmit power should be chosen are not specified by the standard. The selection of such methods must be done by the developer who implements the WLAN protocol stack.

2.4.1 Dynamic Frequency Selection

Dynamic frequency selection means that the frequency channel which is used by a particular BSS can be changed automatically at run-time. In the legacy 802.11 standard, the frequency is fixed unless it is changed by the user. The dynamic selection of the channel is a means to avoid channels with strong interference as it has been discussed in the introduction of the work. To do so, measurements have to be taken to collect information about the interference situation on the available frequency channels. Based on the measurement results, the most suitable channel has to be selected. The standard defines a *DFS owner* which starts the measurements, evaluates the results and informs the stations about an upcoming channel switch. In the infrastructure networks, the DFS owner is the access point. In the ad-hoc mode, a DFS owner has to be found by signalling.

The signalling information for DFS as well as for TPC which is described in the next section is embedded into management frames. The standard specifies the following management packet extensions to control DFS:

- Measurement Request: requests a station to start a measurement. Since the Measurement Request is a unicast packet, for each station, one Measurement Request has to be sent.

- Measurement Report: returns the information gathered in a measurement back to the DFS owner.

- Quiet: asks all stations on the current frequency channel to stop all transmissions for a specified time.

- Channel Switch Announcement: informs the stations inside the BSS.

The format of the Measurement Request/Report action field inside a DFS management packet is given in fig. 2.18. The action field contains the following fields:

- Element ID: identifies the packet as a Measurement Request/Report

- Length: length of the packet

- Measurement Token: a sequence number for the unique identification of the packet

- Measurement Request Mode: identifies a Request or Report

- Measurement Type: three different types of Measurement Request/Reports are available: basic request, CCA request and RPI histogram request.

  - Basic request/report: determines if there has been an OFDM preamble, a radar signal or an unknown signal. If any of the three signals is received, a corresponding flag (one bit) is set.
  - CCA request/report: returns the percentage of measurement time for which the CCA of the station which issued the Measurement Report was busy.
  - RPI histogram request/report: a histogram is returned which contains the percentage of time at which the interference during the measurement time is within a certain interval. There are 6 intervals with a span of $5\,dB$ each, ranging from $-87\,dBm$ to $-57\,dBm$. In addition, there are two open intervals containing values below $-87\,dBm$ and above $-57\,dBm$.
  - Field for the actual Measurement Request/Report with variable length. This field contains the channel to be measured, the starting time of the measurement as well as the duration. The Measurement Report includes an additional field containing the results of the measurement.

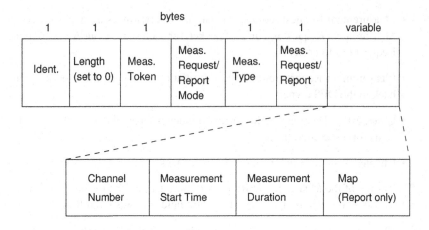

Figure 2.18: Measurement Request/Report action field format

The signalling on the radio channel is necessary to control the measurements and to inform the stations about an upcoming frequency change. An example for the the sequence is shown in figure 2.19.

1. The Station Management Entity (SME) of the DFS owner decides to take a measurement and sends a `MeasurementRequest.req` primitive to the MAC Layer Management Entity (MLME), specifying the station from which the request should be taken and the measurement time interval.

2. The MLME builds a Measurement Request management packet and sends it to the MAC layer.

3. The MAC layer sends the packet to the radio channel.

4. The MAC layer of the receiving station receives the measurement request packet and forwards it to the MLME.

5. The MLME of the receiver evaluates the received packet and sends a `MeasurementRequest.ind` service primitive to the SME.

6. The SME starts the measurement process by switching to the channel specified in the Measurement Request. The station listens to the transmissions of this particular channel for the given time interval.

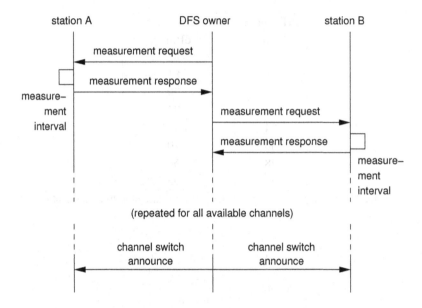

Figure 2.19: Signalling inside a DFS enabled network

7. After the measurement is finished, the SME collects the measurement data.

8. The Measurement Report is sent back to the DFS owner in the same way as the transmission of the Measurement Request.

After all mobile terminals have taken the measurements from all channels, the DFS owner decides if the channel should be changed. If a change is necessary, the channel to which the BSS should change must be determined. The DFS owner then sends a Channel Switch Announcement as a broadcast message. The mobile terminals can then decide to follow the DFS owner to the other channel or to roam to another DFS owner.

2.4.2 Transmit Power Control

The second extension for the spectrum management which is specified in the IEEE 802.11h standard is termed *Transmit Power Control* (TPC). The motivation for TPC is the fact that a signal which is received by a STA is often stronger than needed. This means the C/I is higher than it is necessary to receive the signal with

| PHY mode | receiver sensitivity |
Mbit/s	dBm
6	−82
9	−81
12	−79
18	−77
24	−74
36	−70
48	−66
54	−65

Table 2.4: Minimum receive power levels for the different PHY modes [49]

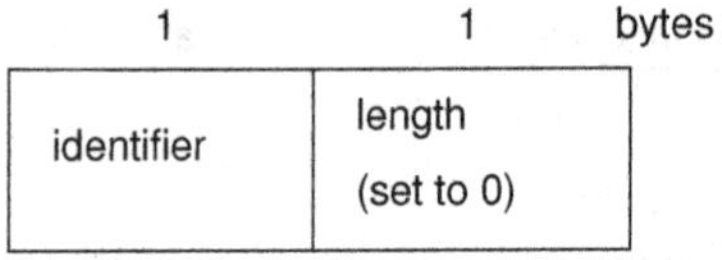

1	1	bytes
identifier	length (set to 0)	

Figure 2.20: Structure of a TPC request field

a bit error rate below a specified limit. By reducing the transmit power, the range of the sender will become smaller which results in less interference to neighbouring stations. The transmit power can be reduced to an amount which is sufficient to provide a minimum C/I at the receiver plus some safety margin. The minimum C/I is dependent on the PHY mode which is currently in use. The higher the physical bit rate of the transmission is, the more sensitive it is against interference. More details about this relationship are discussed in chapter 3.2. Besides the C/I, it also has to be considered that each PHY mode requires a certain minimum signal level at the receiver. A data packet which is received below this level cannot be correctly decoded and is discarded.

Table 2.4 shows the minimum receive power levels for the different PHY modes as specified by the 802.11a standard.

The 802.11h standard specifies two functions for the TPC signalling, TPC Request and TPC Report. These two messages are embedded to and sent as management packets like the DFS messages. The format of the TPC Request field is shown in figure 2.20. It only includes the identifier and the length, which is set to

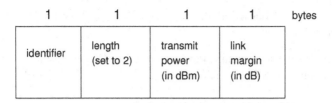

Figure 2.21: Structure of a TPC report field

zero since it does not contain additional information. The length of each field is one byte.

The structure of the TPC Report field is shown in figure 2.21. The TPC Report contains a field indicating the transmit power of the station which sends the TPC Report and a field with the *link margin*. The link margin is the ratio between the level of the received signal and the minimum signal level which is required to receive the signal below a given bit error rate. Each of the fields has a length of one byte.

The way how the receiver should react on the reception of a TPC report, which means which value the transmit power of a station should be set to when the transmit parameters of the communication partner is known, is not specified in the standard and thus left to the developer of the WLAN station's firmware.

2.4.3 Negotiation of Spectrum Management Capabilities

When a mobile terminal roams into a radio cell, a mutual negotiation between the access point and the station takes place as described earlier. The aim of this procedure is to check the match the SSID of the access point and the station and authenticate the station against the access point. In the case of spectrum management enabled stations, it is checked in addition if both the station and the access point fulfil the spectrum management requirements of the other side. The additional information is inserted into the frame bodies of the beacons, the Probe Request/Response and the (Re)Association Request/Response management packets. In particular, the following information fields are added to the beforementioned packets:

- For beacons: Country, Power Constraint, Channel Switch Announcement, Quiet, IBSS DFS, TPC Report.

- Association Request and Reassociation Request: Power Capability, Supported Channels.

- Probe Response: Country, Power Constraint, Channel Switch Announcement, Quiet, IBSS DFS, TPC Report.

In detail, these fields have the following meaning:

- Country. The frequency channels and transmit powers to be used can be dependent on national regulations. Thus, the Country field is provided to identify the location of the station.

- Power Capability. Identifies if the station is capable to control the transmit power.

- Power Constraint. Specifies the interval inside which a station can adjust the transmit power.

- Channel Switch Announcement. Can be set by a DFS owner if it has decided to switch the channel.

- Quiet. Can be set by a DFS owner if it wishes to quiet the channel, for example for measurement purposes.

- IBSS DFS. This element is used in ad-hoc networks to identify the DFS Owner.

- TPC Report. Gives information about the C/I which is observed by the station which supplies the report.

2.5 Centralised Channel Access

The channel access methods discussed in the previous sections were related to the distributed coordination function (DCF) which works without a central station. It was however mentioned that the plain IEEE 802.11 standard supports centralised access controlled by the access point based on the Point Coordination Function (PCF). This extension can be optionally implemented by the Wireless LAN hardware manufacturers, however it was never deployed in WLAN equipment available on the market. In the Point Coordination Function, the channel access is solely controlled by the access point. To initiate a time period controlled by the PCF, called *contention-free period* (CFP), the AP first sends a beacon, which is a broadcast management packet containing information about the duration of the CFP. The

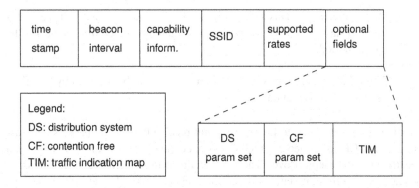

Figure 2.22: Structure of a beacon frame body

header of the packet is the one used for management packets, the elements of the body is shown in fig. 2.22. The optional fields vary according to the mode of operation; for an access point in PCF mode using DSSS transmission, they are as given in the figure.

The elements are:

- Timestamp. The time at which the beacon was transmitted.

- Beacon interval. Beacons are sent periodically at a regular time interval which is specified in this field.

- Capability information. This field informs mobile stations about functionality provided by the access point, for example if encryption is required for access, if spectrum management is provided etc.

- SSID, the name of the radio cell.

- Supported rates. The physical bit rates which are provided by the access point.

After these fields, there can be a combination of other fields depending on the station type (AP or mobile station) and operating mode (FHSS/DSSS, ad-hoc or infrastructure mode). For the operating mode which is considered here, which means infrastructure mode with PCF, the following fields are appended:

- DS parameter set: Describes the characteristics of the DSSS transmission, which is a single value, namely the channel number.

- CF parameter set: This field includes details when the next CF period is going to start, how long one period takes and how much time is left for the current period.

- Traffic Indication Map: specifies if there is data to be received by a station. Used if power-save mode is active.

All stations associated to the access point receive the beacon packets and suspend their DCF controlled channel access once the CFP starts until the time span specified in the beacon is over. The AP then determines the times of transmission of packets for different stations by an internal scheduler. The algorithm for this scheduler which decides which station should be served at what time is not covered by the standard but can be arbitrarily chosen by the hardware manufacturer. The actual data transmission is handled in a different way for the uplink and the downlink. In case of the uplink, the AP assigns airtime to a particular station by sending a CF (contention-free) poll management packet to this particular station. The station then should respond by sending its data packet or by a CF ACK (acknowledgement) packet if there is no data to be sent. For the downlink, the AP sends a data frame in the same way as in the DCF, which has to be acknowledged by the station. In this work, for centralised operation, only the downlink is considered so that details covering the uplink are not elaborated in further detail here. When the CFP is over, the access point sends a CF End packet to indicate that the channel control is taken over by the DCF.

The drawback of plain PCF is that it does not distinguish between different application types or different users; all incoming packets to be transmitted by the AP are treated in the same way, which is still not satisfying because different applications or users might have different requirements. One user might need an audio transmission with a low, but fixed throughput. Another user might be connected to a video stream which requires a higher bandwidth than the audio stream. With the normal PCF, there is only one queue for all users and data flows so that downlink packets are served in a FIFO order; uplink packets are transmitted when the respective station is polled by the AP; the stations are however polled in a round-robin fashion. Since the AP does not have knowledge about how frequently a certain flow should be served and it is not determined to which data flow the packet at the top of the queue which is served next belongs, packets of one data stream still might be served too late, resulting in a delay being too high, while packets for another data stream are served more frequently than it is required. The same problem appears for the uplink, where the round-robin polling order does not consider the urgency of the packets to be transmitted.

To overcome this problem, the standard extension 802.11e was specified which besides other features extends the centralised access of PCF by a number of *traffic classes* (TCs). It is then possible to assign different TCs to different users or different types of applications. For each traffic class, a separate queue is provided so that immediate access to any data flow is always available, in contrast to a single queue, where the access to a packet of a certain flow might be delayed because packets belonging to other flows can be located in front of it inside the queue. These queues can be served according to two different methods. The EDCF (Enhanced DCF) is a decentralised access similar to DCF; it provides a separate backoff process for each queue. For each of these backoff processes, the channel access parameters can be individually configured. The fixed-length DIFS is replaced by an Arbitrary IFS with configurable length which can be set individually for each TC. Also, the minimum and maximum contention window length CW_{min} and CW_{max} are configurable. In this way, a relative weighting between the TCs is possible, because the probability that a contention is won by a particular TC is increased if the AIFS length, CW_{min} and CW_{max} are set to small values.

Besides the EDCF, the system also can be run in a centralised way which is called *Hybrid Coordination Function* (HCF) which performs *HCF Controlled Channel Access* (HCCA). The term *hybrid* indicates that the system can reserve airtime for both contention-free access by centralised MAC and contention-based access by the EDCF described before. The HCF can only be used on an access point inside an infrastructure network which is in the context of HCF termed as *hybrid coordinator* (HC). In HCF, the traffic categories mentioned before are also used. The allocation of airtime to the different TC is controlled by a central scheduler located in the access point. By sending a beacon which was described before, a *contention-free period* (CFP) is initiated inside which the HC has full control on the channel. Within this period, the HC can send downlink packets to mobile terminals or send poll packets to grant airtime to mobile terminals for sending uplink packets. The beacon contains a time stamp which indicates the length of the CFP. Outside the CFP, decentralised access by EDCF is possible. In the investigations in this work, however, only the centralised channel access is considered.

The policy of the scheduler, i.e. for which station it should assign airtime, is not specified by the standard. The design of scheduling strategies is left to the hardware vendor which develops wireless LAN equipment.

2.6 Enhancing Transmission Speed by MIMO: IEEE 802.11n

Another option to enhance the speed of WLAN transmissions considered in this work are parallelised transmissions using *Multiple Input Multiple Output* (MIMO)

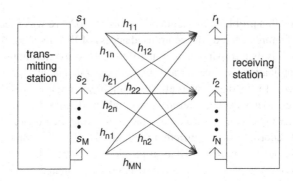

Figure 2.23: $M \times N$ MIMO transmission system

systems, which is proposed in the IEEE standard extension 802.11n. A legacy access point or mobile station has one antenna each so that a *Single Input Single Output* system is formed. MIMO systems allow the parallel transmission of data streams by utilising different spatial transmission paths between transmit and receive antennas as it is shown in figure 2.23: the sender and receiver have M resp. N antennas. Each of the receiving antennas receives the signal of each transmit antenna to some extent. With $s_m(t)$ being the signal of the sending antenna m and $r_n(t)$ being the signal of the receiving antenna n, $1 \leq m \leq M$ and $1 \leq n \leq N$ and assuming a narrow-band channel which is not frequency-selective, the property of that channel at time t can be completely described by a single channel coefficient $h_{mn}(t)$. The t parameter indicates that the channel coefficients are time-dependent. The channel conditions change due to mobility of the stations and moving obstacles in the environment. In a transmission system with M transmit and N receive antennas, a channel matrix $\mathbf{H}$ can be written which is defined as

$$\mathbf{H} = \begin{pmatrix} h_{11} & h_{12} & \ldots & h_{1N} \\ h_{21} & h_{22} & \ldots & h_{2N} \\ \vdots & \vdots & \vdots & \vdots \\ h_{M1} & h_{M2} & \ldots & h_{MN} \end{pmatrix}. \tag{2.11}$$

The number of transmit antennas M can be different from the number of receive antennas N so that the matrix may not be squared. A transmission path between a certain transmit antenna and a certain receive antenna is called a *subchannel*. Assuming $N = M$, the ideal case where the maximum capacity can be achieved would be an orthogonal channel matrix. A special case is a diagonal matrix with

$h_{mn} \neq 0$ for $m = n$ and $h_{mn} \neq 0$ for $m \neq n$, which means that each receive antenna n receives the signal of exactly one transmit antenna $m = n$, so there are $N = M$ separate subchannels available which do not mutually interfere. In practice, this ideal situation of orthogonality cannot be achieved, there is always crosstalk between the subchannels, which results in mutual interference and therefore reduces the capacity of each subchannel as well as the total capacity.

For the calculation of the normalised capacity on a single AWGN channel C_{norm}, i. e. the available bit rate related to the frequency bandwidth of the transmission channel, SHANNON's channel coding theorem is considered with given signal power P_S and noise/interference power P_N [61]:

$$C_{\text{norm}} = \log_2 \left(1 + \frac{P_S}{P_N} \right). \tag{2.12}$$

For a MIMO system, the AWGN channel is extended to $M \cdot N$ AWGN transmission paths, which are however not independent as discussed above. By normalising P_N to 1, C_{norm} can be calculated for a MIMO transmission system as [31, 34]:

$$
\begin{aligned}
C_{\text{norm,MIMO}} &= \log_2 \det \left(\mathbf{I}_N + \frac{P_S}{M} \cdot \mathbf{H}\mathbf{H}^H \right) \\
&= \sum_{i=1}^{r} \log_2 \left(1 + \lambda_i \cdot \frac{P_S}{M} \right) \text{ with } r = \min(M, N).
\end{aligned}
\tag{2.13}
$$

where $\mathbf{H}^H$ is the Hermitian resp. conjugate complex of $\mathbf{H}$ and λ_i is the ith eigenvalue of $\mathbf{H}\mathbf{H}^H$. The equation given above applies for a single-carrier transmission. $\mathbf{I}_N$ is a squared identity matrix with the number of rows resp. columns according to the number of receive antennas N. The result of the equation is the normalised capacity C_{norm} with respect to the RF bandwidth of the channel. Since 802.11a/n is based on an OFDM transmission, the channel is divided into L subcarriers, with $L = 52$ in the 802.11a/n standard. Due to the frequency-selectivity of the channel, this means that in case of a MIMO transmission each of the subcarriers has to be described by a separate channel matrix $\mathbf{H}_i$ with i being the subcarrier number. In case of no channel knowledge at the transmitter, the available transmit power is equally distributed among all subcarriers. When calculating the total available normalised capacity, eq. 2.13 with P_T being the transmitted per-subcarrier power, then rewrites as

$$C_{\text{norm,MIMO}} = \sum_{l=1}^{L} \log_2 \det \left(\mathbf{I}_N + \frac{P_T}{M \cdot L} \cdot \mathbf{H}_l \mathbf{H}_l^H \right). \tag{2.14}$$

The 802.11n standard extension specifies *Time Division Multiple Access* (TDMA) based on MIMO, which means that the bits of a packet are transmitted simultaneously along different subchannels, but the packets of different users are still transmitted consecutively. A parallel transmission of data for different users can enhance the performance furthermore, which is however not specified by the 802.11n standard. One option to do so is to allocate the different subcarriers of an OFDM transmission to different users, which is called *Orthogonal Frequency Devision Multiple Access* (OFDMA). The motivation to do so is that the channel is usually frequency-selective and channel properties differ for each user, even at the same point of time. In case of TDMA, bad subcarriers in the communication path to the currently served user do not contribute to the data throughput. These subcarriers might at a particular point of time be good for another user so that a second transmission can go on in parallel to the first one, which is done by OFDMA to use the channel more efficiently. A further enhancement is provided by *Space Division Multiple Access* (SDMA): it allows to serve more than one user at a time by each of the subcarriers. The basic idea is that users who are separated in the space domain, which means there is a sufficient distance between them, can both be provided a signal on the same frequency and at the same time keeping the mutual interference below a certain threshold. More details about OFDMA and SDMA are given in chapter 5.

An overview about the simulator used in this work which implements the IEEE 802.11 protocol stack along with the different extensions is given in chapter 6.

2.7 Summary

In this chapter, motivations were given why standardisation in communication networks is crucial. In particular, the IEEE 802.11 standard was considered which is the basis for the considerations in this work. Details about the MAC and the PHY layer were given. The spectrum management extension IEEE 802.11h was described which provides the signalling for Dynamic Frequency Selection and Transmit Power Control. Furthermore, the extensions IEEE 802.11e providing quality-of-service by maintaining centralised channel access considering traffic categories and 802.11n providing enhanced transmission speed by the means of MIMO were discussed.

3 Theoretical Aspects of Wireless LAN Performance

In the beginning of this chapter, a survey is given about existing literature concerning the performance of Wireless LAN and the enhancement by spectrum management. After this introduction, theoretical considerations about the capacity and the delay of IEEE 802.11 are discussed in detail starting with a model used in the literature. This model however applies to the case of an ideal, lossless channel, which means that the stations have infinite range, there is no attenuation of the signals on the path between the transmitter and the receiver. In this work, the model which has been introduced for the ideal channel is then extended for a more realistic channel by assuming an exponential attenuation of the signal and requirements for minimum signal levels and signal-to-noise-ratios (SNR) at the receivers. It is discussed how the results of these models apply for Transmit Power Control. Furthermore, novel considerations about the convergence speed of Dynamic Frequency Selection are given. The chapter concludes with calculations to compare the performance of a parallelised transmission for multiple users with a sequential transmission.

3.1 Related Work on Wireless LAN Performance and Spectrum Management

3.1.1 Frequency Channel Selection

Ideas for optimising the behaviour of wireless networks were introduced long before wireless LANs appeared, namely along with the introduction of cellular telephone networks. Such a network consists of a number of base stations with a particular coverage. Similar to wireless LANs, there is mutual interference between neighbouring radio cells which should be reduced. The approaches how to reduce this interference can be the assignment of different frequencies for neighbouring radio cells and the control of the transmit power of the base station. KATZELA and NAGHSINEH give an overview concerning different channel assignment methods used for cellular networks [62]. COMELLAS and OZÓN [20] as well as GARG et al. [32, 33] describe channel assignment methods based on graph colouring. The basic idea is that a network can be mapped to a graph, where the networks are the nodes of the graph and a radio connection between two neighbouring networks is expressed as an edge between two nodes in the graph. Different frequency channels are denoted as different colours of the nodes. The paper describes an algorithm how to distribute colours to the nodes in a way that two adjacent nodes, i. e. two nodes which are connected by a edge, are not assigned the same colour. In the paper, both centralised and deterministic decentralised algorithms are proposed.

GOMES et al. [36] describe a heuristic reactive algorithm which is based on an approach called *Greedy Randomised Adaptive Search Procedure*. This algorithm works in three steps which are repeated until a stopping criterion is satisfied: In the first step, the possible solutions of the given problem are put as elements into a structure termed as *Restricted Candidate List*. In case of wireless terminals, the elements are the antennas, sorted by the number of possible channels which can be assigned to each of them. For the determination of these assignments, it is considered that antennas which are not in mutual coverage can be assigned to the same frequency channel. When building the list is started, all channels are available for all antennas. The algorithm randomly selects one antenna out of the top α percent with the lowest amount of assignable channels and assigns a channel to it. After that, the assignable channels in the list for all other antennas are updated and the list is resorted. The factor α is determined by a heuristic method.

AARDAL et al. [1] provide an overview on a number of frequency assignment models and possible solutions. It is first pointed out that the basic frequency assigning problem can be described as a graph where the networks are the vertices and networks working on the same frequency and overlapping coverages are represented by links between two vertices. Based on such a graph, the frequency assignment problem is described as a linear programming problem where constraints are given by the interference of neighbouring networks; the objective function depends on the optimisation strategy being used. The following optimisations are introduced:

The models are classified according to different optimisation strategies

1. Maximum service: assign as many frequencies as possible.

2. Minimum blocking: optimisation of "maximum service", the unoptimised algorithm tends to neglect some of the edges inside the unoptimised graph.

3. Minimum order: minimise the number of used frequencies.

4. Minimum frequency span: like minimum order, but with the additional constraint that the used frequency channel should be adjacent.

5. Minimum interference: this model takes the interference as the target value for the objective function, which has to be minimised.

A similar way of optimising the frequency allocation, which means describing the network with a neighbourship graph and using linear programming to find a solution, is proposed by KENDALL and MOHAMAD [65]. The same authors propose a *hyper-heuristic* method to minimise the number of frequency channels required for a given number of networks in [63] and [64]. The term hyper-heuristic means that the solution algorithm is completely abstracted from the underlying problem. The interface to the concrete problem is provided by a number of low-level heuristics (LLHs). These LLHs can for example be local search algorithms. The advantage over a single LLH is that the latter, when finding an optimum for an objective function to be minimised/maximised, can run into a local maximum and remain at this point instead of finding the global one. The hyper-heuristic approach evaluates the output of the LLH, it is checked how much improvement the result of the recently called LLH provides compared with the result which was achieved before this step was executed. In each iteration, one LLH is called in a random sequence; the result of that LLH is accepted if it is better than the previous solution at least by a predefined factor.

DANIELS et al. [21] describe dynamic channel assignment in cellular networks considering both geographic locations and interference where the channel utilisation in each network is time-variant. Based on this scenario, a linear programming problem is developed where the constraints are the C/I values between stations and the objective function to be minimised is the number of channels which are used by more than one network. Algorithms are described which determine solutions for a lower and an upper bound for the minimum required number of channels. The lower bound is determined by grouping the radio cells belonging to each network into *clusters*, which is defined here as a group of interfering networks. Interfering networks are here determined from the reuse distance. Each cell inside the cluster must be assigned to a separate frequency. The upper bound is determined from calculations of the cumulative interference, which means for each cell the sum of interferences from neighbouring cells is considered.

FERNANDO and FAPOJUWO [29] describe a frequency selection method based on the VITERBI scheme which initially was designed for the problem of channel coding. VITERBI's approach shows an efficient way how to decode a sequence of bits at the receiver using a *Maximum Likelihood decoder* [61]. The goal of this Viterbi-like algorithm is the minimisation of the number of frequency channels which have to be used to transport a given amount of offered traffic load. In a similar way to the minimum Hamming distance which the Viterbi algorithm uses as a metric to estimate the most probable sequence of received bits, the algorithm in [29] uses the excess frequency factor as the metric to be optimised. The search is in both cases done using a trellis structure. In the original Viterbi algorithm, the value which has to be determined by the trellis search is the most likely received bit sequence, in the Viterbi-like algorithm it is the assignment of channels to networks. A different focus on the problem is shown in the work of JAIN et al. [59]. While the previous works are targetted on mobile telephone networks, this work is related in particular to wireless LANs. A special protocol similar to 802.11 is proposed which includes the dynamic assignment of channels to the mobile stations. The protocol assumes a separate channel for control packets. The basic idea is to negotiate a frequency for each packet to be used by an RTS/CTS sequence which is performed on the control channel; after the frequency has been negotiated in this way, the data transmission itself then takes place on the data channel. The RTS/CTS packets are extended for the signalling of available frequencies. Both the station sending RTS and the station responding with CTS determine a list of suitable frequency channels based on measurements. If there is at least one common channel in the two free-channel lists, the channel with the lowest interference level is selected. If the free-channel list of the station which wants to initiate the transmission by the RTS is empty, then the station enters a backoff and checks the channel availability again after the backoff has expired.

A comparison between different channel selection strategies is shown by PET-TERSSON [105]. The proposed scheme is a local centralised approach, where a *bunch* of antennas is controlled. The controller can for example be a base station which provides coverage by a number of antennas. Knowing the link-gain matrix, different channel selection strategies are examined, such as most-interfered first, least-interfered first, random selection and lowest channel number first. For the channel selected according to these criteria, it is checked if a new station which is added to the channel will reduce the C/I of any of the other stations on the channel below a given threshold. The station is only assigned to the channel if the C/I condition is kept for all stations, otherwise the next channel according to the selection of the algorithm is checked.

The usage of genetic algorithms for Dynamic Frequency Selection is discussed in a paper by WONG and WASSELL for broadband fixed wireless access networks (BFWAs). The concept was extended to Hiperlan/2 by PEETZ [103]. Genetic algorithms are also used as a basis for DFS in 802.11 wireless LANs in this analysis; this is elaborated in detail in chapter 4. Another approach for DFS is the usage of a fuzzy controller, which was also investigated by PEETZ for Hiperlan/2 and in addition by a paper by SHEN, IRVINE and PESCH in general for TDMA based cellular systems [116].

A centralised frequency selection scheme for IEEE 802.11b access points is proposed by YONEZAWA and INOUE [130]. The special aspect about 802.11b is the fact that the available frequency channels are overlapping. In the considered scenario, a group of cooperative access points which change their frequency is exposed to the interference of non-cooperative access points in the environment. A channel separation matrix (CSM) defines what should be the minimum frequency spacing between each pair of access points inside this system. From the CSM, a channel allocation matrix (CAM) is derived which contains the allocation of the cooperative access points to the channels and the minimum separation between the allocated channels. By means of these matrices, the search space to find the optimum channel allocation can be reduced in contrast to the exhaustive search which has to check K_N combinations with K being the number of channels and N being the number of access points.

3.1.2 Power Control

The basic idea of Transmit Power Control is that the signal level which is received at a station does not have to be higher than necessary for a given bit-error rate at the receiver which is determined by the C/I.

SATAPATHY and PEHA propose an abstract algorithm which is independent of the underlying MAC protocol [114]. The work assumes a listen-before-talk MAC layer, similar to the carrier sensing in IEEE 802.11. The proposal introduces two policies: A station is only allowed to transmit if the signal level on the channel is below a given threshold; this is equivalent to the CCA in 802.11. The second policy is that the power at which a signal is transmitted to another station is dependent on the power by which a signal from that station was received. The higher the received power is, the lower is the power with which the receiver sends. The method does not require the knowledge of the opposite station's transmit power.

SHETH and HAN investigate a power control algorithm by tests with real hardware [117]. The tested algorithm assumes a symmetric channel which has the same path loss for the up- and the downlink between two stations. The transmit power of a particular station is the sum of the minimum receive power, the path loss and a safety margin. The path loss is estimated from the receive power of the opposite station, both stations are assumed to use the same transmit power.

An approach for a centralised power control is given by ZANDER in [131]. In this paper, it is shown that a centralised power control is possible if the *link gain matrix* between the different stations is known. By calculating the Eigenvector of this matrix, for each station, the optimum transmit power can be determined. It is shown furthermore that the calculation of the Eigenvector requires a high effort and thus is approached by an iterative method. The algorithm proposed in these papers is described in more detail in chapter 4 since it is used for the power control which is proposed for infrastructure networks in this work. A similar proposal is provided by GRANDHI et al. [38] and by HONGYOU [44]. CHEN et al. [16] suggest an extension to a centralised power control scheme where a central controller predicts path losses based on knowledge about the physical environment of the access points, i.e. the layout and the radio propagation properties of the building.

Investigations on power control in Hiperlan/2 networks are given in [88] and [30]. RADIMIRSCH proposes a combined power control and link adaptation algorithm for Hiperlan/2 which measures the queue filling state, the amount of free space in the MAC frames and the packet loss rate.

Power control can also be used to control the topology of an ad-hoc network, as it is shown by RAMANATHAN [111]. The assumption for the design of the algorithm proposed in this paper is that inside an ad-hoc network it is not necessary that every station has a connection to every other station; it is sufficient if one station has links to two neighbouring stations. The algorithm proposed in the paper assumes the knowledge of the positions of all stations. Based on this knowledge, the transmit power for each link is then successively reduced until the number of links is reduced to the necessary minimum.

The integration of the power control in the signalling of a MAC protocol is investigated by JUNG [60]. All transmissions are initiated using RTS/CTS. The RTS/CTS packets are transmitted at full power while the data and acknowledgement packets are transmitted with the minimum required power. The idea is that if RTS/CTS is included in the power control, collisions can occur despite of RTS/CTS if these packets are not detected by certain stations. A similar proposal is also given by AGARWAL et al. [2].

The work of SHETH and HAN proposes power control using legacy 802.11 like the papers previously mentioned in this section, however it highlights the problem of additional hidden stations due to asymmetric power. The latter term means that unlike legacy network scenarios, the stations have different powers and ranges. Legacy power control protocols reserve the channel by sending an RTS/CTS with maximum power and after that the data/ACK frames with the minimum power needed for the conversation. Due to the RTS/CTS transmitted at high power, the area inside which the RTS/CTS is heard is unnecessarily large. The proposed protocol is reactive, it transmits the RTS, CTS, DATA and ACK packets with optimum power. Only in case of interference, the power is of RTS is adapted so that the interferer can hear it.

The beforementioned algorithm is also discussed by PIRES and REZENDE [106]: based on this algorithm, the paper points out that the power reduction can increase the hidden station problem due to the reduced range of the stations. To increase the performance of the wireless network, it is proposed that even if a station cannot decode the content of an RTS/CTS packet because of a signal level being too low, the station can still detect the carrier. By observing the length of the channel-busy time the station observing the channel can determine if the packet is an RTS or CTS packet. If the signal level of the RTS/CTS packet would be sufficiently high, it would be possible to read the time stamp from the packet so that the station can keep silent for the specified time. In case that only the carrier can be detected, but a decoding of the data is not possible, it is however still possible to add some additional bits to the RTS packet which do not carry information but increase the length of the packet. This length increase can be measured by the station which observes the channel. The variable length can then be used as a coarse indicator for the length of the DATA packet which follows the RTS packet. QIAO et al. [109] introduce an analysis about the optimum combination of power control and PHY mode for the IEEE 802.11 Point Coordination Function. In WANG et al, a combined scheduling and power control scheme is proposed for multicasts in an 802.11 network [127]. The optimum solution is determined by a linear programming problem.

The integration of power management into ad-hoc routing is proposed in [27]. Based on the *connectivity*, which means the number of neighbours to which a station has a physical connection, the power is adjusted. GOMEZ et al. [37] propose a MAC scheme for ad-hoc networks that includes power reduction by optimising the routes. The algorithm includes three functions:

- Overhearing: collect all packets which are received by a certain station and building a list of neighbours with their respective receive power.

- Redirecting: check if the node should claim itself as a redirector; if so, send redirect messages to neighbouring nodes.

- Route maintenance: if there are not sufficient data packets for the regular check of station neighbourship, send dedicated signalling packets.

The power which is required for a particular route is expressed as a cost function which is minimised by the route selection.

LOPEZ et al. [94] study a power control algorithm for IEEE 802.11 cellular networks, which means there is interference between neighbouring radio cells. To adjust the power, it is counted how many consecutively transmitted packets are acknowledged by the communication partner until an acknowledge packet is lost. The proposed extension works with the 802.11 protocol without using the 802.11h extension. The motivation for this protocol design is easy integration into existing hardware.

CHO et al. [17] show a power control algorithm which considers OFDM based transmissions. The proposed algorithm supports OFDMA, which means that each subcarrier is assigned to a different user, and for each subcarrier the power is separately controlled. The algorithm provides reduced complexity compared with the Subcarrier Allocation (WSA) algorithm designed by WONG ET AL. [129]. At the start of the algorithms, the subcarriers are allocated one-by-one to the users. The first user can select any of n subcarriers, the second one any of the remaining n - 1 subcarriers etc., until all subcarriers are allocated. During the run of the algorithm, gain measurements are taken for each subcarrier. According to certain rules, subcarriers are swapped between two users if the transmit power can be reduced in this way. The complexity of the latter algorithm is of the order $O(KN \log N + aN^2)$ where K is the number of users and N is the number of subcarriers. In contrast to this, CHO's algorithm has the complexity $O(aN(K - 1))$ where a is the number of iterations, which is an arbitrary parameter. The higher it is selected, the more precise is the calculated solution.

The publications mentioned above discuss theoretical aspects or simulation results for power control algorithms. In contrast to this, SHRIVASTAVA et al. highlight the implementation of power control in practical hardware [118]. The argumentation in the paper is that a fine adjustment of the power can even be less effective than a coarse adjustment because of external interference.

PARK et al. analyse the dependency between the throughput and the transmission range of WLAN stations in case of ad-hoc multihop networks [102]. In contrast to other investigations with a high node density, a relatively low number of wireless stations related to a given area is considered here, which the authors consider as the typical case for the application of wireless LANs.

For the throughput Γ in a multihop network, the relation

$$\Gamma \propto \frac{r \cdot D \cdot \lambda}{N_f} \qquad (3.1)$$

is given, where r is the transmission range, D is the border length of the squared area inside which the stations are located λ is the physical bit rate and N_f is the number of data flows. The equation shows that the throughput is increased proportionally to the transmission range which is opposite to the usual effect, where a range reduction is needed to increase the throughput of a WLAN station population.

SARAYDAR et al. is one of several works which propose a *game theoretical* approach for the power control inside a CDMA system [113]. The wireless terminals are self-optimising within a *non-cooperative power control game*. Another example for using the game theory in DFS is presented by NEEL and REED [101]. LEUNG describes a solution for the power control problem in CDMA networks using a Kalman filter [92].

Power control has also become important for wireless sensor networks, where distributed algorithms are used as shown by KUBISCH et al. [89].

3.1.3 Link Adaptation

There are different approaches introduced in the literature how to perform Link Adaptation: DEL PRADO PAVON and CHOI present a link adaptation method for Wireless LANs which is based on measuring the signal strength at the receiver [108]. The aim of the algorithm is that no changes are required for the existing 802.11 protocol. It assumes that the transmit power of the access point is constant so that a receiving station can determine relative changes of the signal strength. Furthermore, it can determine if its transmissions to the AP were successful depending on the reception of acknowledgement packets. Based on these two parameters, thresholds for the signal strength are computed which trigger a change of the PHY mode if the current signal strength becomes higher resp. lower than the threshold. POLLIN et al. show a cross-layer based strategy where the link adaptation algorithm for an OFDM-based WLAN system is provided control information from the transport layer [107]. The metrics for the algorithm are the throughput and the energy per bit. The throughput is determined from the physical transmission rate by considering the overhead of the IEEE MAC protocol in an analytical way and the effects of TCP by means of simulation. The tradeoff is to minimise the energy per bit on the one hand and maximise the throughput on the other hand. LEUNG and WANG [93] present an integrated link adaptation and power control approach for cellular telephone networks. The terminals are grouped according to their signal path gain. For the power control, a Kalman filter is applied. The modulation scheme is adjusted for each group by measuring the average BER and the link margin of the received power. In case of the BER exceeding a threshold, the modulation scheme is switched to a slower and thus more robust PHY mode; in case of a sufficient amount of link margin, the modulation scheme is switched to a faster PHY mode. A combined optimisation scheme for the transmit power and the physical bit rate is introduced by KRISHNASWAMY for an Extended GPRS (EGPRS) network with a number of base stations. An optimum working point for the target SNR at the receiver is determined for each of the available PHY modes using a set of sigmoid functions which describe the available throughput as a function of the SNR with the PHY mode as parameter. With the knowledge of these working points, the path loss information between a user and neighbouring base stations and the transmit power of these base stations, the optimum setting for the PHY mode and the transmit power is determined.

3.1.4 Cross-Layer Design

There are various ways how to enhance the performance of Wireless LANs. The way how the performance is enhanced by exchange of cross-layer information between the different protocol layers is discussed by WIJTING and PRASAD; possible options are additional packet headers or a special signalling scheme [128]. In the approach presented here, additional signalling is used as described in section 5. Crosslayer designs that are specialised on video applications [90, 104, 66, 18] take the quality of the video image at the mobile station as the metric for optimisation. In contrast to these works, the approach given in this work is independent of the particular application, however QoS requirements specified by the application are considered.

In [132], it is pointed out by ZHAI that Video-On-Demand can cope with relatively large delays which should, however, be constant. For this reason, a scheduling scheme which in particular also aims to reduce the jitter is discussed in this paper. The scheduling concept presented by HALEEM and CHANDRAMOULI in [41, 40] is specially designed for OFDM-TDMA transmissions; it integrates the channel state into the MAC layer scheduling. In the approach presented here, the PHY scheduling is separated from the MAC scheduling. The schedulers communicate through an abstract interface, i. e. providing an importance metric instead of giving detailed information about packet lifetime etc.

In the paper of KAWADIA and KUMAR, the power control problem is investigated from the view of cross-layer design. The interactions between the behaviour of the MAC layer and the transmit power are discussed, for example that a reduction of the power reduces the average contention between stations.

MERLIN et al. discuss different aspects of cross-layer design: in [5] the importance of channel knowledge for the MAC layer in WiMAX (IEEE 802.16) is discussed. [99] and [98] investigate cross-layer based resource allocation methods inside a cellular OFDMA transmission system. The subcarriers of the OFDM signal do not only have to be shared between users inside the same radio cell, but also between neighbouring cells with overlapping coverage zones. Three algorithms are investigated: Linear optimisation, power minimisation with greedy heuristics and efficiency maximisation.

Two scheduling concepts are analysed in [15] by CHEN et al., where one has a better support for QoS and the other one has a better support for the total throughput. In this work, a cross-layer scheduler is proposed which satisfies the QoS requirements for a maximum number of users, because meeting the QoS requirements is the criteria which results in the highest satisfaction for the user. There is a tradeoff between user and operator requirements: The operator wants to maximise the total network utilisation, which means the overall throughput. The user on the other hand wishes to get a good performance of the application which he runs, even in case of bad channel conditions. Achieving the this goal can conflict with the optimisation criteria of the network operator. TRIANTAFYLLOPOULOU et al. propose a cross-layer scheduling scheme for IEEE 802.16 which combines the physical layer with the application layer [123]. The scheme proposes three steps for the cross-layer scheduling, which is the abstraction of layer-specific parameters, parameter optimisation and reconfiguration of the parameters according to the scheduler decision. KOBRAVI and SHIKH-BAHAEI do an analytical investigation of the tradeoff between adaptive ARQ on the MAC layer and the modulation scheme on the physical layer [68]. If a higher modulation scheme is selected, more data can be transmitted in a time unit, however, there is a higher probability for packet loss because the higher modulation scheme is more sensitive against bad channel conditions. BOKHARI et al. discuss a cross-layer based scheduling scheme based on a token bank [12]: each data flow has a certain deposit which is filled up according to the data rate of the particular flow; the tokens are consumed by the transmission of data. The priority of the flow with respect to the physical layer is dependent on the amount of tokens on the bank. Flows with the highest priorities get the highest amount of OFDM subcarriers resp. transmission time. ALONSO et al. highlight the tradeoff between the cross-layer overhead and the efficiency [3]. A cross-layer manager is proposed in order to maintain the communication between the different layers. Finally, a cross-layer approach between the MAC and the PHY layer is proposed for CDMA and WLANs, where the MAC layer selects the spreading factor – and thus the data rate – dependent on the number of users in the environment; furthermore the channel state is included into the scheduling decision, which means that the service of users with a bad channel is delayed assuming that they face better conditions later on.

Cross-Layer and MIMO

When designing a MIMO transmission with multi-user access, it is not useful to maximise the sum rate over all users. In this case, the fair assignment of data flows according to the application requirements is more important, as described in BANG et al. [6], where it is also combined with a prediction of the channel quality. The latter work highlights that even though the scheduler determines an entire vector which gives the transmission order for each user in case of given channel characteristics, the scheduling process should be repeated after each packet which has been transmitted, because no reliable long-term predictions for the channel exist. ANTON-HARO et al. discuss cross-layer scheduling approaches for

MIMO systems [4]. The authors distinguish between channel-aware scheduling and channel/queue-aware scheduling for single-carrier systems, which is further extended by space-frequency scheduling for multi-carrier systems where the sub-carriers are an additional degree of freedom for the resource allocation. Another scheduling criteria which can be included into a cross-layer scheduler is the probability of a queue overflow according to BOCHE and WICZANOWSKI [10, 11]. Alternatively, the waiting time of the oldest packet in the queue can be observed which results in shorter delays as described by WANG and MURCH [126]. BOSISIO et al. investigate the interaction between scheduling and linear precoding for an SDMA transmission in [13]: different criteria are considered for the long-term fairness for the allocation of transmission time between data flows, such as the ratio between the maximum and minimum served flow as well as a service which is proportional to the weighting factors in the long-term average.

3.2 Performance of IEEE 802.11 Wireless LANs

When considering the performance of wireless LANs, it is important which type of channel model is used. In the easiest case, there is no limited range for the stations, every station has an infinite range, so each receiving station detects the channel as busy if there is a sending station, regardless of the distance to the sender.

When considering the range of a WLAN station, in the most simple model, a station has an exactly determined range inside which a perfect reception without errors is possible and outside which the station cannot be heard. In more realistic models, however, different types of ranges have to be distinguished.

The *transmission range* r_g is the range of a station inside which a neighbouring station can receive the transmitting station's signal and decode the transmitted data. Since there is no ideal error-free transmission, the criteria bit errors or no bit errors is not suitable to determine the transmission range. Instead, a certain maximum bit error rate has to be defined for which the communication is considered as successful. For this particular bit error rate, a certain Carrier-to-Interference ratio (C/I) can be specified at which the receiver must receive the signal to decode it with the given maximum bit error rate (BER). The transmission range is important concerning the power control. It is useless to increase the transmit power of the sender arbitrarily in order to improve the signal quality at the receiver because some residual bit error rate always remains as mentioned above. Instead, a maximum bit error rate (BER) can be specified which should be achieved to consider the connection as being good. A numeric value can for example be 10^{-4}. To achieve this value, a minimum C/I is needed which is dependent on the used PHY mode. An example for the dependence of the BER on the C/I is shown in fig. 3.1. In this figure, the BER is shown as a function of the S/N (signal to noise ratio). The function which describes the dependency between the C/I and the resulting BER can be determined analytically for simple modulation schemes [95], otherwise it is determined by simulations.

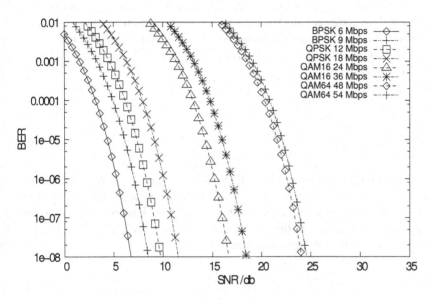

Figure 3.1: BER as a function of the C/I for different modulation schemes [96]

The *carrier sense range* r_c is the range of a transmitting station inside which other stations sense the channel as busy while the transmission is going on. Hence, the carrier sense range is vital for considerations about the capacity of a wireless LAN since a transmitting station prevents all stations inside its carrier sense range from transmitting simultaneously. The negative effect on the performance can be illustrated by the following example: A station transmits data to a station which is only a few meters away and has a line-of-sight connection. For successful communication, a low transmit power is sufficient. Any additional amount of transmit power does not improve the communication, but just increases the carrier sense range and the interference to neighbouring stations.

According to the IEEE 802.11 standard, the carrier is considered as busy by another IEEE 802.11 compliant station if a signal with a level higher than a given threshold is detected. If an 802.11 compliant preamble is detected in addition, it is assumed that the signal is sent by another 802.11 compliant station [50]; the

threshold for a busy carrier is for this reason specified by a relatively low value of
$-82\,\mathrm{dBm}$. If no valid preamble was detected, the signal is considered as interference, the threshold for a busy carrier is therefore higher, namely $-62\,\mathrm{dBm}$.

A simple model called *log-distance path loss model* [112] for the carrier sense
range of a station assumes omnidirectional antenna characteristics and omnidirectional signal propagation. The antenna is considered as the centre of a sphere
with the radius r. The transmitted power P_T is distributed over a spherical surface
$A = 4\pi r^2$ at the distance r from the transmitting station. The received power P_R
can then be written as

$$P_\mathrm{R} = \frac{P_\mathrm{T}}{Gr^2} \tag{3.2}$$

where

$$G = \frac{1}{(c/4\pi f)^2}. \tag{3.3}$$

The equation for G shows that the ratio between P_R and P_T is dependent on the
carrier frequency f. The attenuation increases when f becomes higher. The expo-
nent of 2 for r refers to the ideal case which only considers the attenuation due
to geometric conditions. In the general case, the power by which r is taken is a
variable referred to as the attenuation factor γ:

$$P_\mathrm{R} = \frac{P_\mathrm{T}}{Gr^\gamma}. \tag{3.4}$$

The reason to introduce γ is that the signal suffers from additional attenuation of
the RF due to obstacles, where parts of the signal can be absorbed, reflected or
refracted. In case of absorption, the absorbed signal power is transformed to heat.
The effect of reflection and refraction is that different components of the signal
travel along different paths, which is termed as *multipath propagation*. Due to
varying path lengths, two or more signal components superimpose with each other
which can result in constructive or destructive interference. This problem appears
in particular in indoor environments, where the signal is affected basically by the
walls of the building. This additional signal attenuation is considered by assuming
a mean statistical value which is approximated by γ.

To give a numeric example, for $P_\mathrm{T} = 50\,\mathrm{mW}$ and a receiver sensitivity of
$-82\,\mathrm{dBm}$, the resulting carrier sense range is $r_s = 31\,\mathrm{m}$.

The *interference range* r_i specifies inside which range a station can interfere
ongoing transmissions. r_i is not only dependent on the transmitting station, but
also on the receiving station and its communication partner. Both the absolute
value and the C/I of a received signal are important for the consideration if the

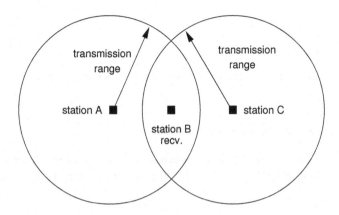

Figure 3.2: Hidden station problem

signal has been successfully received or not. Interference which superimposes the received goodput signal reduces the C/I.

An example is illustrated in fig. 3.2. Station B receives a goodput signal by station A and is at the same time interfered by station C. If the signal from C is increased by a certain factor, the interference may be increased by the same factor to keep the resulting C/I at station B.

3.2.1 Throughput

In this chapter, a theoretical approach to calculate the capacity of wireless LANs is given. First, a simple case with two stations and unidirectional data flow is considered. After that, the capacity is calculated for the general case with n stations. In the last part of the section, it is considered how power control affects the network capacity.

3.2.1.1 Network with Two Stations

In the simple case, there are two stations, one sending data packets and the other one responding to these data packets with acknowledgements. In this case, no collision can occur since the second station only responds to the first one and does not send data packets on its own. To calculate the available throughput, the transmission phases according to the DCF scheme are considered. The sequence for the transmission of a packet was illustrated in chapter 2:

1. DIFS,

2. random backoff,

3. transmission of the data packet with size D which requires the time t_{data},

4. SIFS,

5. transmission of acknowledgement needing t_{ACK}.

The maximum throughput S which can be achieved with this setup is determined by summing up the delays for the different phases of the transmission:

$$S = \frac{D}{t_{\text{DIFS}} + t_{\text{backoff}} + t_{\text{data}} + t_{\text{SIFS}} + t_{\text{ACK}}}. \tag{3.5}$$

D is the amount of payload contained in the packet, t_{DIFS} and t_{SIFS} are the time for a DIFS and SIFS, respectively. The particular values are dependent on the physical layer characteristics and hence differ in the various 802.11 PHY extensions. For 802.11a, they are specified with $t_{\text{DIFS}} = 34\,\mu\text{s}$ and $t_{\text{SIFS}} = 16\,\mu\text{s}$. t_{data} includes two parts: t_{header} and t_{payload}. t_{header} is fixed and includes the time for the PHY and the MAC header. t_{payload} depends on the amount of data to be transferred (1 to 2312 bytes) and the PHY mode (6 to 54 Mbit/s). t_{backoff} is $n \cdot \sigma$, where n is a random number of contention time slots and σ is the length of a contention window time slot. The value σ is fixed and given by the standard. n is randomly selected according to a uniform distribution within the contention window size W: $0 \leq n \leq W$. To calculate the throughput, a large number of packet transmissions has to be considered, thus the average value of n is taken for the calculation, which is $n = \frac{W}{2}$. Since there are no collisions and considering an ideal channel without packet loss, there are no retransmissions of data packets. Thus the minimum contention window size $W = W_{\text{min}}$ applies which is given by the 802.11 standard. The average backoff time then is:

$$t_{\text{backoff}} = n\sigma = \frac{W}{2}\sigma. \tag{3.6}$$

With D being the user payload of one packet, Eqn. 3.5 then becomes:

$$S = \frac{D}{t_{\text{DIFS}} + \frac{W}{2}\sigma + t_{\text{data}} + t_{\text{SIFS}} + t_{\text{ack}}}. \tag{3.7}$$

For 802.11, the standard specifies:

- $W_{\text{min}} = 15$,

- $\sigma = 9\,\mu s$,

- $t_{SIFS} = 16\,\mu s$,

- $t_{DIFS} = t_{SIFS} + 2\,\sigma = 34\,\mu s$,

- user payload size: max. 2314 bytes,

- physical bit rate: 6 to 54 Mbit/s (IEEE 802.11a/g).

3.2.1.2 General Case: Network with n Stations

In the general case with n transmitting stations, collisions have to be considered. An analytical consideration of this problem has been presented by BIANCHI in [8] and is summarised here.

The aim of the calculation is to deduce the capacity of a wireless LAN, which is in this case the total throughput of all stations inside a scenario. The deduction of the capacity is done in two steps: first, the probability τ is calculated with which a station starts transmitting in a particular time slot of the contention window. After that, the per-connection throughput is determined as a function of τ.

The basic problem of specifying τ is that the process of accessing a time slot in the contention window is not Markovian because the transmissions of different stations are not independent. If a station starts sending, then the backoff timers of the other stations are stopped and continued once the transmission of the currently sending station is over. If a collision occurs, the station will select another backoff window size which once again affects the transmit probability.

The assumption which is taken to allow the modelling of a Markovian system is to consider the average value of τ over a long period of time, meaning the stationary probability. With this constant τ, the transmit events become statistically independent of each other so that the system can be modeled with a Markov chain which includes two statistical processes: On the one hand, a station decrements the backoff counter $b(t)$ during the ongoing backoff process where $b(t)$ and $b(t+1)$ denote two consecutive time slots. On the other hand, for each backoff process, the system selects a certain contention window size $s(t)$, dependent on the number of retransmissions of a particular packet. The index t which identifies a particular size of the backoff window is called the *backoff stage* in this context. The state of the system can be described by a value pair $(b(t), s(t))$. The state changes along with the corresponding transition probabilities can be modeled by a two-dimensional Markov chain shown in fig. 3.3. Each horizontal line shows the states $b(i), s(k)$ for a certain backoff stage, where the system advances according to a descending index i from the right side of the diagram to the left side. In case of retransmissions, the system moves from the upper horizontal line in the figure to the horizontal lines below as the backoff stage k is increasing.

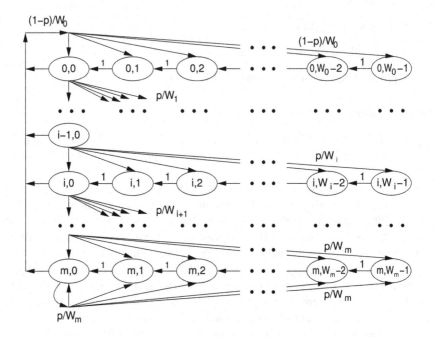

Figure 3.3: Markov chain to model the 802.11a backoff states [8]

It can be observed from the diagram that four types of transitions are possible. The first two apply to a successful (re)transmission, the last two for an unsuccessful one.

1. Inside a backoff stage, the backoff counter is decreased. This is equivalent to a transition to state k to the left-neighbouring state $k-1$ with a probability of 1.

2. After a packet has been successfully transmitted, the system will always return to the initial state, which means with a probability of 1, change to the lowest backoff stage $i=0$ for the transmission of the next packet. Inside the backoff stage, the starting value k_{start} for the backoff counter is randomly selected by a uniform distribution between 0 and W_i-1.

W is the contention window size. The index of W indicates the different sizes of the contention window dependent on the backoff stage. Possible values for the index range from 0 for the first attempt to send a packet and the backoff window has the minimum size up to the mth attempt when the maximum contention window size has been reached.

3. After an unsuccessful transmission, the system will switch to the next higher backoff stage $k+1$, provided that the highest stage has not yet been reached. The probability to select the starting state is determined in the same way as for case 2.

4. If the system is in the highest backoff stage and another retransmission is needed, the system will re-enter this highest stage again. The starting state inside the backoff stage is determined as in case 2.

The transitions which above have been described in words can be formally expressed as follows:

$$
\begin{aligned}
&1. \ p^*\{i,k|i,k+1\} = 1 && k \in (0, W_i - 2) && i \in (0, m) \\
&2. \ p^*\{0,k|i,0\} = (1-p)/W_0 && k \in (0, W_0 - 1) && i \in (0, m) \\
&3. \ p^*\{i,k|i-1,0\} = p/W_i && k \in (0, W_i - 1) && i \in (0, m) \\
&4. \ p^*\{m,k|m,0\} = p/W_m.
\end{aligned}
\tag{3.8}
$$

For further calculations, the stationary distribution $b_{i,k}$ is defined which describes the probability that the system will enter the kth time slot in the ith backoff stage measured over a large number of events:

$$
b_{i,k} = \lim_{t \to \infty} p^*\{b(t) = i, s(t) = k\}, i \in (0, m), k \in (0, W_{i-1}). \tag{3.9}
$$

The following two equations describe the stationary probabilities for the change between the backoff stages.

If the system is in backoff stage $i-1$ and the backoff counter has expired ($k=0$), the transmission of the packet will be started. With a probability p, the packet will collide so that the system enters the next higher backoff stage i. In this higher backoff stage, it counts down the backoff until $k=0$ is reached:

$$
b_{i-1,0} \cdot p = b_{i,0}, \quad 0 < i < m. \tag{3.10}
$$

From this recursive expression, $b_{i,0}$ can be written as a function of $b_{0,0}$:

$$
b_{i,0} = p^i b_{0,0}. \tag{3.11}
$$

When the system enters the highest backoff stage m, there are two ways to do so. It can enter from the lower backoff stage m - 1, which was considered in eqn. 3.10, or it can re-enter from the highest backoff stage, since there is no higher backoff stage available:

$$b_{m-1,0} \cdot p = (1 - p)b_{m,0} \rightarrow b_{m,0} = \frac{p^m}{1-p}b_{0,0}. \tag{3.12}$$

Furthermore, with the probability that there is no collision 1 - p, the system returns to the lowest backoff state $b_{0,0}$ from any other state $b_{i,0}$:

$$\sum_{i=0}^{m} b_{i,0} = \frac{b_{0,0}}{1 - p}. \tag{3.13}$$

The following equations describe the stationary probabilities for the individual backoff counter settings inside each backoff stage: The part $\frac{W_i-k}{W_i}$ is the probability that the system will run into a particular state $b_{i,k}$ conditioned by the fact that the backoff stage was changed. The parts of the equation right to the curly brace are the probabilities that a particular backoff stage is entered. They mean in particular:

- $i = 0$: the lowest backoff stage 0 is entered from any backoff stage (including itself) with the probability of a successful transmission $1 - p$.

- $i < 1 < m$: a backoff stage i between the lowest and the highest one is entered with the collision probability p from the stage $i - 1$ below it.

- $i = m$: The highest backoff stage m is entered either from the backoff stage $m - 1$ below it or from itself, each with the collision probability p.

$$b_{i,k} = \frac{W_i - k}{W_i} \cdot \left\{ \begin{array}{ll} 1 - p & i = 0 \\ p \cdot b_{i-1,0} & 0 < i < m \\ p \cdot (b_{m-1,0} + b_{m,0}) & i = m \end{array} \right. \tag{3.14}$$

From 3.12, 3.13 and 3.14, there yields:

$$b_{i,k} = \frac{W_i - k}{W_i}b_{i,0} \quad i \in (0, m) \quad k \in (0, W_i - 1) \tag{3.15}$$

The sum of all stationary probabilities $b_{i,j}$ must be 1:

$$1 = \sum_{i=0}^{m} \sum_{k=0}^{W_i-1} b_{i,k} = \sum_{i=0}^{m} b_{i,0} \sum_{k=0}^{W_i-1} \frac{W_i - k}{W_i} = \sum_{i=0}^{m} b_{i,0} \frac{W_i + 1}{2} \tag{3.16}$$

This sum can be transformed into a closed expression which gives $b_{0,0}$ as a function of W and p:

$$b_{0,0} = \frac{2(1-2p)(1-p)}{(1-2p)(W+1) + pW(1-(2p)^\tau)} \quad (3.17)$$

The steady state transmit probability τ is the sum of all probabilities that the backoff counter has decreased to 0 inside a backoff stage and the station is ready to start the transmission.

$$\tau = \sum_{i=0}^{m} b_{i,0} \quad (3.18)$$

This can be written as

$$\tau = \frac{b_{0,0}}{1-p} \quad (3.19)$$

and with eqn. 3.17 as

$$\tau = \frac{2(1-2p)}{(1-2p)(W+1) + pW(1-(2p)^m)} \quad (3.20)$$

This equation contains the probability p for a collision which can be calculated by considering the fact that a collision occurs if at least two stations are transmitting simultaneously. Since τ is the probability that a particular station is transmitting, $1-\tau$ is the probability that this particular station is not transmitting. $(1-\tau)^{n-1}$ is the probability that $n-1$ stations are not transmitting, hence

$$p = 1 - (1-\tau)^{n-1} \quad (3.21)$$

is the probability that two or more stations are transmitting.

Equations 3.20 and 3.21 form a nonlinear equation system in τ and p which must be solved by numerical methods. Figure 3.4 gives the values of the function for the minimum contention window size $W_{min} = 16$ and the maximum backoff stage $m = 7$ as specified in the IEEE 802.11 standard. For increasing number of stations, τ converges against 0 while p converges against 1. This means it gets less likely with more stations that a particular station transmits, however the probability for a collision increases.

In the special case that the contention window size W is constant, which means it is not increased in case of a failed transmission, it is shown in [43]:

$$\tau = \frac{2}{W+1}. \quad (3.22)$$

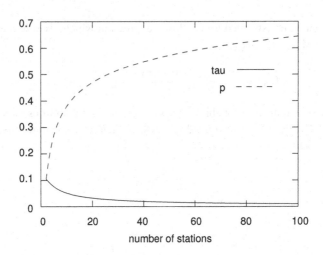

Figure 3.4: τ and p for $W_{\min} = 16$ and $m = 7$

In the next step, the probability p_{tr} is calculated that one of n stations transmits in a particular time slot. With a probability of τ, a particular station transmits in a certain time slot, with a probability of $1 - \tau$ it does not do so and with a probability $(1 - \tau)^n$ none of the n stations transmit in a certain time slot. With

$$p_{\text{tr}} = 1 - (1 - \tau)^n \qquad (3.23)$$

at least one station transmits.

From p_{tr}, the conditional probability p_{s} can be calculated that one of the n stations inside the scenario transmits successfully. With $\tau(1 - \tau)^{n-1}$, exactly one particular station transmits. With $p_n = n\tau(1 - \tau)^{n-1}$, one arbitrary station out of n stations transmits. The conditional probability p_{s} related to p_{tr} is

$$
\begin{aligned}
p_{\text{s}} &= p\{\text{one station transmits} \mid \text{at least one station transmits}\} \\
&= \frac{p_n}{p_{\text{tr}}} = \frac{n\tau(1 - \tau)^{n-1}}{1 - (1 - \tau)^n}.
\end{aligned}
\qquad (3.24)
$$

With the achieved values, the relative throughput S can now be calculated. Considering a time interval T inside which the payload D is transmitted, S is defined as:

$$S = \frac{E[D]}{E[T]}.$$

S can now be written as:

$$S = \frac{p_s p_{tr} E[D]}{(1 - p_{tr})\sigma + p_{tr} p_s T_s + p_{tr}(1 - p_s)T_c}. \tag{3.25}$$

D is the payload size measured in bits. $E[D]$ considers traffic with variable packet size so that an expected value is determined. In case of constant packet size, there is $E[D] = D$. T_s is the time needed for a successful transmission, T_c is the time which elapses if a collision occurs.

The three terms of the sum in the denominator have to be interpreted as follows: $(1 - p_{tr})\sigma$ applies for the case that the stations are waiting until their contention window expires and none of the stations is transmitting. The probability that no station transmits is $1 - p_{tr}$, they wait for a time slot with the duration σ. The second element of the sum considers the case of a successful transmission which requires the time T_s, including the transmission of the user data, SIFS, acknowledgement and the following DIFS. A transmission takes place with the probability p_{tr}, weighted with the conditional probability p_s that the transmission was successful. The last element of the sum is related to the case of an unsuccessful transmission due to a collision. The time T_c elapsing in case of a collision includes the data packet and the following EIFS. A collision takes place with the probability p_{tr}, weighted with the conditional probability $(1 - p_s)$ for an unsuccessful transmission.

The formula is independent of the particular DCF scheme which is used, i. e. without or with RTS/CTS. The usage of RTS/CTS affects the values for T_s and T_c, which have to be set according to the DCF scheme considered.

For the basic operation without RTS/CTS, T_s and T_c are:

$$\begin{aligned} T_s &= t_{\text{DIFS}} + t_{\text{H}} + E[t_{\text{D}}] + t_{\text{SIFS}} + t_{\text{ACK}} \\ T_c &= t_{\text{H}} + E[t_{\text{D*}}] + t_{\text{DIFS}}. \end{aligned} \tag{3.26}$$

t_{H} is the transmission duration of the user data packet header. The time needed to transmit the user payload of a packet is denoted as t_{D} in case of a successfully transmitted packet with payload size D, respectively $t_{\text{D*}}$ for a collided packet. In the special case of constant size, there is $E[t_{\text{D}}] = E[t_{\text{D*}}] = t_{\text{D}}$. In the general case, the probability density function $F(D)$ for the packet size has to be considered. There are n stations, out of which k transmit simultaneously. From the k

collided packets, the one with the maximum length $\max(D_1, \ldots, D_k)$ has to be considered. After a collision, the channel becomes free after the transmission of the longest packet is finished, which means it is busy with the collision according to the transmission time of the longest packet. For a randomly distributed value of D, the expected value is:

$$\frac{\sum_{k=2}^{n} \binom{n}{k} \tau^k (1-\tau)^{n-k} \int_0^{D_{\max}} (1 - F(D)^k) dD}{1 - (1-\tau)^n - n\tau(1-\tau)^{n-1}}. \tag{3.27}$$

The probability for 3 or more colliding packets can be neglected because it is small compared with the probability for 2 collided packets, then $E[D]$ can be written as:

$$\int_0^{D_{\max}} (1 - F(D)^k) dD \tag{3.28}$$

with $D_{\max}$ being the maximum payload size. It can now be shown that eqn. 3.25 given for the general case of the throughput becomes eqn. 3.5 if there is only one transmitting station and thus no collision can occur. Considering again 3.25:

$$S = \frac{p_s p_{tr} E[D]}{(1 - p_{tr})\sigma + p_{tr} p_s T_s + p_{tr}(1 - p_s) T_c}$$

In the collision free case and assuming there is no packet loss due to bad channel conditions, the probability p_s for a successful transmission is always 1. Furthermore, if constant packet size is assumed, there is $E[D] = D$. S is then calculated as:

$$S = \frac{p_{tr} \cdot D}{(1 - p_{tr})\sigma + p_{tr} T_s} = \frac{D}{(1/p_{tr} - 1)\sigma + T_s} \tag{3.29}$$

According to eqn. 3.23, the probability for a transmission in a certain time slot is $p_{tr} = 1 - (1 - \tau)^n$ where n is the number of transmitting stations. With $n = 1$, there is $p_{tr} = \tau = 2/(W + 1)$ according to 3.22. W is the contention window size which is always set to the minimum W_0 because the transmissions are always successful. From this there yields:

$$S = \frac{D}{(W_0 - 1)/2 \cdot \sigma + T_s} \tag{3.30}$$

which was deduced earlier for the collision-free case.

In the case of RTS/CTS, the additional time taken by the RTS/CTS handshake has to be considered:

$$T_{s,\mathrm{RTS}} = t_{\mathrm{RTS}} + t_{\mathrm{SIFS}} + \delta + t_{\mathrm{CTS}} + t_{\mathrm{SIFS}} + \delta + t_{\mathrm{H}}$$
$$+ E[D] + t_{\mathrm{SIFS}} + \delta + t_{\mathrm{ACK}} + t_{\mathrm{DIFS}} + \delta, \tag{3.31}$$

$$T_{c,\mathrm{RTS}} = t_{\mathrm{RTS}} + t_{\mathrm{DIFS}} + \delta. \tag{3.32}$$

δ is the propagation delay of the signal between the sender and the receiver.

3.2.2 Delay in Case of Ideal Channel

In a paper by CARVALHO and GARCIA-LUNA-ACEVES [14], the average delay inside a single-hop 802.11 network is deducted, again assuming a lossless channel. This means there are three mutual exclusive events, which means an idle channel, a successful transmission of exactly one station and a collision. A backoff process is considered where a station has selected a waiting period of n time slots. For each slot, there is a probability p_s for a successful transmission, p_i for an idle channel and p_c for a collision. There is $p_i + p_s + p_c = 1$. Inside the waiting period of n slots, r_i, r_s and r_c are the number of slots where the channel is idle, where a successful transmission occurs and where a collision occurs, respectively. There are, respectively, $r_i!$, $r_c!$ and $r_c!$ possibilities to group r_i, r_s, r_c into the n time slots. For a given combination of r_i, r_s, r_c events, the probabilities p_i, p_s, p_c have to be raised by the respective powers r_i, r_s, r_c. The probability for the event occurrence r_i, r_s, r_c is then expressed by the multinomial probability distribution

$$p(r_i, r_s, r_c | n, p_i, p_s, p_c) = \frac{n_k}{r_i! r_c! r_s!} p_i^{r_i} p_c^{r_c} p_s^{r_s}. \tag{3.33}$$

The paper then shows that the average time a node spends in a backoff period with n timeslots is

$$T_B(n) = n(\sigma p_i + t_c p_c + t_s p_s). \tag{3.34}$$

The average number of backoff steps drawn by the (uniformly distributed) random generator is $n = (W-1)/2$, the average waiting time for constant backoff window size W hence is

$$T_B(n) = (W - 1)(\sigma p_i + t_c p_c + t_s p_s)/2. \tag{3.35}$$

Due to collisions, it can happen that a packet has to be retransmitted. In case of a stationary collision probability p, the probability for a successful transmission can be written as $q = 1 - p$. In case of a constant backoff window size W, the average total backoff time which includes all times due to retransmission is

$$T_{\text{B}} = \frac{\alpha(W-1)}{2q} + \frac{1-q}{q}t_{\text{c}} \qquad (3.36)$$

with

$$\alpha = \sigma p_{\text{i}} + t_{\text{c}}p_{\text{c}} + t_{\text{s}}p_{\text{s}}. \qquad (3.37)$$

In case of an exponential backoff with minimum contention window size W_{min} and m backoff stages, the average backoff time is

$$T_{\text{B}} = \frac{\alpha(W_{\text{min}}\beta - 1)}{2q} + \frac{(1-q)}{q}t_{\text{c}}, \qquad (3.38)$$

$$\beta = \frac{q - 2^m(1-q)^{m+1}}{1 - 2(1-q)}. \qquad (3.39)$$

q is the probability for a successful transmission within a certain backoff stage i, which is assumed to be independent of the particular value of i. The average service time is then

$$T = T_{\text{B}} + t_{\text{s}} \qquad (3.40)$$

where t_{s} is the time for a successful packet transmission.

3.3 Performance in Case of Limited Transmission Ranges

In the previous sections, investigations about the throughput S and the delay of a wireless network in an ideal channel case with unlimited transmission range of the stations were shown, which means that the carrier sense and interference ranges are unlimited as well. In this analysis, the models for the ideal channel are extended to a more realistic channel with limited range.

The assumption of the ideal channel model which was used for the previously discussed calculations was that there are no range limitations; any station can communicate with any other station inside the scenario regardless of the distance between them. Whenever a station is transmitting, all other stations stop their backoff process or they collide with the transmitting station, dependent on the situation. In case of a collision, the signals of the colliding stations are lost. This model assumes that the attenuation factor γ of the frequency channel is zero. In real systems, the factor γ cannot be smaller than 2 due to the isotropic radiation of the signal which distributes the radiated power on a spherical surface. In practice, the factor is assumed to be higher to consider the attenuation due to obstacles or multipath propagation. Due to these limited ranges which includes limited carrier sense ranges, not all stations inside a scenario necessarily have knowledge about the transmissions of neighbouring stations. Since the CCA is not triggered in this case, there can be transmissions which are overlapping in the time domain. Dependent on the interference range of the transmitting stations and the positions of the receiving stations, these transmissions can be successful. Even if the transmitting stations are inside each other's carrier sense range, they can perform a simultaneous transmission without colliding, which means, the receivers can successfully decode the signal. This is again dependent on the position of the respective stations. This shows that in the case of limited range, a general analytical expression which is only dependent on the number of stations n and the transmission probability τ can no longer be given. Instead, the positions of the stations and the resulting distances must be considered. This means that an analytic expression has to be individually developed for a given scenario, which is done in this section for a number of examples.

3.3.1 Concurrent Transmissions

A simple example arrangement of two networks with two stations each is shown in figure 3.5. The stations are located in a square with the edge length $a = b$. The absolute value of a is not important for this scenario. The same applies for the absolute value of the transmit power, it just has to be high enough so that the signal level at the receiver is at least $-82\,\mathrm{dBm}$. It is assumed that all stations transmit with the same power and the lowest PHY mode of 6 Mbit/s which is specified by IEEE 802.11a. It is now assumed that stations 1 and 3 transmit simultaneously. In case of an unlimited range of the stations, $\gamma = 0$, this would mean a collision and packet loss for both stations. In case of limited range, $\gamma > 0$, the situation is different as the following calculation shows: the distance from station 1 to 2 is a, the distance from station 3 to 2 and resp. 1 to 4 is $\sqrt{2}a$. At station 2, the ratio of the signal powers from station 1 P_{R1} and station 3 P_{R3} is

$$\frac{P_{R1}}{P_{R3}} = \frac{\frac{P_T}{A \cdot a^\gamma}}{\frac{P_T}{A \cdot \sqrt{2}a^\gamma}} = 2^{\frac{\gamma}{2}}. \tag{3.41}$$

For $\gamma = 3.5$, this yields a C/I of $3.364 = 5.27\,\mathrm{dB}$ at station 2. For a 1500 byte data packet, this means a packet loss probability of approx. 2%. This means that despite of the simultaneous transmission, there is a high probability that both packets can

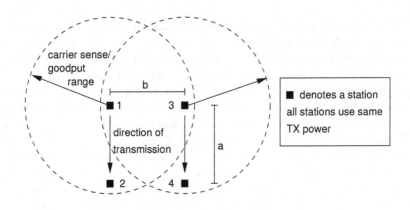

Figure 3.5: Simple scenario with simultaneous transmission

nevertheless be successfully received, so there is no collision. For any higher modulation scheme, there would be a collision, because the C/I at the receivers is too low. However, the C/I increases if γ is increased: $2^{\frac{\gamma}{2}}$ is an exponential function of γ whose base 2 is greater than 1, which means the function is strictly increasing. For $\gamma = 5$, the C/I is $5.659 = 7.53\,\mathrm{dB}$, which yields a packet error rate of about 20% for the second lowest PHY mode of 9 Mbit/s, so still a fair amount of packets can be transmitted.

If the stations are arranged in a rectangle with $b > a$, the C/I at the receivers increases. Eqn. 3.41 is then modified as

$$\frac{P_{\mathrm{R1}}}{P_{\mathrm{R3}}} = \frac{\frac{P_{\mathrm{T}}}{A \cdot a^{\gamma}}}{\frac{P_{\mathrm{T}}}{A \cdot (\sqrt{a^2+b^2})^{\gamma}}} = \left(1 + \frac{b^2}{a^2}\right)^{\frac{\gamma}{2}}. \tag{3.42}$$

The expression right to the equality sign is strictly monotonic increasing when considered as a function of b/a. Increasing b means that the distance between the neighbouring networks is increased so that the interference is reduced.

It is now calculated how the effect of simultaneous transmissions increases the throughput of the total system. In case of unlimited range resp. a lossless channel, the throughput can be calculated according to eqn. 3.25 for $n = 4$. Furthermore, for simplicity of the following calculation, a constant backoff window size is assumed. For constant backoff window size, the throughput can then be calculated out of eqn. 3.20, 3.21 and 3.25. In case of an exponentially increasing backoff window size, the value τ can be taken from fig. 3.4.

When the model is extended to consider the effects of the limited range, eqn. 3.20 remains unchanged because τ is only dependent on the contention window size. Eqn. 3.21 also does not change: In the model with unlimited range, p denotes the collision probability. Even though in the model with limited range there are no collisions in certain cases, eqn. 3.21 gives the probability that two stations transmit simultaneously, which might or might not result in a collision. Eqn. 3.23 gives the probability that at least one station transmits. This equation is used to calculate the conditional probability of a successful transmission. For the limited-range model, a similar equation is introduced which gives the probability that at least two stations transmit at the same time. This probability $p_{\mathrm{tr}2}$ is

$$p_{\mathrm{tr}2} = 1 - (1 - \tau)^n - n(1 - \tau)^{n-1}. \tag{3.43}$$

Expressed in words, eqn. 3.43 means that from 1, the probability that no station transmits and the probability that exactly one station transmits is subtracted.

In the same way like in the ideal-channel model, the probability $p_{\mathrm{s}2}$ is calculated that the simultaneous transmission of two stations is successful. For the ideal-channel model, the transmission is successful if exactly one station transmits. For the limited-range model, a transmission is successful if exactly one station transmits or if two stations transmit with the boundary condition that not *any* pair of two stations may transmit, but only *particular* pairs of two stations. In the example above, the stations 1 and 3 can transmit simultaneously or the stations 2 and 4 can do so. In general, if there are n stations inside the scenario, out of which k stations can form a pair which is able to perform a successful simultaneous transmission, then there are $\binom{n}{k}$ possible pairs of stations. The probability for a successful transmission is

$$p_{\mathrm{s}1} = \binom{n}{k} \tau^k (1 - \tau)^{n-k}. \tag{3.44}$$

To determine the throughput S, eqn. 3.29 is rewritten. Instead of distinguishing the transmission probability p_{tr} and the conditional probability for a successful transmission p_s which is related to p_{tr}, the absolute probability p_1 is considered that exactly one out of n stations transmits successfully. Analogously, an absolute probability p_2 is defined that two stations perform a successful simultaneous transmission as well as a probability p_c for collisions. In case of an ideal channel with unlimited range, the probability of an idle wireless media then is $1 - p_1 - p_c$; in case of a network where a maximum of two stations can perform a successful transmission, the probability for the idle media is $1 - p_1 - p_2 - p_c$.

With these prerequisites, now the expression for the throughput S is rewritten. In the idealised case of unlimited range, when only one transmission at a time is possible, the equation is

$$S = \frac{p_1 D}{(1 - p_1 - p_c)\sigma + p_1 T_s + p_c T_c}. \tag{3.45}$$

In case of up to two simultaneously transmitting stations, the equation is with T_s, T_c as specified in 3.26:

$$S = \frac{p_1 D + 2p_2 D}{(1 - p_1 - p_2 - p_c)\sigma + (p_1 + p_2)T_s + p_c T_c}. \tag{3.46}$$

In case of up to m simultaneously transmitting stations, there is:

$$S = \frac{\sum_{i=1}^{m} i p_i D}{(1 - (\sum_{i=1}^{m} p_m) - p_c)\sigma + (\sum_{i=1}^{m} p_m)T_s + p_c T_c}. \tag{3.47}$$

The probabilities p_i for successful parallel transmissions of i stations have to be determined according to the given scenario. Out of all combinations of i stations inside a scenario, parallel transmissions might be possible only for a subset of combinations. Any combinations of stations which result in a collision increase the collision probability P_c. Since every successful transmission requires a sender and a receiver, m is always an even number, as shown in the previous example with four stations. Further examples how to calculate the probabilities for a given arrangement of stations are given in sections 3.3.2 and 3.3.3.

Delay Considerations

For the delay calculation, in the ideal channel model, there are three mutual exclusive events, which is idle channel, busy channel and collision. The extension for the limited range is similar as in the throughput consideration, which means that there is now a fourth possible event which is simultaneous transmission of two or more stations. For this reason, the probabilities $p_2, p_3, \ldots$ were introduced in the throughput calculation which give the probability for two, three, etc. concurrent transmissions. These probabilities can be applied as well for the delay calculation, in the way that occurrences that the collision probability p_c in the equations has to be reduced by $p_2, p_3, \ldots$. The multinomial probability distribution function needs to be extended by the probabilities of successful simultaneous transmissions and by the number of time slots inside which these simultaneous transmissions take place. The probability for a successful transmission p_s in the original calculation is substituted by the probabilities for $1, 2, \ldots$ simultaneous transmissions

$p_1, p_2, \ldots$ and by the number of time slots $r_1, r_2, \ldots$ inside which the respective transmissions take place.

$$p\{(r_\mathrm{i}, r_1, r_2, \ldots, r_\mathrm{c})|n, (p_\mathrm{i}, p_1, p_2, \ldots, p_\mathrm{c})\} = \frac{n_k}{r_\mathrm{i}! r_\mathrm{c}! r_1! r_2! \ldots} p_\mathrm{i}^{r_\mathrm{i}} p_\mathrm{c}^{r_\mathrm{c}} p_1^{r_1} p_2^{r_2} \ldots .$$

(3.48)

For calculating the time of simultaneous successful transmissions, it has to be considered that the time spent in collisions is reduced, because certain parallel transmissions which collide in case of unlimited range can be performed in a normal way if the range is limited. Hence the probability p_c which is a weighting factor for the collision time t_c is reduced by p_2, p_3 etc. On the other hand, the probabilities $p_2, p_3, \ldots$ are *not* added to p_s which is a weighting factor for the time for a successful transmission t_s, because for the parallel transmissions, no *additional* time is needed in comparison to the case of one single successful transmission. The probability for idle times does not change either: if in case of unlimited range the channel is idle, this does not change due to the limitation of the ranges since no transmission takes place.

Regarding these considerations, the average time spent in a backoff period with n time slots is

$$T_\mathrm{B}(n) = n(\sigma p_\mathrm{i} + t_\mathrm{c}(p_\mathrm{c} - p_2 - p_3 - \ldots) + t_s p_s)$$

(3.49)

where p_c is the conditional collision probability in case of unlimited range and $p_2, p_3, \ldots$ are the probabilities for the transmissions of $2, 3, \ldots$ stations. Analogously to eqn. 3.37, the term α is then calculated as

$$\alpha = \sigma p_\mathrm{i} + t_\mathrm{c}(p_\mathrm{c} - p_2 - p_3 - \ldots) + t_s p_s.$$

(3.50)

The second parameter which needs to be considered for the calculations is the conditional probability q for a successful transmission, which includes the probabilities for one, two or more transmissions dependent on the scenario. In case that only transmissions of a single station are considered, the probability is conditioned by the probability p_tr that at least one station transmits. In the considerations for parallel transmissions, the probabilities for simultaneous transmissions of two or more stations have to be considered as well. Since they have to be added as conditional probabilities, they are related to p_tr as well. q is then calculated as

$$q = \frac{p_1 + p_2 + \ldots}{p_\mathrm{tr}}.$$

(3.51)

3.3.2 Effect of the CCA Threshold

In the case of IEEE 802.11 WLAN, an additional effect has to be considered. The 802.11 standard requires a check of the preamble when the reception of a signal starts. If the preamble is detected, the received packet is considered as a valid OFDM-modulated 802.11 signal. In this case, the threshold value of the CCA is set to -82 dBm. If a signal is received for which no preamble is detected, the threshold value is set to -62 dBm. An example for this situation is discussed in figure 3.6. Three networks include two stations each with bidirectional data flow between the stations. It is assumed that the network in the middle is inside the carrier-sense range of both the left and the right network, whereas the left and the right network are not inside each other's carrier sense range. The CCA of the stations in the left and in the right network will then only be triggered by the stations in the middle network. This means that, given that the stations in the middle are not transmitting at a particular moment, stations in left and the right network can start transmitting simultaneously, which leads to a superposition of the signals at the receivers of the network in the middle. Since in this case the middle network cannot detect the preambles, it sets the CCA threshold to -62 dBm. In the given scenario, it hence will then start transmitting even if there are ongoing transmissions in the neighbouring networks. This can, in return, result in collisions with the networks on both sides.

For the given example, first the signal levels are calculated. The distance d between two neighbouring stations is 5 m. All stations transmit with a power of 50 mW. The stations 3 and 4 in the middle receive signals from the outer stations with -68.9 dBm and -76.4 dBm, which is both above the CCA threshold of -82 dBm. When both signals superimpose, this results at maximum in -65.9 dBm which is above the CCA threshold of -82 dBm, however it is below the CCA threshold for non-802.11 signals at -62 dBm.

The stations $(1,2)$ receive signals from the stations $(5,6)$ at max. -81.6 dBm and vice versa, so they are inside each other's CCA range. The throughput can now be calculated as follows:

Setting a constant backoff window size W, the probability p that a station transmits in the next time slot is again assumed to be independent of the number of stations. As described in the previous scenario, there is a probability p_{tr2} for the simultaneous transmission of two stations, where n is now 6. A successful simultaneous transmission occurs if the ratio of the distances between the two transmitting stations and the respective receiving stations is greater than the required signal-to-noise ratio. There are in total $\binom{6}{2} = 15$ possible pairs, out of which 12 are suitable for a simultaneous transmission, which means all except the three possible cases

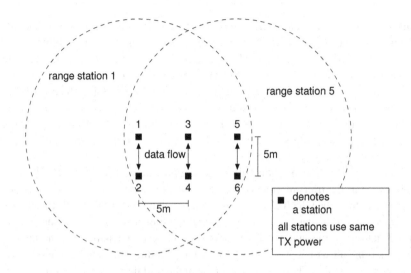

Figure 3.6: Scenario to demonstrate the variable CCA threshold effect

(1,2), (3,4) and (5,6). The probability p_{s2} for a successful simultaneous transmission can be determined as described above. However, if one station out of (1,2) and one station out of (5,6) is transmitting simultaneously, then the stations 3 and 4 do not detect this transmission. The reason is that the superimposing signals from stations (1,2) and (5,6) destroy each other's preamble, so the stations 3 and 4 increase the CCA threshold to $-62\,\mathrm{dBm}$. Since the signals from (1,2) and (5,6) are below $-62\,\mathrm{dBm}$ as shown above, the stations 3 and 4 can start a transmission while the stations (1,2) and (5,6) are transmitting so that in this case three transmissions take place at the same time without colliding. In a more general case where the distances between the stations vary, three transmissions are possible if the received signal between opposite stations (1,2), (3,4) and (5,6) is at least stronger than signals from other stations by a factor of the minimum C/I needed for a transmission with the lowest bit rate of 6 Mbit/s is possible.

To describe this effect analytically, the probability p_{1256} is calculated that for the station pairs (1,2) and (5,6), one station from each pair transmits simultaneously, conditioned with the probability p_{tr2} that two stations transmit which is already known. There are four out of 15 possibilities that this happens, described by the 2-tuples (1,5), (1,6), (2,5), (2,6), so $p_{1256} = \frac{4/15}{p_{tr2}}$. The probability $p_{1256}p_{tr2}$ must then be multiplied by the probability that a station (in this case 3 or 4) transmits within this time. From the view of the stations 3 and 4, there is a silence period with the length of a data packet which is equal to m time periods of a backoff slot time δ. Since the probability to transmit in one slot is τ, the probability p_{34} to start a transmission with these m slots is $p_{34} = 1 - (1 - \tau)^m$. Hence the absolute probability that the stations 3 or 4 transmit is $p_{1256}p_{tr2}p_{34}$.

The throughput S can now be calculated according to eqn. 3.47. The probability that two stations successfully transmit simultaneously is $p_2 = p_{1256}p_{tr2}$. For three stations, the probability is $p_3 = p_{1256}p_{tr2}p_{34}$. Considering the probability for the transmission of a single station $p_1 = \tau(1 - \tau)^5$, the collision probability p_c is $1 - p_1 - p_2 - p_3$.

For the parallel transmission with three stations, the station in the middle network can start the transmission at any time while the outer networks are transmitting. Hence the time which elapses to finish a parallel transmission of three stations is longer than in the cases for one or two parallel transmissions. When the signals of the stations in the outer two networks superimpose, the stations in the middle network transmit with a probability of τ. After each time slot δ, it is re-determined if a station transmits. There are two stations in the middle network; the probability that exactly one of them transmits after m tries is

$$p_m = (1 - \tau)^{2(m-1)} \cdot \tau(1 - \tau). \tag{3.52}$$

Neglecting the factor on the right, the left factor is a geometric distribution with the mean value $\mu = 1/\tau$. With known time slot length δ, the mean delay of the packet transmitted by the middle network can then be calculated. With $W = 16$, there is $\tau = 0.11$ and $\mu = 1/\tau = 9$. The length of a time slot is 9 μs, so the average delay is 90 μs. It can be seen that the delay is small compared with a packet length of 2 ms which is assumed in the considerations here (6 Mbit/s PHY mode and 1500 bytes = 12000 bit packet length).

3.3.3 Stations Outside Each Other's CCA Range

In the examples given up to now, all stations are inside each other's CCA range. Simultaneous transmissions hence can only occur if two or more stations start a transmission *at the same time*. In any other case, the channel is sensed busy by a station if another station transmits. In the following example, it is now assumed that the outer networks are outside each other's CCA range, see fig. 3.7. This figure is similar to fig. 3.6 with the difference that the range of the outer stations is smaller; only the stations in the middle are inside the range. This means their backoff counters are only stopped if the network (3,4) transmits, but not if the respective other outer network is doing so. Since the outer networks cannot hear each other, the probability that they transmit simultaneously P_{tr2} differs from the

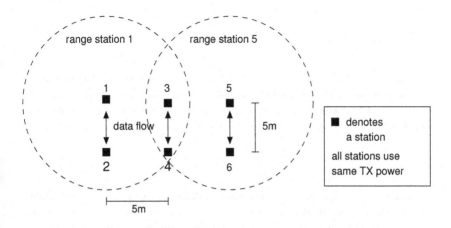

Figure 3.7: Example arrangement of stations to demonstrate minimum CCA threshold effect

previous cases, where a simultaneous transmission is only possible if both stations start transmitting in the same time slot.

Like in the previous examples, the calculation is done in the way that the probabilities for one, two or three simultaneous transmissions are determined, as well as the time which elapses for each of these transmissions. For p_1, it must be considered that the outer networks transmit independently. Each station always has a packet to transmit, so the probability that one of the outer networks transmits while the other one is doing so is

$$p_{12} = 1 - (1 - \tau)^{(D/\sigma)}, \qquad (3.53)$$

where D is the duration of a data packet and σ is the duration of a time slot in a backoff window. With $\sigma = 9\,\mu s$ and D being 1500 bytes = 12000 bit, there is $D = 2\,ms$ for the 6 Mbit/s PHY mode. p_{12} is almost 1, which means that the outer networks will always transmit simultaneously. This happens if one of the outer networks is transmitting, but not if the middle network transmits. Out of three possible networks which transmit, for two of them (the outer ones), there will be a simultaneous transmission of the other outer network. In this case, the double payload compared to a single transmission is transported. To calculate the payload in the enumerator of eqn. 3.47, this means that the probability for a single transmission is multiplied by 2/3 for 2 out of 3 possible networks and by a factor 2 for two parallel transmissions:

$$p_{\text{suc}} p_{\text{tr}} \left(1 + \frac{2}{3} \cdot 2 \right). \tag{3.54}$$

p_2 is determined considering the fact that there are eight possible pairs of stations which can successfully transmit at the same time: (1,3), (1,4), (2,3), (2,4), (3,5), (3,6), (4,5), (4,6); the parallel transmissions of the outer networks, which would be (1,5), (1,6), (2,5), (2,6), are already considered in the previous calculation. There is

$$p_2 = 8 \cdot \tau^2 (1 - \tau)^4. \tag{3.55}$$

The probability for three transmissions is calculated considering the simultaneous start of transmissions by the two outer networks. Only in this case, the preambles become unreadable from the view of the middle network so that is sets the CCA threshold to $-62\,\text{dBm}$. If the outer networks start at different times, the middle network detects the CCA and hence considers the channel as busy as long as any of the outer networks is transmitting. This situation suggests that the throughput of the middle network is lower than the one of the outer networks.

Similar to the previous case, the packet transmitted by the middle network overlaps with the packets transmitted by the outer networks. The average amount of time by which the packet is delayed is calculated in the same way that as the previous case where all networks are overlapping. As in the case described in section 3.3.2, all three transmissions can take place in parallel without colliding, provided that the C/I ratio is sufficient, which in case of variable distances depends on the locations of the stations.

This example and the one in the previous section shows that in certain scenarios, simultaneous transmissions are possible due to the limited range of the stations and the effect of the CCA. This means that the sum throughput is higher than in case of the idealised channel with unlimited range.

3.3.4 Hidden Stations

Up to now, effects were discussed where due to the limited range of a station, simultaneous transmissions become possible which means the performance was *increased*. On the other hand, there is an effect called the *hidden station problem* which was already discussed in chapter 2. In this case, the throughput is *reduced* in comparison to unlimited ranges. The problem occurs, as mentioned earlier, if two stations A and C are outside each other's carrier sense or CCA range, respectively. The difference to the problem described in the previous section where the

CCA range causes an increase of the throughput is that the arrangement of stations is different. The station B in the middle is inside the goodput range of A and C. Since A and C cannot hear each other, they can start transmissions at any time. In the hidden station problem, however, both outer stations have the same destination station so that a collision occurs. For the outer stations, the probability for a successful transmission is lower than in the case of unlimited range, because while one of these stations is transmitting, it can still occur that the other outer station starts transmitting as well. While one station is transmitting, the other one senses the channel as idle. The probability that a station transmits in a given idle time slot is τ. The probability that the second station transmits while the first one is currently transmitting is dependent on how many idle time slots of the second station with the length σ fit into the transmission duration t_{data} of the first station. τ is the transmission probability of a particular station inside a given time slot, so $(1 - \tau)^{\frac{t_{\text{data}}}{\sigma}}$ is the probability that the second station does not transmit during the $\lfloor \frac{t_{\text{data}}}{\sigma} \rfloor$ idle timeslots which elapse from its view while the first station is transmitting. The probability that it does transmit is then

$$p_c = 1 - (1 - \tau)^{\lfloor \frac{t_{\text{data}}}{\sigma} \rfloor}. \qquad (3.56)$$

The time for such an incident is the time for the transmission of two colliding and thus overlapping data packets without acknowledgement. Assuming constant packet size, in case of a collision the packets overlap in average by 50% of their length. For this reason, the average elapsed time in case of a collision is the time to transmit a single packet multiplied by 1.5. To this term, the probability for a collision between the middle station and one of the outer stations must be added, which is

$$p_{c2} = 2\tau^2(1 - \tau). \qquad (3.57)$$

The probability for a successful transmission of the middle station is

$$p_{s,m} = \tau(1 - \tau)^2. \qquad (3.58)$$

The probability for a successful transmission of the outer stations is conditioned on the fact that the other outer station does not start transmitting at the same time

$$p_{s,0} = \tau(1 - \tau)^{\frac{T_{\text{DATA}}}{\sigma}}. \qquad (3.59)$$

The throughput S is

$$S = \frac{(p_{s,m} + p_{s,0})D}{p_i\sigma + (p_{s,m} + p_{s,0})T_s + p_cT_c + 1.5p_{c2}T_{c2}}. \qquad (3.60)$$

A comparison of theoretical results determined according to the previous sections and simulated results is given in section 7.1.3.1.

3.4 Effects of Spectrum Management on the Capacity

In the previous section, it was discussed how the positioning of stations and the limited ranges affect the performance of a wireless network. With this knowledge, a closer look can now be taken at the effects of spectrum management on the capacity.

3.4.1 Power Control

A particular transmit power of a station results in certain goodput, carrier sense and interference ranges as discussed before. The application of power control results in the change of these ranges during an ongoing communication. For a particular network scenario, this can mean that the carrier sense range of stations is reduced. A station which sees less neighbours senses the channel as free more often, so it can transmit packets more frequently. However, the carrier sense range reduction can also result in the hidden station problem which did not exist before the power was reduced. Another effect can be that the interference level at a certain station which currently has the CCA threshold set to -62 dBm is reduced below this level so that the station considers the channel as free and may start a transmission. This results in the effects described in section 3.3.2. Therefore, analytic descriptions of throughput or delay enhancements achieved by power control have to be developed by considering the powers of the stations before the controlling process was started and after it was finished. For the situation before and after the control, it has to be checked how many neighbours the station sees and at what levels their signals are received. From this, the probabilities for successful transmissions of a single station, for successful simultaneous transmission, for collisions and for idle stations can then be calculated for each station. When these probabilities are known, the throughputs and delays for the stations can be calculated.

The question arises what the optimum power settings are. The algorithms discussed later are "blind" algorithms in the sense that they do not have knowledge about the positions of the stations; they have to estimate power settings based on interference measurements. When the station positions are known, the minimum powers are dependent on the particular scenario. If all stations are inside each other's CCA range, no station starts transmitting if another one is already doing so because the channel is sensed busy (except for the collision case if both stations start transmitting simultaneously). In this case, interference is only caused by the receiver noise. The minimum required power at the transmitter is then the product of the receiver noise and the minimum C/I which the selected PHY mode needs for a successful transmission. The term *successful* can be defined as a maximum bit error rate which should not be exceeded, for example 0.001. In practice, an additional link margin is included to consider the time-variant characteristics of the channel, which are neglected in the idealised models presented here.

In the CCA scenario, there is an effect by power reduction if the received powers of interfering signals are reduced below $-62\,\text{dBm}$. Due to the principle of the CCA, this may allow a station to transmit which detects the channel as free if interfering signals overlay whose preamble cannot be detected. However, the station which is now transmitting in addition might prevent other stations from doing so or collide with them.

As it can be seen, there are a large number of interactions so that analytic considerations are difficult for large networks. The theoretical considerations can however be used to validate simulation results, which is done in chapter 7 for some examples.

3.4.2 Dynamic Frequency Selection

3.4.2.1 Effects on the Performance

The application of Dynamic Frequency Selection reduces the number of stations per channel. In this section, an analytic description is introduced to investigate the effect of DFS on the throughput which can be achieved by stations inside a scenario.

It is assumed that there are n stations inside a system with unlimited range which transmit on the same frequency channel at the beginning of a considered scenario. Using Dynamic Frequency Selection, in the ideal case they are distributed homogeneously over all m available frequency channels, meaning that after the DFS procedure has reached the final state, in each channel there are $\lfloor \frac{n}{m} \rfloor$ or $\lceil \frac{n}{m} \rceil$ stations. Due to the reduced number of stations, both the total throughput and the per-station throughput increase. To prove this fact analytically, eqn. 3.25 is again considered:

$$S = \frac{p_s p_{\text{tr}} E[D]}{(1 - p_{\text{tr}})\sigma p_{\text{tr}} p_s T_s + p_{\text{tr}}(1 - p_s)T_c}$$

This equation can be rewritten as:

$$S = \frac{D}{\frac{1}{p_s p_{\text{tr}}}\sigma + \frac{1}{p_s}(T_c - \sigma) + T_s - T_c} \tag{3.61}$$

To prove that the throughput S increases when the number of station decreases, the expressions $p_s p_{tr}$ and p_s are discussed; only these two expressions are a function of n. $p_s p_{tr}$ is the absolute probability for a successful transmission, which is

$$p_s p_{tr} = n\tau(1 - \tau)^{n-1}. \tag{3.62}$$

The derivative of this expression with respect to n is

$$\frac{dp_s p_{tr}}{dn} = \ln(1 - \tau)(1 - \tau)^{n-1}\tau n + (1 - \tau)^{n-1}\tau. \tag{3.63}$$

For large n, eqn. 3.63 becomes $\ln(1 - \tau)$ which is a negative value, because τ is a probability with $0 < \tau < 1$, so the argument of the ln function is smaller than 1. It can also be easily shown that the expression never becomes zero which means it is negative for all n so that eqn. 3.62 is strictly decreasing.

The other expression to discuss is the conditional probability for a successful transmission p_s which is

$$p_s = \frac{n\tau(1 - \tau)^{n-1}}{1 - (1 - \tau)^n}. \tag{3.64}$$

The enumerator of the fraction is equal to $p_s p_{tr}$, the derivative was given above in eqn. 3.63 and was shown to be negative, so the enumerator is strictly monotonic decreasing. The denominator $1 - (1 - \tau)^n$ is the probability p_{tr} that at least one station transmits. The derivative is

$$\frac{d}{dn}\left(1 - (1 - \tau)^n\right) = -\ln(1 - \tau)(1 - \tau)^n \tag{3.65}$$

which is always positive so that the denominator is strictly increasing. Hence the entire fraction in eqn. 3.64 is strictly decreasing.

Both expressions 3.62 and 3.24 are inside the denominator of the fractions $\frac{\sigma}{p_s p_{tr}}$ and $\frac{T_c - \sigma}{p_s}$, respectively. These two fractions are themselves inside the dominator of the fraction of eqn. 3.25. Since the expressions are strictly decreasing, the large fraction is strictly decreasing as well, which proves that S increases if n gets smaller.

The amount of increase can be calculated as follows: without DFS, there are n stations inside one network; after the stations have been distributed over m frequency channels, there are n_i stations on frequency channel i with $1 \leq i \leq m$. In the optimum case, n_i is either $\lceil \frac{n}{m} \rceil$ or $\lfloor \frac{n}{m} \rfloor$ as described earlier.

3.4.2.2 DFS Convergence Characteristics

Dynamic Frequency Selection means the change of the frequency channel if the currently used one is occupied by other WLAN stations or other types of radio applications. A scenario is considered where at the beginning n networks share the same frequency channel. During the ongoing DFS process, the networks should distribute over n available frequency channels so that finally each channel is occupied by exactly one network. In this section, an analytic description is given how fast the stations distribute over the frequency channels. In case of DFS algorithms which do not use a central instance which can coordinate the stations and distribute them uniformly over the channels, each network has to take a decision without negotiations with neighbouring networks according to interference measurements which were previously taken. Due to the lack of knowledge to which channels other networks will change, it can happen that more than one network switches to the same frequency channel even if the number of channels is equal to the number of networks. On the other hand, some of the available frequency channels might remain unused. In this case, the networks which are sharing their channels with other networks run the frequency selection algorithm again in order to change to another channel which is still free. In this way, it might be required that the algorithm is run several times until the final state has been reached. The problem under discussion here is how many runs are needed until each channel is occupied by exactly one network. In this work, an analytic method is developed to determine the number of turns which have to be executed by the frequency selection algorithm until each network found a channel of its own.

For the calculation, it is assumed that a network which shares the channel with another network will select one of the available free channels including the currently used one in a uniform random way. Once it has found a channel which is not used by another network, it remains on this channel. In this idealised scenario, the method how a network knows which channels are free or occupied is not considered; time needed for measuring channels and signalling is left out.

In the beginning of the algorithm, all networks are on the same channel, meaning they will all try to find an alternative one. After the first run, k out of n networks have found a channel of their own, while $n - k$ networks share the newly selected channel with at least one other network. In the most extreme case that all these $n - k$ networks select the same channel, $n - k - 1$ channels remain unused.

To illustrate the calculation, a small scenario with two networks is considered; there are two frequency channels available so that at the end of the allocation process each network has a frequency channel which is not occupied by another network. Each mapping between the stations and the channels is denoted by one

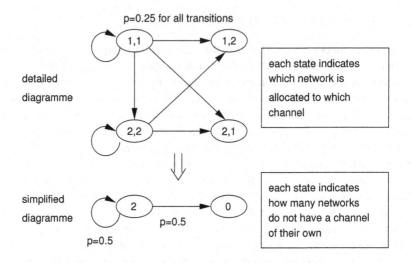

Figure 3.8: Diagram with channel allocations for a 2-network scenario

state in the upper diagram of figure 3.8. For two networks and two different channels, which each network can select, there are four states. The random generator of each network has Laplacian property which means that each channel is selected with the same probability $\frac{1}{2}$. The probability for a state transition is $p = \frac{1}{2} \cdot \frac{1}{2} = \frac{1}{4}$. The probability to get to one of the final states after one transition is $p_1 = \frac{1}{4} + \frac{1}{4}$, because there are two alternative paths to the states (1,2) and (2,1) as shown in the diagram. For traversals with two transitions, there are four possible options: the system can either remain in the current state (1,1) or move to the state (2,2). From either of these states, the system can move to one of the final states (1,2) or (2,1). The probability for two transitions is hence $P_2 = 4 \cdot \frac{1}{4} \cdot \frac{1}{4} = \frac{1}{4}$. In case of the probability of traversals with three transitions, the probability for one particular traversal is $\frac{1}{4} \cdot \frac{1}{4} \cdot \frac{1}{4}$; there are eight possible traversals, because for the first two transitions, there are the states (1,1) or (2,2) which can be selected; for the final transition, there are the states (1,2) and (2,1). The probability for three transitions is hence $8 \cdot \frac{1}{64} = \frac{1}{8}$. In general, in case of n transitions, there are n decisions to be taken to select a state. This means there are 2^n ways how to traverse the state diagram. The probability for n transitions is

$$p_n = 2^n \cdot \frac{1}{4^n} = \frac{1}{2^n}. \tag{3.66}$$

The state diagram as it is considered up to now defines one state for each possible channel combination. For the analysis of the system it is, however, not important which networks allocate which channel. It is sufficient to know how many networks have not yet found a free channel and thus still participate in the channel search process. For the system with 2 stations, the allocations (1,1) and (2,2) indicate that none of the networks has yet been assigned a free channel, which is equivalent to the state in which 2 networks are still searching for a channel. The allocations (1,2) and (2,1) indicate each station has found a free channel, which is equivalent that no station is left which is searching for a channel. In the diagram, this state only has an entry but no exits because the algorithm stops at this point. The situation that one network is left which is searching for a channel cannot occur. The reason is the assumption that the number of channels is equal to the number of stations. This means if there is one network left, then there is exactly one channel which can be occupied by this network. Based on these assumptions, a simplified diagram can then be drawn as shown in the lower part of fig. 3.8. Starting at state 2, there are two options: either the system remains in state 2 or it transits to state 0. The transition probabilities are calculated based on the detailed diagram in the upper part of the figure. Starting with (1,1), there is a probability of 0.25 that the system remains in state (1,1) and another 0.25 that the system changes to (2,2). Both of these states are mapped to state 2 in the simplified diagram, which means that with a probability of 0.5 the simplified system remains in the current state. The two other states are (1,2) and (2,1), meaning that there is no station left which searches a channel. In the simplified diagram, this is equivalent to state 0. In the detailed diagram, the system can transit from each of the states (1,1) and (2,2) to either of the states (1,2) or (2,1) with a probability of 0.25. In the simplified diagram, this means a transition probability of 0.5 from state 2 to state 0. This shows that in the simplified diagram, all transition probabilities are equal, which means 0.5.

In case of more than two networks, a closed expression for the transition probabilities becomes complex. For this reason, an algorithm is used to determine the transition probabilities in the general case. At the start of the algorithm, it is assumed that all networks occupy the same channel. If there are n networks resp. channels, each network decides with a probability $p = \frac{1}{n}$ to switch to a certain channel. A system of n networks hence selects a certain combination of channels with the probability $p = \frac{1}{n^n}$. For each of these combinations, it can be counted how many channels are occupied by only one network and how many stations are still searching a channel. In this way, similar to fig. 3.8, again a detailed state diagram can be drawn and mapped to a simplified state diagram. For three stations, there are 3^3 possible states in the detailed diagram, each station can select one out

detailed	simple	detailed	simple	detailed	simple
111	3	211	2	311	2
112	2	212	2	312	0
113	2	213	0	313	2
121	2	221	2	321	0
122	2	222	3	322	2
123	0	223	2	323	2
131	2	231	0	331	2
132	0	232	2	332	2
133	2	233	2	333	3

Table 3.1: Mapping between detailed and simplified diagram for 3 networks. The numbers in the column labelled "detailled" give the channel allocation for each of the three networks, the number in the "simple" column gives the number of stations which has not yet found a free channel.

of 3 channels. In the simplified diagram, there are 3 states (3 stations, 2 stations or no station is searching a free channel). The mapping between the states in the detailed diagram and the simplified diagram is shown in table 3.1.

The table shows there are 3 states with 3 networks which did not yet find a free channel, 18 states with 2 networks and 6 states with 0 networks. When displaying the possible states in a detailed diagram similar to the one in fig. 3.8, the transition probability between two states is constant; it is $p = 1/3^3$ because each of the three stations can select any of the three channels. The transition probabilities between the states in the simplified diagram are, however, not equal because each of them is equivalent to a different number of states in the detailed diagram. For this reason, the transition probabilities between states in the simplified diagram have to be determined by counting the number of corresponding transitions in the detailed diagram and multiplying the number by the probability for a transition in the detailed diagram.

Once a number of networks has found channels which are not occupied by other networks, the remaining number of networks which still searches a channel forms a smaller system with less states. If the scenario starts for example with 5 networks, out of which 2 find an unoccupied channel after the first step of the algorithm, these two networks no longer have to be considered in the next steps. The remaining system then can be treated as a system of 3 networks. Written in pseudocode, the algorithm works as follows:

n=no. of networks before a transition
k=no. of networks after a transition
calculate transition probabilities:
n_0 total number of networks inside the scenario at start of algorithm
for $n=2$ **to** n_0 **do**
    calculate probability for a transition inside the detailed diagram:
    $p \leftarrow 1/(n^n)$
    for all possible combinations of channels after the transition **do**
        determine number of stations k
        which do not yet have a channel of their own
        increase number of possible transitions a_k to state with k
        stations without a free channel (in simplified diagram)
        $a_k \leftarrow a_k + 1$
    end for
    for all possible k **do**
        calculate probability for a transition inside the simplified diagram:
        $p_{n,k} \leftarrow p \cdot a_k$
    end for
end for
Calculate probabilities:
μ_{NC}: expected value for number of networks which change
the channel within a traversal
for all possible traversals **do**
    $p_{trav} = 1$
    numChanges: number of networks which changed the channel inside one
    transition
    for all transitions inside the traversal **do**
        $p_{trav} \leftarrow p_{trav} \cdot P_{n,k}$
        numChanges $\leftarrow$ numChanges $+$ changes in current transition
    end for
    i=number of transitions
    $p_{sumtrav}[i] \leftarrow p_{sumtrav}[i] + p_{trav};$
    calculate expected value for number of networks
    $\mu_{NC} \leftarrow \mu_{NC} + p_{trav} \cdot$ numChanges
end for
Calculate expected value for number of transitions:
for all $p_{sumtrav}[i]$ **do**
    $\mu \leftarrow \mu + p_{sumtrav}[i] \cdot i$
end for

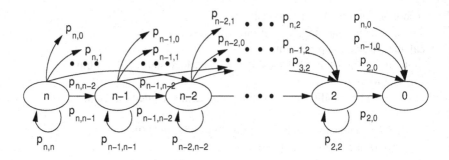

Figure 3.9: Markov chain for change of the allocated channels

The algorithm first computes all probabilities $p_{n,k}$ with which the system changes from a state with k unallocated channels resp. networks to a state with exactly k allocated channels. For fixed n, this yields a probability function with n as the input variable. After the calculation of the transition probabilities inside the simplified diagram, the algorithm calculates the probability for each possible traversal from state n to state 0 inside the simplified diagram. In the first step, the probability for a transition from n to $n - k$ unassigned channels is considered. In the next step, only the remaining $n - k$ channels have to be considered. For the probability calculation, one can assign $n_{(i+1)} \leftarrow n_{(i)} - k_{(i)}$, which means the value of $n - k$ of the previous calculation with the number i is renamed to n in the $(i + 1)$st calculation.

The procedure ends when all channels have been assigned exactly one network, which means $n_{(i)} = 0$, i.e. there are no unallocated networks left.

The transitions inside a traversal are illustrated in figure 3.9 by a Markov chain: The next state $n_{(i+1)}$ is only dependent on the previous state $n_{(i)}$ and the number of channels k which were assigned to a single network. The traversal starts on the left of the chain where $n = n_0$. A change of the states can only happen from left to right or to the state itself. For each change, there is a certain probability $p_{n_{old}, n_{new}}$.

The goal of these investigations is the calculation of the average number, or in other words the expected value of the number of transitions inside a traversal. To do so, for each traversal the individual probability has to be calculated first, which is the product of all transition probabilities inside the traversal.

For $n = n_0$ as the starting state, there are $\sum_{i=1}^{n} \binom{n}{i}$ possible traversals, which means for a traversal with i steps there are $\binom{n}{i}$ possibilities which states are entered during the traversal if state changes to the current state are neglected. For the probability calculations, changes to the current state must, however, be considered because these transitions contribute to the probability. The number of possible traversals then becomes infinite, because it can happen arbitrarily often that the system returns to the same state which it came from.

The probabilities of all transitions which are included into the traversal must be multiplied. The probability for a traversal of n steps is then

$$\sum_i^m p_{i_1,j_1} p_{i_2,j_2} \cdots p_{i_n,j_n} \qquad (3.67)$$

where p_{i_l,j_l} is the transition probability in the lth step from state i to state j.

In the next step, the probabilities for all traversals with the same number of transitions need to be added. After that, each of these probabilities is multiplied with the respective number of traversals; the sum of these products yield the expected value.

Since the number of transitions within a traversal can converge against infinity, it is impossible to calculate the expected value for k precisely. Hence, the maximum k which is considered for the calculation must be limited, the expected value $E[k]$ has then to be specified by a lower boundary. The boundary is a lower one because each element of the sum which contributes to the expected value is positive and increases the sum.

The left graph in fig. 3.10 shows a comparison of $E[k]$ between the analytically calculated number of transitions and the average number of transitions determined by a stochastic simulation of the discussed network scenario. The graph on the right shows how many channel changes occur in total during the simulation run. The simulation determines the mean values for 2000 traversals. For the calculated results, traversals with a maximum of eight transitions are considered due to the exponentially growing execution time of the calculation algorithm. It can be seen that the calculated results are close to the simulated results, however they are slightly lower than the simulated results due to the limitation of traversals with up to eight transitions. The gap between the calculated and simulated results gets larger with increasing number of stations. The reason is that $E[k]$ gets higher with increasing k; because of this, there are more traversals with a high number of transitions which are not considered in the analytical calculation.

A comparison between results deduced from the theory given in this chapter and simulation results is given in section 7.1.2.2.

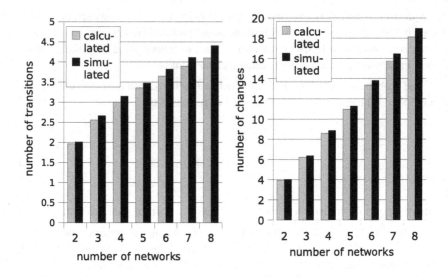

Figure 3.10: Comparison between calculated and simulated results

3.5 Assigning Airtime in Centralised Operation

In this section, the centralised operation of a QoS enabled access point is considered. The access point has full control on the radio channel, it serves a number of stations with one data flow per station. It is assumed that there are only data flows in the downlink. Analytical considerations are developed in this work to show the amount of enhancement that can be achieved for the throughput of the individual flows when using parallelised transmissions in contrast to sequential transmissions in case of TDMA.

3.5.1 Sequential Transmission

In the first step, the total throughput for the system is calculated. It is assumed that the packet size D is constant and equal for each flow i, however the channel capacity C_i is variable for each flow. For the calculation of the total throughput S_{total} of a system with n flows it is assumed that C_i is uniformly distributed between a minimum $C_{\min,i}$ and a maximum $C_{\max,i}$, where $C_{\min,i}=C_{\min}$ and $C_{\min,i}=C_{\max}$ for all flows. A TDMA transmission is assumed where the policy of the access point is the selection of the packet with the highest C_i. The total throughput yields

$$S_{\text{total}} = \frac{\text{total amount of data}}{\text{total elapsed time}} \tag{3.68}$$

Considering the assumption of constant packet length, S_{total} is rewritten as:

$$S_{\text{total}} = \frac{D}{T_{\text{mean}}} \tag{3.69}$$

where T_{mean} is the mean time for the packet transmission. The flow j_k for which a packet is selected and transmitted at the point of time k is always the one for which the transmission time is minimum:

$$j_k = \arg\min\{T_{1,k}, T_{2,k}, \ldots, T_{n,k}\} \tag{3.70}$$

where $T_{j,k}$ is the transmission time for flow j at the point of time k. The mean transmission time is then calculated as

$$T_{\text{mean}} = \frac{1}{m} \sum_{k=1}^{m} \min\{T_{1,k}, T_{2,k}, \ldots, T_{n,k}\} \tag{3.71}$$

with n being the number of flows and m being the number of points of time at which a new transmission is started. The individual transmission times $T_{i,k}$ are not known in an analytical consideration, but only in a simulation. In the analytical calculation, the minimum transmission time must be determined by the CCDFs for $T_1, \ldots, T_n$. The probability that the transmission time for each of the n flows is above the time t is

$$
\begin{aligned}
P(T_i > t) &= P(T_1 > t, T_2 > t, \ldots, T_n > t) \\
&= P(T_1 > t) \cdot P(T_2 > t) \ldots P(T_n > t) \\
&= G_1(t) \cdot G_2(t) \cdot \ldots \cdot G_n(t)
\end{aligned} \tag{3.72}
$$

where G_i is the CCDF for flow i. Since it was assumed that all flows are distributed in the same way, $G_i = G$. Eqn. 3.72 then becomes

$$P(T_i > t) = G(t)^n. \tag{3.73}$$

It is assumed that the PDF for the transmission time $f(t)$ is uniformly distributed between $T_{\min}$ and $T_{\max}$:

$$
f(t) = \begin{cases} \frac{1}{T_{\max} - T_{\min}} & \text{for} \quad T_{\min} \le t \le T_{\max}, \\ 0 & \text{else.} \end{cases} \tag{3.74}
$$

The CCDF is then

$$
\begin{aligned}
G(t) &= \int_t^\infty f(t)\,\mathrm{d}t \\
&= \int_t^{T_{\max}} \frac{1}{T_{\max} - T_{\min}}\,\mathrm{d}t.
\end{aligned}
\tag{3.75}
$$

where $T_{\min} \le t \le T_{\max}$. From the previous equation, it follows

$$
G(t) = \frac{T_{\max} - t}{T_{\max} - T_{\min}}.
\tag{3.76}
$$

The relationship between the CCDF $G(t)$ and the corresponding PDF $f(t)$ is

$$
\begin{aligned}
\tfrac{\mathrm{d}}{\mathrm{d}t} G(t) &= \tfrac{\mathrm{d}}{\mathrm{d}t}(1 - F(t)) \\
&= -f(t).
\end{aligned}
\tag{3.77}
$$

From the total CCDF $G_{\text{total}}(t) = (G(t))^n$, the PDF $f_{\text{total}}(t)$ is calculated as

$$
\begin{aligned}
f_{\text{total}}(t) &= \tfrac{\mathrm{d}}{\mathrm{d}t}(G(t))^n \\
&= -f(t) \cdot n(G(t))^{n-1}.
\end{aligned}
\tag{3.78}
$$

T_{mean} can then be calculated as

$$
T_{\text{mean}} = \int f_{\text{total}}(t) \cdot t\,\mathrm{d}t.
\tag{3.79}
$$

From 3.76, 3.78 and 3.79 there follows:

$$
\begin{aligned}
T_{\text{mean}} &= \int -f(t) \cdot n(G(t))^{n-1} \cdot t\,\mathrm{d}t \\
&= \int_{T_{\min}}^{T_{\max}} \frac{-1}{T_{\max} - T_{\min}} n \left(\frac{T_{\max} - t}{T_{\max} - T_{\min}} \right)^{n-1} t\,\mathrm{d}t \\
&= \left[\frac{1}{n+1} \left(\frac{T_{\max} - t}{T_{\max} - T_{\min}} \right)^n \cdot (T_{\max} + nt) \right]_{T_{\min}}^{T_{\max}} \\
&= \frac{T_{\max} + nT_{\min}}{n+1}.
\end{aligned}
\tag{3.80}
$$

For $n \to \infty$, T_{mean} converges against $T_{\min}$. With known T_{mean}, the mean throughput is then determined according to eqn. 3.69.

In the next step, the probability for the service of a particular flow is calculated considering that the flow is assigned airtime if its current transmission duration T_i is lower than the duration for any of the other flows. In average, this happens whenever $T_i < T_{\text{mean},n-1}$, the mean minimum transmission time for the remaining $n-1$

flows. In eqn. 3.80, the mean minimum transmission duration was calculated for n flows; this equation can be modified for $n - 1$ flows which then yields:

$$T_{\text{mean,n}-1} = \frac{T_{\max} + (n - 1)T_{\min}}{n}. \tag{3.81}$$

The probability p_i that a flow i is served with the shortest transmission time out of all flows is determined by calculating the CCDF of $T_{\text{mean,n}-1}$ analogously to T_{mean} where the CCDF was determined in eqn. 3.76:

$$p_i = \text{CCDF}(T_{\text{mean,n}-1}) = \frac{T_{\max} - T_{\text{mean,n}-1}}{T_{\max} - T_{\min}}. \tag{3.82}$$

Inserting 3.81 into 3.82 then yields:

$$p_i = \frac{1}{n}. \tag{3.83}$$

The results from eqn. 3.80 and 3.83 are compared against a simulation with 1,000,000 trials with $T_{\min} = 1$ time unit, $T_{\max} = 2$ time units and a variable number of data flows in table 3.2. In the table, for different numbers of data flows, the mean transmission time and the number of services for the least frequently and the most frequently served flow is given. The simulated results confirm the analytic calculation.

In an extension of the model given above, the flows have now different data rates while all other conditions remain unchanged. Then assigning the channel to flow i with the probability P_i as previously described is not optimum because all flows get the same service rate; different traffic loads resp. packet interarrival times of the individual flows are not considered. To overcome this problem, weighting factors a_i for each flow i are introduced which weigh the transmission duration in the following way:

$$T_i' = \frac{T_i}{a_i}. \tag{3.84}$$

To analyse the effect of weighting, a large number n of stations is considered. For large n, it can be assumed that T_{mean} is not changed if one of the flows changes the channel access probability. If one station uses a weighting factor a_i, then the PDF for that station is

$$f(x) = \begin{array}{ll} \frac{a}{(T_{\max} - T_{\min})} & \text{for} \quad \frac{T_{\min}}{a} \leq x \leq \frac{T_{\max}}{a}, \\ 0 & \text{else.} \end{array} \tag{3.85}$$

no. of flows	mean TX time analytic	mean TX time simulated	no. of services analytic	no. of services least served flow	no. of services most served flow
2	1.333333	1.333473	500000	499341	500658
3	1.250000	1.249883	333333	332861	334075
4	1.200000	1.199939	250000	249590	250402
5	1.166667	1.166560	200000	199375	200678
10	1.090909	1.090863	100000	99022	100376
20	1.047619	1.047622	50000	49358	50350
50	1.019608	1.019490	20000	19539	20374
100	1.009900	1.009851	10000	9780	10283

Table 3.2: Mean transmission time and number of occurrences for n data flows with uniformly distributed individual transmission times between $T_{\min} = 1$ time unit and $T_{\max} = 2$ time units in case of TDMA, considering the policy that always the flow with the shortest transmission time is selected

The goal is to calculate the probability that the weighted transmission duration is smaller than $T_{\min}$. To do so, the CDF for the weighted transmission duration is calculated.

$$
\begin{aligned}
F(x) &= \int_{T_{min}/a}^{T} \frac{a}{(T_{\max} - T_{\min})} dx \\
&= \left[\frac{ax}{(T_{\max} - T_{\min})} \right]_{T_{min}/a}^{T} \\
&= \frac{aT - T_{min}}{(T_{\max} - T_{\min})}.
\end{aligned}
\tag{3.86}
$$

The flow whose PDF is weighted has to be compared against the mean value of the $n - 1$ other flows, which yields

$$
\begin{aligned}
F(T_{min}) &= (a - 1) \cdot \frac{T_{\mathrm{mean},n-1}}{T_{\max} - T_{\min}} \\
&= (a - 1) \cdot \frac{T_{\max} + (n-1)T_{\min}}{n(T_{\max} - T_{\min})}
\end{aligned}
\tag{3.87}
$$

For a large number n, the change of the transmission probability of a single flow does not significantly change the mean value T_{mean} so that the transmission probabilities for the other flows are not changed. The situation changes for small n where T_{mean} is increased if a flow gets a higher weight. The reason for the increase is that the flow with the higher weight gets more chances to access the channel also when its transmission time is relatively large. Because of the mutual dependence between $F(T_{\text{mean}})$ of the weighted flow and T_{mean}, the change of T_{mean} cannot be expressed analytically, but only investigated in a simulation.

3.5.2 Parallelised Transmission

In case of parallelised transmission, n flows are served simultaneously. It is assumed that each flow always has a packet to transmit, i.e. the system is saturated. For an individual flow, the transmission time for one packet is uniformly distributed between T_{min} and T_{max}. It is assumed that all flows start transmitting a packet at the same time. Flows with a short transmission time wait until flows with a longer transmission time have completed their transmission before starting the next transmission.

To calculate the mean throughput for such a scenario, the mean time for one transmission cycle is calculated. This time is determined by the flow with the longest transmission time in a particular cycle,

$$T_{\text{mean,par}} = \frac{1}{m} \sum_{k=1}^{m} \max \{T_{1,k}, T_{2,k}, \ldots, T_{n,k}\} \qquad (3.88)$$

where m is the number of flows. This equation has the same structure than eqn. 3.71 with the difference that the minimum operator is replaced by the maximum operator. Hence the way of calculating $T_{\text{mean,par}}$ is done in a way similar to the calculation of T_{mean} which yields the result

$$T_{\text{mean,par}} = \frac{nT_{\text{max}} + T_{\text{min}}}{n + 1}. \qquad (3.89)$$

To determine the total throughput, it is considered that in each transmission cycle, each of the n flows sends a packet. The packet length is again assumed as constant and equal for all flows as in the case of sequential transmissions which was discussed in the previous section. The total throughput is then

$$S_{\text{total,par}} = \frac{nD}{T_{\text{mean,par}}} \qquad (3.90)$$

where D is the packet size.

The factor by which the parallelised transmission increases the throughput is the ratio between $S_{\text{total,par}}$ and S_{total}:

$$\frac{S_{\text{total,par}}}{S_{\text{total}}} = n \frac{T_{\max} + nT_{\min}}{nT_{\max} + T_{\min}}. \tag{3.91}$$

The fraction behind n is smaller than 1, which means the gain achieved by parallelisation grows smaller than the number of stations in the system. The maximum value of the fraction is 1 if $T_{\max} = T_{\min}$ which means an ideal transmission channel without changes of the capacity. In case of a channel with highly variable channel capacity, $T_{\max} \gg T_{\min}$, the expression becomes 1, so that the performance gets the same as for a sequential transmission. For a high number of users, n gets large, in this case this expression converges against $n \frac{T_{\min}}{T_{\max}}$, i. e. the throughput is enhanced proportionally to n by the parallelised transmission.

Practical methods for the assignment of airtime by a scheduler are given in chapter 5.

3.6 Summary

In this chapter, an overview about related work regarding the topics of spectrum management and scheduling was given.

A theoretical model from the literature describing the performance of Wireless LANs were discussed in detail which show that for infinite range of the stations, the achievable throughput decreases and the delay increases if the number of stations is increased. The contribution of this work is an analytical extension of the beforementioned models which considers the limited range of the stations, which results in a limited number of interacting stations so that concurrent transmissions become possible. Even stations which are located inside each other's carrier sense range can transmit simultaneously if the transmission starts at the same time. In this case, the success of the transmission is dependent on the positions and transmit powers of the stations.

Another novel investigation is an analytical method to calculate the average number of steps to assign frequency channels to a number of stations based on Markov chains. Finally, new considerations were given about the performance enhancement of a transmission which serves multiple users in parallel in comparison to a sequential transmission.

The theoretical results given in this chapter are validated in chap. 7 by a comparison with simulated results.

4 Spectrum Management Algorithms

The aim of this work is the investigation of spectrum management methods for IEEE 802.11a based networks, as they are introduced by the 802.11 h standard. As shown in the previous chapter, the standard defines *Dynamic Frequency Selection* and *Transmit Power Control*. The standard, however, only defines the signalling which is needed to maintain these spectrum management extensions. It does not specify the decision algorithms which select the frequency channel and the transmit power to be used. The standard only covers the topics which are important for the interoperability between hardware of different manufacturers. In this chapter, different methods to maintain Dynamic Frequency Selection (DFS) and Transmit Power Control (TPC) are introduced. The Transmit Power Control is extended by Link Adaptation (LA), which is not specified in the standard as well. Existing WLAN hardware rarely supports spectrum management by DFS and TPC according to the 802.11h standard. Link Adaptation is usually provided as a proprietary extension.

In this section, algorithms for DFS and TPC are discussed; in case of TPC, two algorithms with a centralised and a distributed control are shown which rely on channel measurements and signalling between the access points and the mobile stations as provided by the 802.11 standard. For TPC, the extension by Link Adaptation is introduced. Error recovery for the 802.11h based operation is considered which is not defined by the standard, however required for a proper function of the spectrum management algorithms. The algorithms discussed here are implemented in a simulator for validation which is described in detail in chapter 6.

4.1 Dynamic Frequency Selection

The purpose of the Dynamic Frequency Selection is the automatic selection and, if necessary, the automatic change of the frequency channel of all stations inside a BSS without user intervention. In legacy 802.11a networks, a BSS will remain on the same channel unless the configuration of the stations is changed by hand, which has to be done for all stations inside the BSS. If more than one network have to share the same channel, the available airtime for each network is reduced because some of the airtime is occupied by the other networks. Moreover, collisions can occur if at the receiver, the signal from the corresponding station is interfered by another station which transmits at the same time. These effects can result in a severe performance degradation of the network, in particular in an increase of the delay and a reduction of the throughput. To cope with this problem, the network measures the interference situation on the currently used and the other channels. If measurement results have been collected for all channels, the DFS algorithm decides either to keep the current channel or to switch to another one.

Since the acquisition of measurements plays a vital role in the DFS mechanism, this topic is discussed first. After that, different DFS algorithms are introduced.

4.1.1 Acquisition of Measurements

4.1.1.1 Measuring Sequence

Measurements of the individual frequency channels are the basis for the DFS algorithms to select the most suitable channel. Channel measurements can either be taken on demand, for example if the quality-of-service parameters like delay and throughput become too low, or on a regular basis. The disadvantage of measurements on demand is that the delay between a change of the channel conditions and the response of the system can be too slow. This can result in a reduced link quality or an entire link disruption for an unnecessary long time. Hence, for this analysis, a regular interference measurement is supported. The DFS owner, see section 2.4.1 regularly sends Measurement Requests to each of the MTs for each frequency channel. The Measurement Requests are sent as unicast packets, so all stations are polled in turn. This polling is done for each of the available frequency channels. Each station to which a Measurement Request is sent executes the measurement on the specified frequency channel and for the specified time; during the ongoing measurement process, the station suspends all sending activity. After having taken the measurement, the station reports the results back to the DFS owner by a Measurement Report. The details of the signalling were introduced earlier in section 2.4.1. This signalling scheme is used in the DFS procedure to query the measurements from the stations. The Figure 2.19 in the mentioned chapter shows the sequence how the DFS owner polls the different stations.

In the measurement process, two cases have to be distinguished: measurements on the currently used frequency channel and on other frequency channels. If a station is requested to measure on another frequency channel, it switches to this channel, takes the measurement and returns to the currently used channel. All other stations in the network can continue their activities without restrictions. The situation is different if the measurement has to be taken on the currently used channel: in this case, no stations of the network should be transmitting, otherwise the signals of these stations would be considered as interference. This means that a measurement on the currently used channel results in a link disruption for all stations of a network, while a measurement on another channel only results in a link disruption for the station which executes the measurements.

To stop all activities inside the network which is controlled by the DFS owner, additional signalling is required. The IEEE standard defines the Quiet message for this purpose, as it was discussed in chapter 2. A Quiet message is sent as a broadcast signal and is thus simultaneously processed by all stations inside the network. During the quiet period, the interference measurement is taken.

4.1.1.2 Measurement Values

When measuring a channel, values indicating the radio link quality are the interference level and the carrier-to-interference ratio (C/I). The interference level P_{int} is an individual value for each station. It is the sum of the powers P_i of all signals which are received by a station from other stations in neighbouring networks; in addition, also the receiver noise with the power P_N contributes to the interference signal. At a given time t, $P_{int}(t)$ can be written as:

$$P_{int}(t) = \sum_i P_i(t) + P_N. \tag{4.1}$$

with $1 \le i \le n$, n is the number of interfering stations inside the environment.

For the simple radio propagation model used in this work, the equation for the received power P_R,

$$P_R = \frac{P_T}{4\pi r^\gamma}, \tag{4.2}$$

was deduced in section 3.2 where P_T is the transmit power, r is the radius of the sphere and γ the attenuation factor.

The measurement of the interference level on a given frequency channel is done within a user-configurable time interval. In each of these time intervals, one of the available frequency channels will be measured, including the one which is currently in use for normal operation. If the currently used channel is measured, all stations inside the network have to stop their transmission in order to avoid their signals being measured as interference.

During the measurement interval, P_{int} is not constant. Changes occur when an interfering station starts or stops transmitting a packet. These changes are discrete, i. e. they occur at certain points of time. On the other hand, continuous changes of interference can also occur due to the movement of stations.

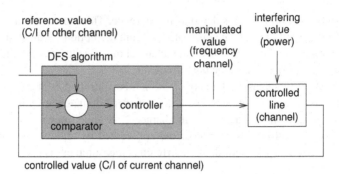

Figure 4.1: General structure of a controller

As an alternative to the interference level, the C/I can be used for the measurements on which the DFS algorithms rely. The C/I also considers the power of the carrier signal which is received from the communication partner in addition to the interference level. The received user-data signal power C is dependent on the position of the communication partner and on obstacles between the two communicating stations. As mentioned earlier, obstacles are not considered in the propagation model used in this analysis. The C/I at a given time can then be expressed as:

$$C/I = \frac{C}{P_{\text{int}} + P_{\text{N}}}. \tag{4.3}$$

In this work, the term signal-to-noise ratio S/N or SNR is sometimes used as a synonym to the carrier-to-interference ratio C/I. The C/I considers the quality of the radio frequency signal at the receiver, whereas the S/N is a measurement value taken at the baseband stage of the receiver after the RF demodulation. In case of real hardware, the S/N can differ from the C/I due to imperfections of the digital signal generation at the transmitter and signal analysis at the receiver [19]. In the simulations used in this work, ideal hardware is assumed so that the baseband signal processing is assumed as noise-free. In this case C/I and S/N are equal.

4.1.2 Principle of Controllers

In section 3.1, the effect of DFS on the performance of wireless LANs is considered analytically. In this section, algorithms for DFS are discussed. One of them is to maintain DFS by imposing *controllers* which is discussed in this work. The general structure of a controller [25] is shown in fig. 4.1.

The *controlling value* is one of the input values for the controller. In the case of DFS, it is the interference level or the C/I which is measured on the currently used frequency channel. The aim of the controller is to increase this value as far as possible under the current conditions.

The *reference value* is the value against which the controlling value is compared. In the case of DFS, the reference value is the interference or C/I of the other channels, which are possible alternatives to the channel which is currently in use.

The *controlled line* is the system inside which the controlling value is measured. In the context of DFS, this is the radio channel.

The *comparator* compares the controlling value against the reference value and provides an output signal which is related to the measured difference.

The *manipulated value* is the output value which is set by the controller. For DFS, this is the frequency channel which is selected by the decision algorithm.

Inside a wireless LAN, the controller is located inside the DFS owner. The terminals, however, also participate in the controlling process because they measure the controlling value.

4.1.3 Decision Algorithms

After the measurements have been performed, a decision has to be taken about the optimum frequency channel to be used by the BSS. The challenge which the algorithms have to meet is that there is no central coordination among the networks. Each of the networks has to observe its environment by taking interference measurements on the different frequency channels and draw conclusions what channel is the optimum one to be used. The DFS algorithms discussed here were investigated by PEETZ [103] for Hiperlan/2 and have been adapted for IEEE 802.11a/h in this work.

The task of the DFS algorithm is to find an optimum solution how to distribute n stations over m channels. In order to calculate the number of possibilities for the distribution, this situation is considered as drawing one out of m numbers n times where repetitions are allowed and the order is considered, so one gets m^n combinations.

Considering and example with $n = 3$ networks A, B, C and the frequency channels 1 and 2, there are following $2^3 = 8$ possibilities, where each digit represents the number of the selected frequency channel, as shown in table 4.1. The table can be resorted in the way that it is written which networks are assigned to each available channels as given in table 4.2. The 8 combinations can thus be reduced to 4 permutations, i.e. the channel number is no longer considered, as described in table 4.3.

network A	network B	network C
1	1	1
1	1	2
1	2	1
1	2	2
2	1	1
2	1	2
2	2	1
2	2	2

Table 4.1: Possible combinations when assigning 3 networks to 2 channels

channel 1	channel 2
A, B, C	–
A, B	C
A, C	B
B, C	A
A	B, C
B	A, C
C	A, B
–	A, B, C

Table 4.2: Distribution of 3 networks to 2 particular channels

any channel	the other channel
A, B, C	–
A, B	C
A, C	B
B, C	A

Table 4.3: Distribution of three networks to two channels independent of channel number

In the general case, n^m combinations are reduced to $\binom{n+m-1}{n}$ permutations without repetition.

The algorithms can be divided into two groups:

- *A priori* algorithms are memoryless, they take their decision based on the current measurement values. In this work, two algorithms of this type are discussed: Least Interfered and Fuzzy Logic.

- *A posteriori* algorithms include a memory, they learn from events in the past and draw conclusions for the future. In this work, the Genetic Algorithm is discussed as an example for a posteriori algorithms.

4.1.3.1 Least Interfered

Least Interfered is the most basic DFS algorithm discussed here. The principle of operation is the selection of the frequency channel with the lowest amount of interference I. In the other algorithms discussed later in this chapter, the signal-to-noise (S/N) ratio is measured, which is in the context of the work assumed to be the same as the carrier-to-interference ratio (C/I). This approach is easy to implement; however, different problems are expected when applying this algorithm:

- A frequency switch will occur even if a channel is only better by a small amount compared to the current one. If there are frequency channels with similar interference levels, this can lead to a channel switch after each measurement. Each channel switch will disrupt the communication link until both ends of the connection have changed the channel.

- An unstable situation can occur if a number of networks measure similar interference situations and all networks decide to switch to the same channel. In this case, they will always mutually block each other.

- The algorithm only considers the interference. A more realistic measurement is obtained by determining the carrier-to-interference ratio C/I which is used by the other algorithms presented here.

4.1.3.2 Fuzzy Logic

Fuzzy Logic is like Least Interfered an a-priori method. Unlike calculation methods which are based on precise (sharp) sets, fuzzy logic works with *fuzzified* sets. When values are assigned to sets, there is no sharp limit which assigns a value exactly to one particular set. A value can belong to more than one set by some

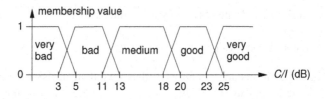

Figure 4.2: Example for a membership function

particular amount. In the human language, many effects are described by fuzzy attributes. For example, temperatures can be measured as precise values like +17 C or −5 C. In human language, however, temperatures are often expressed in ways like "cold", "cool", "warm", "hot", where no exact limits are given and e.g. +20 C can belong to the set "cool" and "warm".

A fuzzy calculation includes three steps:

- In the *fuzzification*, a sharp input value ("the temperature is 25 C") is assigned to a fuzzy set ("warm").

- The *inference* is a set of rules which describe how to calculate a fuzzy output value from a number of fuzzy input values: "The weather was cool before and is warm now → it has become warmer".

- In the *defuzzification*, the result of the inference is mapped to a sharp value: "The weather has become warmer, so the heating can be turned off."

The three steps of the fuzzy controlling process are now discussed in a formal way.

Fuzzification

The sharp input values are mapped to fuzzy classes by *membership functions*. A membership function gives an amount by which a given value belongs to a particular class. An example for membership functions to classify the quality of a radio channel is given in figure 4.2. Due to the finite gradients of the membership functions, the amount value can achieve any value between between 0 and 1, where 0 means that the value does not belong to the class and 1 means that it fully belongs to the class. There is exactly one membership function for each class. Because of this property of fuzzy logic, a value can belong to more than one class by a particular percentage. This distinguishes fuzzy logic from sharp logic where the membership functions only take the values 0 and 1: a value exactly either fully belongs to the class or it does not belong to the class at all.

For each input value x and n membership functions, the sum of all membership degrees $m_i(x)$ is 1:

$$\sum_i^n m_i(x) = 1 \tag{4.4}$$

In the fuzzy algorithm considered here, the shapes of the membership functions are trapezoids as shown in fig. 4.2. The outer two trapezoids are half-open, they can be described by two values x_1 and x_2 with $x_1 < x_2$. For the left open trapezoid tagged as "very bad", $m(x)$ is defined as follows:

$$m(x) = \begin{cases} 1 & x \leq x_1 \\ 1 - \frac{x-x_1}{x_2-x_1} & x_1 < x < x_2 \\ 0 & x \geq x_2 \end{cases} \tag{4.5}$$

For the right open trapezoid tagged as "very good", there is:

$$m(x) = \begin{cases} 0 & x \leq x_1 \\ \frac{x-x_1}{x_2-x_1} & x_1 < x < x_2 \\ 1 & x \geq x_2 \end{cases} \tag{4.6}$$

The inner trapezoids can be described by four values x_1, x_2, x_3, x_4:

$$m(x) = \begin{cases} 0 & x \leq x_1 \\ \frac{x-x_1}{x_2-x_1} & x_1 < x < x_2 \\ 1 & x_2 \leq x \leq x_3 \\ 1 - \frac{x-x_3}{x_4-x_3} & x_3 < x < x_4 \\ 0 & x \geq x_4 \end{cases} \tag{4.7}$$

These fuzzy input values are classes which roughly describe the quality of a channel with attributes like *very bad, bad, medium, good, very good*, as shown in the example in fig. 4.2.

Inferences

An inference is a rule which derives a fuzzy output value from two or more fuzzy input values. In the context of the fuzzy controller discussed here, the input values are quality classes both of the current channel and of a channel which has been measured.

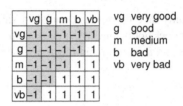

Figure 4.3: Fuzzy Associative Memory (FAM) matrix

In a formal description, the fuzzy operators are defined as follows. The fuzzy OR operator calculates the maximum of two membership values:

$$\mathrm{OR}(y_1, y_2) = \max(y_1, y_2). \tag{4.8}$$

If y_1, y_2 is set to 0 or 1, the fuzzy OR operator is identical to the binary OR operator.

The fuzzy AND operator calculates the minimum of two membership values:

$$\mathrm{AND}(y_1, y_2) = \min(y_1, y_2). \tag{4.9}$$

If y_1, y_2 is set to 0 or 1, the fuzzy AND operator is identical to the binary AND operator.

Based on these definitions, an inference rule can for example be: IF the current channel is *poor* AND the measured channel is *good* THEN change the channel.

In the DFS fuzzy algorithm, the inference is calculated as follows based on the C/I measurements of the channels. As described earlier, a membership function includes n classes. Hence, for the C/I of the currently used channel, n membership values can be written as a_i, for another measured channel the n membership values can be written as b_j, where i, j, each ranging from 1 to n, are the indices for the different membership classes.

- For each pair (i, j), determine $c_{ij} = \min(a_i, b_j)$. This operation represents the fuzzy AND operator.

- In case of n classes, assume the worst class (very poor) is indexed as 0 and the best one (very good) is indexed as $n - 1$. Calculate the sum

$$d = \sum_{i,j} S_{ij} c_{ij} \tag{4.10}$$

where S_{ij} is $+1$ for $j > i$, otherwise -1. Expressed in words, this means:

- Add any value S_{ij} where the class j of the new channel represents better channel conditions than the class i of the old channel.
- Subtract any value S_{ij} where the class j of the new channel represents equal or worse channel conditions than the class i of the old channel.

This calculation of d is done for each combination of the current channel and of another available channel, which results in a set of values

$$d_1, \ldots, d_{k-1}, d_{k+1}, \ldots, d_n,$$

n being the number of available channels and k being the number of the current channel. The matrix $\mathbf{S} = \{S_{ij}\}$ is called *Fuzzy Associative Memory* (FAM)-Matrix. As it is shown in figure 4.3, it is divided into two triangles; inside one triangle, the matrix elements S_{ij} are filled with the value 1 which indicates a channel change, the other one is filled with the value -1 for no channel change.

Defuzzification

In the defuzzification process, a sharp output value (i. e. change the frequency or not) must be determined from the fuzzy output values. This is done in the way that the frequency is changed to the channel with the highest positive value d. If there is no positive value d, the channel will not be changed. d can be interpreted as the gain which will be achieved when changing the channel: the higher d, the better is the new channel compared to the current one.

4.1.3.3 Genetic Algorithm

The previously discussed algorithms are a-priori algorithms which are memory-less; in contrast to this, the Genetic Algorithm which is described in this section represents the class of a-posteriori algorithms, i. e. it has a memory to store earlier events, from which it can take assumptions of the future development of a system. In the context of the genetic algorithm, these events are C/I measurements on the different frequency channels. The C/I measurements are considered as individuals of a population which perform the steps mutation, crossover and selection.

The task of the DFS algorithm is to distribute the wireless networks among the available frequency channels. The way how the networks are mapped to the different channels is called a *constellation*. Since the discussed DFS algorithms are decentralised, there is no central instance which can determine the optimum constellation for all networks. Each of the networks has to decide itself based on the interference measurements to which frequency channel it should change. Each network measures the interference on all frequency channels as described in section 4.1.1.1.

Due to the lack of a central coordination, a deadlock can result as it was discussed earlier in section 4.1.3.1: two networks which interfere with each other measure a better interference situation on another channel than on their own. Each of them will then decide to change to this particular channel so the interference conflict cannot be resolved. An algorithm with memory which learns from the past might such as the genetic algorithm not always immediately changes the channel if another one with less interference is available; due to the memory, earlier interference situations are considered so that a new channel is only selected if that new channel yields more benefit in long terms.

A radio cell with an access point and a number of mobile terminals is considered. On each of the available frequency channels, each mobile terminal experiences a certain amount of interference from neighbouring WLAN radio cells or other radio applications which results in a particular C/I value. These values are regularly measured by the mobile stations and reported to the access point. Let $q_{i,j,k}$ be the ith C/I measurement on channel j by station k. After the access point has collected a set of measurements from all n stations on a particular frequency channel j, it stores the measurements as a measurement vector $\mathbf{q}_{i,j} := (q_{i,j,1}, \ldots, q_{i,j,n})$.

If some mobile stations inside a wireless network scenario are mobile or change their transmit powers, this leads to varying interference conditions. Thus, in consecutive measurements, a C/I pattern which was measured on a channel will differ from the previous pattern. However, they are not entirely different, some amount of similarity still remains. Due to this, it is required that similar vectors can be identified, which means that there must be a metric for the similarity of vectors. In the DFS context, the Euclidean distance of the vectors is used for this purpose. The Euclidean distance d of two n-element vectors $\mathbf{q}_1, \mathbf{q}_2$ with the elements $\mathbf{q}_{1,i}$ resp. $\mathbf{q}_{2,i}$ is defined as:

$$d = \sqrt{\sum_{i=1}^{n} (\mathbf{q}_{1,i} - \mathbf{q}_{2,i})^2} \qquad (4.11)$$

The genetic algorithm measures the C/I vector $\mathbf{q}$ for each frequency channel to form a population. Similar vectors are then grouped into classes according to the following scheme which is known in the literature as *adaptive resonance theory* (ART), which is taken from the area of neural networks [39]. This method is repeated until all vectors inside a population have been grouped into a class.

1. Take any vector $\mathbf{q}$ of the population as the initial vector.

2. Define the selected vector as the *prototype* of a new class: $\mathbf{p}_1 := \mathbf{q}$.

3. Select any of the remaining vectors $\mathbf{q}_i$.

4. Check if the Euclidean distance between the $\mathbf{q}$ and the prototype $\mathbf{p}$ is smaller than a threshold called *vigilance* ρ.

5. If yes, add the vector to the class and recalculate the prototype with a weighted sum which includes the old prototype and the newly inserted vector:

$$\mathbf{p}_{i+1} = \alpha j \cdot \mathbf{q} + (1 - \alpha)\mathbf{p}_i \qquad (4.12)$$

The factor α, which can be selected between 0 and 1, is called learning rate. The higher it is, the more quickly the system will adapt to changed conditions, however it might become less stable because the weighting of previous events $1 - \alpha$ is reduced, so it "forgets" previous data more quickly. Finally return to step 3.

6. If the new vector is outside the Euclidean distance around the class, return to step 2.

After the definition of the classification, the genetic algorithm for DFS can now be specified which is illustrated in fig. 4.4. The algorithm is decentralised, it is executed by each DFS owner without signalling between neighbouring networks.

In the following list, the numbers refer to the numbers given in the figure. In the first three steps, the system is initialised:

1. A starting population of n vectors is determined by measuring the interference patterns on all n frequency channels by the mobile stations. Each element of the vector is the measurement result by one mobile station. The vector $\mathbf{q}$ with the highest fitness is selected according to eqn. 4.13 and the frequency channel is switched according to the selected vector. The fitness metric F is the mean value of $q_1, \ldots, q_n$ calculated over all mobile terminals k, i.e. the mean C/I which was measured by the n stations:

$$F = \frac{1}{n}\sum_{k=1}^{n} q_k. \qquad (4.13)$$

2. The starting population is now grouped into classes according to the ART method which has been described before. Each class contains a prototype vector $\mathbf{p}$.

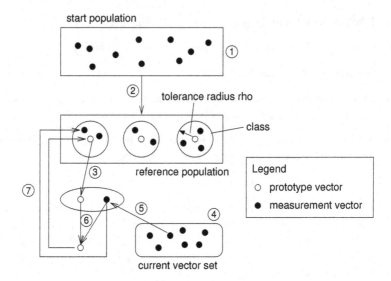

Figure 4.4: Principle of the genetic algorithm

3. Out of the classes which have been formed by ART, the one including the prototype with the highest fitness is selected.

The following steps which are continued repeatedly after the first three steps are completed implement the features of genetic processes, i. e. mutation, selection, crossover:

4. A new measurement of vectors resp. interference patterns is taken at a later point of time by repeating the measurements of all mobile stations. Again, each DFS owner initiates such a measurement inside the network which it controls. These patterns may differ from the patterns taken in earlier measurements which can be considered as the *mutation*.

5. One of these vectors is selected according to the ART algorithm, i. e. the one which has the smallest Euclidean distance to the previously selected prototype. This step refers to the *selection*. In this step, the frequency channel which corresponds to the selected vector is chosen.

6. Out of the prototype **p** and the selected vector **q**, a new prototype vector is calculated according to the ART equation 4.12. This step corresponds to the *crossover*.

7. The measured vector $\mathbf{q}_{i+1}$ is added to the class selected in step 5. The old prototype vector of that class $\mathbf{p}_i$ is replaced by the new one $\mathbf{p}_{i+1}$.

4.1.3.4 Introduction of Randomness

In the genetic algorithm as described above always selects the optimum vector, which is done in a deterministic way by choosing the vector with the smallest Euclidean distance to the prototype. However, this method implies two problems:

- If always the best vector is chosen, the search might run into a local maximum, which provides optimum conditions for the particular network inside the scenario which took the measurement, but which is not optimal for the other networks.

- If the conditions in the network change rapidly due to high mobility of the stations, the system might detect this with a long delay.

A random component which selects a less suitable vector with a certain probability can increase the reaction speed of the system to adapt to changing channel conditions. The method used to extend the genetic algorithm is called *roulette wheel selection*; it selects the prototype with a probability p_x which is the quotient F_x of the fitness of the considered vector and the sum of the fitness values of all prototypes:

$$p_x = \frac{F_x}{\sum\limits_{i=1}^{n} F_i}. \tag{4.14}$$

In this equation, F_x is the fitness, i. e. the C/I rating of the prototype to be examined, F_i is the fitness of the prototype i in the reference population.

For DFS, the application of roulette wheel selection provide a better adaptivity of the system: If the genetic algorithm which selects the frequency for each network is not extended by randomness, the vector resp. the channel which is chosen by each network is optimum for the considered network, but the behaviour of the network might not be optimum for the other networks. The DFS algorithm is decentralised so that there is no central control which can find an optimum solution for all networks. By introduction of randomness, a probability is introduced that a network selects a vector resp. channel which is not optimum for the considered network, but a better solution for the entire system.

4.1.4 Simulated Annealing

Like the genetic algorithm, *simulated annealing* [67] is an a-posteriori method with memory which is taken from the area of thermodynamics. It considers the behaviour of atoms inside a slowly cooling down liquid with a temperature close to the freezing point. In case of liquid metal, this process is called "annealing". Each atom inside the annealing liquid has a certain energy which is dependent on its location in the crystal grid. A displacement of the atom due to thermal movement changes its energy. A large amount of atoms inside a given volume always in average always takes the state with the lowest possible energy. In case of an individual atom, when denoting the energies before resp. after state change with E_1 and E_2, the atom will always change the state if $E_2 < E_1$. However, in case of $E_2 > E_1$, a transition can occur as well with a probability p dependent on the temperature T and the energy difference $E_2 - E_1$.

$$p = \left\{ \begin{array}{ll} \exp\left(\frac{-E_2 - E_1}{kT}\right) & \text{for } E_2 > E_1, \\ 1 & \text{else} \end{array} \right\}, \tag{4.15}$$

where k is the Boltzmann constant, $k = 1.38 \cdot 10^{-23}$J/K.

For the application on DFS, the carrier-to-interference values C/I_i for the n available frequency channels are the values analogue to the energies of an atom dependent on its location. Being

$$C/I_{\max} = \max\left\{C/I_1, C/I_2, \ldots, C/I_n\right\} \tag{4.16}$$

and

$$i_{\max} = \operatorname{argmax}_i\left\{C/I_1, \ldots, C/I_i, \ldots, C/I_n\right\} \tag{4.17}$$

the difference $d_i = C/I_{\max} - C/I_i$ is calculated for each pair of $(i_{\max}, i \neq i_{\max})$.

For each d_i, the transition probability is calculated as $p_i = 0.5 - e^{-d_i/kT}$, i. e. the probability function is modified in comparison to the physical annealing in the sense that for energy reductions ($E2 > E1$), the transition is probabilistic instead of deterministic ($p = 1$). T has to be selected in a suitable way so that the result of the exponential function ranges within -0.5 and 0.5 for typical C/I values. The channels i are sorted according to descending C/I. Starting with $i = 1$, p_i is compared against a uniformly distributed random variable which is redrawn for each channel i. By this method, the channel with the highest C/I gets the highest chance to be selected as the next channel to be used. However, there is a certain probability that a channel with a smaller C/I is selected. The reason to do so is the same as in case of the genetic algorithms which is modified by the roulette wheel selection, which is the increase of adaptivity in case of changing channel conditions; a channel which is currently not optimum, i. e. does not have the best C/I, can become optimum later due to the frequency changes of networks or due to mobility.

4.1.5 Error Recovery

The management packets used for signalling DFS messages can be lost due to congestion or poor channel conditions. Therefore, some means have to be provided how the protocol stack copes with such conditions. The standard does not specify how errors should be recovered. In this work, methods for the error recovery are proposed considering different error situations which are listed as follows:

- A Measurement Request is sent by the DFS owner, but the station does not receive it. This problem is coped with in the way that the DFS owner sets a timer after the Measurement Request has been sent. If there is no Measurement Report within the interval given by the timer, the Measurement Request is resent. Setting this timer is a tradeoff: if it is too short, the system will react quickly on a loss of a Measurement Request; however, in case of a high round trip delay it can happen that the Measurement Report arrives after the timer has expired, so that another Measurement Request already has been sent. If the retransmission timeout is high, retransmissions can be avoided, however the reaction of the system on a packet loss is very slow. Thus, the time has to be set to a compromise, which means some duplicate Measurement Requests have to be accepted. In this case, the protocol stack of the mobile terminal resends the Measurement Report. The reason for this is clarified in the next section.

- A Measurement Report sent by a station is not received by the DFS owner. This results, like in the previous case, in a retransmission of the Measurement Request by the DFS owner since no Measurement Report was received. Since in this case the terminal has received the previous Measurement Request, it sees a duplicate Measurement Request. However, the terminal cannot identify if a Measurement Request is retransmitted due to a delayed Measurement Report or due to a loss of the Measurement Report. Because of this, a Measurement Report is sent in any case whenever a Measurement Request was received. Another issue which has to be considered here is the quieting of the channel by the DFS owner in case that the frequency to be observed is the one currently in use by the network. As it has been mentioned before, the DFS owner quiets the channel in this case. If no Measurement Report is received, this quieting must be stopped to submit the next Measurement Request.

- A Channel Switch Announcement is not received by a station. In this case, the station which could not hear the Channel Switch Announcement remains on the previous channel while the other stations and the DFS owner switch to the new channel. To tackle this problem, all stations observe the packets received from the DFS owner. If no packets have been received for a certain amount of time, it is assumed that the DFS owner has changed the channel. Thus, the terminal switches to the next frequency channel and observes this channel for a certain amount of time. If packets from the DFS owner can be observed here, it is assumed it has switched to this particular channel, so that the mobile terminal will remain here. Otherwise, it continues searching all channels until the DFS owner is found. The fact that the mobile terminal cannot receive packets from the DFS owner can have a second cause besides the change of the channel described above, which is that the DFS owner has quieted the channel to do a measurement on the current channel. The mobile terminal can identify this situation by receiving the Measurement Request. Hence, after the terminal has submitted the Measurement Report and the channel remains quiet, it assumes that the DFS owner did not receive the Measurement Report and thus waits for another Measurement Request. However, this process also has to be limited by a timer. After this timer has expired, the mobile terminal starts searching the channel as described above.

Simulation results about the performance of DFS are found in section 7.1.2.

4.2 Transmit Power Control

The Transmit Power Control adjusts the power at which a station transmits during an ongoing communication. In contrast to the Dynamic Frequency Selection which tries to find optimum conditions for a network by escaping from channels which are occupied by neighbouring networks, the aim of TPC is the improvement of the conditions for the neighbouring networks by reducing the interference which is caused by the controlled network.

Two algorithms for Transmit Power Control are discussed in this work. The first one evaluates the link gain matrix between a number of access points and mobile terminals. It relies on an infrastructure network because it sends control information over the backbone channel which connects the access points inside an EBSS.

It is used as a comparison to a second algorithm which is also suitable for ad-hoc networks; this latter algorithm is based on a fuzzy controller. Both algorithms are discussed in detail in this section.

4.2.1 Infrastructure Networks

The algorithm for infrastructure networks has been adapted from a power control strategy for cellular telephone radio networks which has been proposed by ZANDER [131]. Instead of base stations, in the scope of this analysis wireless access points are considered which are connected by a wired backbone. This backbone is used for negotiations between the access points. In the centralised algorithm, two concepts are introduced:

- Co-channel set. A co-channel set is a set of BSSes which use the same frequency channel. The access points which control the particular BSSes announce by signalling over the wired backbone which frequency channel they are using. This information is used to form co-channel sets.

- TPC owner. In this work, the co-channel set is extended by a central station which requests measurements from all BSSes inside the co-channel set and collects the measurement results. This central station is called TPC owner; the service is provided by one of the access points inside the co-channel set. The TPC owner is determined by signalling on the wired backbone; inside a given co-channel set, the access point with the lowest MAC address acts as the TPC owner.

The acquisition of C/I measurements which are needed to control the transmission power is maintained by the TPC owner. The signalling includes two types of management packets which are defined in the 802.11h standard, TPC Request and TPC Response.

The TPC owner regularly sends a signal over the backbone channel which indicates that the APs inside the co-channel set are requested to send a TPC request management packet to the mobile stations. The TPC request is defined in the 802.11h standard. When a mobile terminal receives a TPC Request, it takes a measurement of the channel for the time specified in the TPC request. Due to the centralised initiation of the TPC request, all APs send it within a short time. In this way, the mobile terminal can quickly collect the C/I measurements of the signal for the network it belongs to and for neighbouring access points. These measurements are reported to the AP using a TPC report. The AP forwards the report to the TPC owner by the wired backbone. Based on the data contained in the report, the

TPC owner calculates the new power which has to be set for each mobile terminal. Once it has received the reports from all APs, it sends the calculated data inside the new TPC request to the BSSes. Thus the TPC request is on the one hand a request to take the next measurement and on the other hand a request to adjust the transmission power.

After the TPC owner has collected all measurement data for the co-channel set, it calculates the new TX power for each of the mobile terminals. A number of n radio cells is considered, where each of them contains a transmitting and a receiving station. In [131], the case that a base station serves multiple mobile stations is not considered. In this work, it is proposed that in this case the power is adjusted to satisfy the most distant station which is assumed to be the one which has the highest path loss on the link between base station and mobile station. In the channel model used in this analysis, the received power P_{rec} can be expressed as $P_{\text{rec}} \propto P_{\text{trans}}^{-\gamma}$, which means the relation between P_{rec} and P_{trans} is strictly monotonic decreasing. Hence the most distant station can always be identified. Adjusting the power to a closer station is not useful because all stations which are covered by the same base station need to hear the base stations's transmissions to avoid hidden station problems.

The ratio between the transmitted power P_{T}, i from cell i and the received power P_{rec}, j received in cell j is called *link gain* with $G_{ij} = \frac{P_{\text{T},i}}{P_{\text{R},j}}$. This means that G_{ii} denotes the link gain for the signal from the communication partner inside the same radio cell whereas G_{ij} with $i \neq j$ identifies interference from another cell. All link gains inside a system of n networks form a squared link gain matrix $\mathbf{G}$ with size n:

$$\mathbf{G} = \begin{pmatrix} G_{11} & G_{12} & \cdots & G_{1n} \\ G_{21} & G_{22} & \cdots & G_{2n} \\ \vdots & \vdots & \cdots & \cdots \\ G_{n1} & G_{n2} & \cdots & G_{nn} \end{pmatrix} \tag{4.18}$$

This matrix is normalised by dividing all values $G_{ij}, i \neq j$ by the gain G_{ii} of the link which transports the goodput data:

$$Z_{ij} = \frac{G_{ij}}{G_{ii}} \tag{4.19}$$

According to the definition of Z_{ij}, all Z_{ii} are equal to 1.

The value C/I_i also considers the noise N_i which is observed by terminal i. The noise is also normalised:

$$N_i' = \frac{N_i}{G_{ii}} \tag{4.20}$$

The C/I_i for station i can then be calculated as follows:

$$\left(\frac{C}{I}\right)_i = \frac{P_i}{\sum_{j=1}^n P_j Z_{ij} - P_i + N_i'} \tag{4.21}$$

P_i is the power of the signal transmitted by station i. From these C/I_i, the TPC owner determines the TX power for each station which should be used next:

$$P^{(0)} = P_0; P_0 > 0; P_i^{(n+1)} = \beta P_i^{(n)} \left(\frac{1}{(C/I)_i^{(n)}}\right). \tag{4.22}$$

P_0 is a starting value which can for example be set to the maximum transmit power which is allowed by the IEEE 802.11 standard to make sure that there is connectivity between all stations when the system is started. β is a value $0 < \beta < 1$; the optimum value for β has to be found by simulation experiments.

When the algorithm is run, the C/Is of the different stations converge against a constant limit. The transmit powers, however, become smaller in a strictly monotonic fashion. Assuming a constant C/I which is achieved due to the convergence characteristics of the algorithm, the power after iteration n is approximately

$$P^{(n)} = P_0 \cdot (\beta(C/I)_\infty)^n, \tag{4.23}$$

where

$$C/I_\infty = \lim_{n \to \infty} C/I^{(n)}. \tag{4.24}$$

P_0 is the starting power, $P^{(n)}$ is the power at iteration n.

Equation 4.23 shows that the power is reduced according to a geometric sequence. For this reason, a lower boundary is introduced in this work because in reality the power cannot be set infinitely small; if the power assigned to any station falls below this boundary, the powers for all stations need to be adjusted in the following way: If p_a is the power of the station whose power is too low and p_0 is the required minimum power, then the powers for all stations need to be multiplied by p_0/p_a. This multiplication by a constant factor does not affect the C/Is which are ratios whose enumerator and denominator are multiplied by the same factor.

The convergence of the algorithm is demonstrated by a simplified example where no signalling is considered. There are three pairs of a transmitting and a receiving station as shown in fig. 4.5. The time is divided into slots, where each

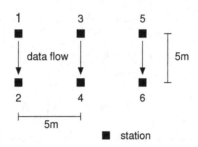

Figure 4.5: Infrastructure TPC example scenario. All stations start with 50 mW TX power

station alters the transmit power according to the measurements taken in the previous slot. The starting transmit power in the first time slot is 50 mW, while the minimum required power is 1 mW. Fig. 4.6 depicts the transmit power for station 4 as a function of time with $\beta = 0.6$. It is shown that the algorithm rapidly reduces the power so that the limitation of the power by the lower boundary already comes into effect after a few iterations. The power values are reduced in each iteration according to eqn. 4.22 which is approx. 10 in the example given here, so that after each iteration the transmit power becomes smaller by a factor of 10. The starting value of 50 mW is not visible in fig. 4.6 because for overview reasons the value range of the y axis is limited to 4 mW. The figure on the right shows the C/I seen by station 4. The graphs for stations 2 and 6 look similar, with the difference that the oscillation reaches its maximum when it is minimum for station 4 and vice versa.

In order to evaluate the influence of β, simulations were also run with $\beta=0.1$ and $\beta=1$. The variation of β affects the reduction speed for the transmit powers, as it can be seen from eqn. 4.23. For the C/I convergence, the results are almost the same as for $\beta=0.6$.

The proposed power control algorithm adjusts the transmit powers for the stations so that each receiver experiences the same C/I and in this way provides a fair distribution of the channel ressources among the stations. In addition, there is a second effect of power control which improves the transmission conditions. According to the standard, a station only transmits if the signal level on the channel is below -82 dBm. If in the scenario given above station 1 transmits with 50 mW, then it can be calculated that the signal level at station 6 is -73 dBm which is above the -82 dBm threshold so that station 6 does not transmit because the channel is considered busy. By reduction of the transmit power, the received power of station 1's signal at station 6 eventually falls below -82 dBm so that station 6 can then

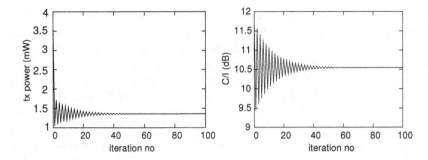

Figure 4.6: Results for TPC example scenario in fig. 4.5. Left: power of TX signal at station 4, right: C/I of RX signal at station 4. The transmit power of the 0-th iteration (50 mW) is not visible in the graph.

start transmitting parallel to station 1. In section 3.3.1, it was demonstrated how these parallel transmissions enhance the throughput for a connection. Once the received signal powers for the outer stations fall below -82 dBm and they transmit simultaneously, then there are also chances that the stations in the middle experience the superimposed signals of the outer stations. As it was described in section 3.3.2, this means that the preambles of the signals are destroyed from the view of the middle stations so that the CCA threshold is then set to -62 dBm. In this case, the middle stations can transmit as well.

4.2.2 Ad-Hoc Networks

The distributed algorithm which is discussed here was investigated by PEETZ and is adapted for IEEE 802.11h in this work. The algorithm works on a point-to-point basis, which means no central station is needed; the transmission power is adjusted between neighbouring stations which are connected by a direct link. The principle of fuzzy controllers has already been discussed in section 4.1.3.2. The controller used for TPC is a *relational* fuzzy controller. As it was shown earlier, a fuzzy controller is useful if the controlled value is non-deterministic, which also applies for the radio channel. Due to the mobility of the station under consideration and the neighbouring stations and obstacles between the stations, the dependency of the C/I on the time is non-deterministic.

Along with the transmission power control, the controller also supports link adaptation. This means that the physical bit rate (the PHY mode) is changed according to the load of the link and the C/I of the channel. The term *link* means the exchange of data packets between a sending and a receiving station. Other stations in the neighbourhood which also receive the packets from the sending stations consider these packets as interference. These two values are conflicting: A particular data load on the connection requires a PHY mode with a certain minimum bit rate to make sure that all data can be transmitted without congestion. On the other hand, a particular C/I on the channel requires a PHY mode whose minimum required C/I is smaller than the C/I on the channel. Since the minimum required C/I increases with the increasing bit rate of the PHY mode, the C/I on the channel limits the speed of the PHY mode which can be used. However, the C/I can be increased by increasing the TX power of the stations, provided that the TX power is not already set to the possible maximum. From this, it can be seen that the controller has to find an optimum adjustment between the TX power and the PHY mode. Methods of Link Adaptation were discussed in the literature survey in chapter 3.

The controller is implemented as a finite state machine, which means it changes between four different states during the ongoing controlling process: Initialisation, testing, controlling and monitoring. A change between the states takes place on external events, i. e. a change of the controller input values. These values which are evaluated by the controller are the queue load and the C/I on the channel.

4.2.2.1 Initialisation State

For each link which is newly opened by a STA, a separate entity of the TPC fuzzy controller is created in the 802.11h protocol stack which starts in the initialisation state. A connection is opened when a station receives a packet from a corresponding station for the first time. Since the power control is implemented on the receiver side which reports the results of the control back to the sender, a connection is opened when a station receives a packet from a corresponding station for the first time. The station which received the packet requests the corresponding station to send the packets at the maximum transmission power and measures the performance of the transmission which can be achieved under these conditions. The values which are measured are the throughput, the interference level and the queue load. The measurements are taken within a specified time interval called settling time. The average of the values which have been measured in this interval are used as a reference value for the following control process. After the settling time has expired, the controller switches to the testing state.

4.2.2.2 Testing State

It was mentioned earlier that the controller has to find a tradeoff between the transmit power and the PHY mode to be used. This task is performed by the testing state. After entering the testing state, the fastest PHY mode according to the mean C/I measured in the initialisation state is selected. After that, the C/I is further observed to estimate the behaviour of the neighbouring networks. If the interference power is reduced in comparison to the reference values taken in the initialisation state, it is assumed that the neighbouring stations have reduced their transmit power. The station then decreases its transmit power by 3 dB. After the reduction, the C/I of the connection is checked again. Further, it is checked if the PHY mode of the station can be reduced. The minimum PHY mode depends on the payload which has to be transported on the link. The bit rate of the selected PHY mode must always be higher than the user payload because of the protocol overhead. Selecting a slower PHY mode supports the power control because it requires a lower C/I and hence a lower transmit power. If the interference power of the neighbouring stations is again reduced, the station continues the reduction of is own TX power and the measurements until the minimum C/I along with the most robust PHY mode has been reached.

If the neighbouring networks do not decrease their TX power, this means they do not react on the TX power reduction of the station. In this case, the station remains in the testing state until the C/I is sufficient for the PHY mode which is at least needed to transfer the full data load of the connection.

At this point, another tradeoff becomes evident: reducing the PHY mode minimises the interference, but increases the time for which the channel is occupied. This means for other connections that they might have to switch to a higher PHY mode, since otherwise the airtime on the channel to transmit the data might not be sufficient and the queue load will increase. A higher PHY mode means the requirement for a higher C/I and thus higher transmit power.

4.2.2.3 Controlling State

When the station enters the controlling state, at first the interference is checked against the reference value which has been determined in the testing state. If the interference does not exceed the reference value in more than three consecutive measurement processes, the fuzzy controller takes over the control, otherwise the controller returns to the testing state. The input values for the controller are the Packet Error Rate, which is deduced from the C/I, and the queue load. For the fuzzification, the slowest possible PHY mode is again selected according to the current C/I; after that, fuzzy sets corresponding to the particular PHY modes are chosen to compute the fuzzy memberships for the particular queue load and C/I measurements. The C/I fuzzy set has three linguistic variables (high, medium, low); the queue load fuzzy set has four variables (very low, low, high, very high).

In the inference calculation, for each combination of the C/I membership value p_i and the queue load membership value q_j, the fuzzy AND operation is performed, yielding a 3×4 matrix with elements a_{ij}:

$$a_{ij} = \min(p_i, q_j); 1 \geq i \geq 3; 1 \geq j \geq 4 \qquad (4.25)$$

In the next step, a fuzzy OR operation is performed on each row of the matrix which determines the maximum element of the row. All other elements are set to zero.

$$a'_{ij} = \begin{cases} a_{ij} & \text{if } a_{ij} = \max(a_{i0}, a_{i1}, a_{i2}, a_{i3}) \\ 0 & \text{else.} \end{cases} \qquad (4.26)$$

The remaining elements are weighted by a so-called FAM matrix with the weighting factors f_{ij}:

$$b_{ij} = a'_{ij} f_{ij} \qquad (4.27)$$

Finally, with the so-called maximum height method, the computed fuzzy output values are defuzzified. The highest of the four non-zero values b_{ij} is selected. The indexes i and j of this value are used to select a power offset p_{ij} from the power offset matrix. The values for the power offset are 0.5 (reduce power by $-3\,\text{dB}$), 0.75 (reduce power by $-1.5\,\text{dB}$), 1 (keep power unchanged) and 2 (increase power by $3\,\text{dB}$).

4.2.2.4 Monitoring State

After the fuzzy controller has found an optimum setting for the transmit power, the controller enters the monitoring state in which the queue load and the interference are observed. If the interference power exceeds the reference value for three consecutive measurements, the controller waits for a certain time interval, which is short if the TX power is currently high and long if the TX power is low. The reason for the longer delay in case of a low TX power is that the testing state tries to further reduce the transmit power, which should be done with care if it is already low. During this time interval, the interference is further observed. If the interference still exceeds the reference value after the time interval has expired, the controller switches to the testing state. This is done to check if the station itself is the cause for the increased interference. This can happen if the station, due to its transmission, causes additional interference which leads to an increase of the transmit power at the neighbouring stations. In the testing state, the station waits for a certain number of cycles given in table 4.4 which depends on the current PHY mode.

PHY Mode Mbit/s	Cycles
6	0
9	0
12	1
18	1
24	2
36	3
48	3
54	4

Table 4.4: Number of monitoring state cycles for different PHY modes

Simulation results demonstrating the performance of TPC are given in sections 7.1.3.3 to 7.1.3.5. Results for the combination of DFS and TPC are shown in 7.1.5.

4.3 Signalling Issues for Power Control

Similar to DFS, in the case of power control, signalling issues must also be considered. By default, all data and management packets which have to be transmitted are put into the same transmit queue inside the MAC layer where they are kept until they are transmitted. If the offered load of user traffic is higher than the average service rate of the queue, the queue is filled up to its maximum size. Since the queue is managed in a FIFO way, a packet which is inserted at the end of the queue must wait until all previous packets were transmitted, which results in a high queueing delay. In case of a completely filled queue, there is an additional problem, which is that any packet arriving at the queue is discarded until a slot in the queue becomes free again.

Due to the losses, retransmissions and timeouts have to be scheduled to continue the correct operation of the signalling. However, the reaction speed of the system can become slow in case that the power has to be changed. For a frequency change, this could result in a long link disruption in the case that the DFS owner decides to switch the channel and the associated stations do not detect the Channel Switch Announcement. For power control, the result of lost signals is less critical. A link disruption only occurs if a power level is too low and not increased quickly enough so that the two involved stations lose the communication.

If the response time of the signalling is too slow, the time which DFS or TPC needs to adapt to a given situation can be unacceptably slow. In case of queue overflow losses which are in particular likely for high channel load, signalling packets can be lost repeatedly so that the algorithm cannot continue. A packet which was successfully queued still suffers from a long queueing delay. When the packet arrives at the receiver after some seconds, any informational content inside this packet such as measurements might already have become too old to be useful. It can be said that these control packets have quality-of-service requirements regarding the delay, which can hardly be satisfied by a system which does not distinguish priorities of different flows. For this reason it is, beyond the specifications of the 802.11h standard, proposed in this work that spectrum management packets are prioritised. One way to realise this feature is assigning a separate prioritised queue for these packets. This queue is always served once a packet is available in the queue and the station is ready to transmit the next packet. Since the amount of signalling packets is low, the risk of a queue overflow is very small so that queue losses are almost eliminated. Furthermore, the queueing delay is also reduced. Another way of prioritising the packet is prepending it at the beginning of the existing queue, which can make implementation easier because no second queue is needed. The packet is then also transmitted once the transmission of the previous packet is complete. The reduction of the queueing delay can be determined as follows: Assuming a saturated system, i.e. the traffic load is higher than the service rate of the queue, the queue is always filled up to the maximum. In this case, a packet has to travel across the entire queue length before being transmitted. Assuming the packet size D, a mean transmission bit rate R and a queue length L, the mean queueing delay is

$$t_{\text{delay}} = \left(\frac{D}{R} + t_{\text{backoff}} \right) \cdot L \tag{4.28}$$

In case of a single transmitting station, i.e. the channel does not get busy by other stations, the mean backoff time is

$$t_{\text{overhead}} = t_{\text{DIFS}} + CW_{\text{min}}/2 \cdot \sigma + t_{\text{SIFS}} + t_{\text{ACK}}. \tag{4.29}$$

where t_{DIFS} is the time for the interframe spacing before the transmission of the data packet, CW_{min} is the minimum contention window size and σ is the backoff slot time.

In a practical example, with $t_{\mathrm{DIFS}} = 25\,\mu\mathrm{s}$, $t_{\mathrm{SIFS}} = 9\,\mu\mathrm{s}$, $R = 6\,\mathrm{Mbit/s}$, $CW_{\mathrm{min}} = 16$ a packet size of 1000 Byte and a queue length of 50, the delay is approx. 45 ms. In practice, with a number of stations inside the scenario and high delays due to retransmissions and busy channels, the delay can become 500 ms and higher.

4.4 Link Adaptation

Besides DFS and TPC, *Link Adaptation* (LA) is an additional means of maintaining spectrum management which is introduced in this work. While DFS controls the frequency and TPC controls the power, LA selects the PHY mode to be used. The selection of the PHY mode is done according to the the minimum C/I which the selected transmission rate requires and the C/I which is available on the channel. The bit rate provided by a particular PHY mode is the result of the modulation scheme and the amount of forward error correction which is applied to the user data, as discussed in section 2.3.1. The information to select the PHY mode is already provided by the TPC signalling: the receiver returns the C/I of the received signal back to the sender. According to the C/I, the PHY mode can then be set. Since both TPC and LA are controlled by the same input value, i. e. the available C/I, they are tightly related so that it is useful to to combine them in the same algorithm. In this work, Link Adaptation has been added to the simulator which is used for the investigation of spectrum management, both for infrastructure and ad-hoc power control. Simulation results including Link Adaptation are shown in section 7.1.5.

Link Adaptation is also widely used in available Wireless LAN hardware. However, due to the lack of spectrum management signalling, there is no information about the receiver's C/I available at the sender for the proper setting of the PHY mode. Hence the PHY mode has to be estimated by some indirect means such as the packet loss rate.

The spectrum management algorithms described above as well as the necessary signalling have been implemented in the simulator which was used for the spectrum management investigations as described in section 6.3. Section 7.1.5 shows simulation results for different combinations of DFS, TPC and LA.

4.5 Summary

This section discussed different spectrum management algorithms for Wireless LANs. For Dynamic Frequency Selection, different channel assignment strategies without and with memory were discussed. In case of transmit power control, both a centralised and a decentralised method was introduced. Signalling and error recovery schemes needed to deploy DFS and TPC in 802.11 networks were developed in this chapter to provide a reliable operation of spectrum-managed wireless LAN stations.

5 Cross-Layer Architecture

5.1 Introduction

In the previous chapters, spectrum management methods were discussed which enhance the performance of wireless LANs based on the dynamic selection of transmit frequencies, transmit power and physical bit rate. These methods are applicable to optimise the coexistence between neighbouring networks. However, also in case of a single network with an access point which serves a number of stations, optimisations are possible.

A prerequisite which is assumed for the further investigations in this chapter is that the access point has full control of the channel access. It allocates airtime to the different mobile stations inside its range. In case of the uplink, this is done by sending polling packets which request a mobile station to transmit any data which might be available. As long as no poll packets are sent, the mobile stations are not allowed to transmit as it was described in chapter 2; during this time, the access point can send packets in the downlink direction.

Another feature of the resource allocation method discussed in this chapter is the *cross-layer architecture*: Legacy protocol stacks strictly separate the different layers inside the protocol stack, as proposed by the OSI reference model. There is no communication between the layers to exchange control information; only the user payload is transferred between the layers through the Service Access Points (SAPs), cf. section 2.1. The transmission of packets can be optimised by lifting this separation; a cooperation between the layers can increase the performance. The cross-layer approach allows requirements of the application layer to be considered in the MAC scheduling. Moreover, information about PHY layer capabilities for a certain user and the transmission channel are provided which can be used in the application layer to adapt accordingly. The exchange of MAC and PHY layer information can significantly increase system and user performance. If, for example, information is exchanged about the importance of packets belonging to different flows and about the channel conditions, the order of transmission can be determined as a compromise between the packet priority and the channel capacity. The physical access can be enhanced in several steps, starting with the legacy single-antenna transmission which is extended to a MIMO transmission combined with SDMA and OFDMA. The PHY scheduler considers both the Quality-of-Service (QoS) requirements of the MAC layer and the availability of resources on the PHY layer (space, time, frequency), assigning the PHY resources to the users on a per-packet basis.

The separation of the layers is in particular problematic for the design of the two lowest layers, which is the MAC and the PHY layer, because there are close mutual dependencies between these two layers. QoS requirements do not only have to be considered when selecting a certain data flow on the MAC layer, but also on the physical layer when ordering the packets according to their transmission priority. The PHY layer has to combine this ordering policy with information about the current channel state when taking the decision in which order a number of packets should be transmitted. A cross-layer approach between these two layers is also relatively easy to implement because the MAC and the PHY layer are usually implemented inside the same hardware device, so that the effort for signalling between the two layers is low. If signalling is needed between different hardware devices to transfer cross-layer related control information, suitable protocols have to be designed which allow to exchange this cross-layer information between the devices.

In this chapter, first the concept of the cross-layer scheduler is introduced which has been developed in the framework of this work. After that, different scheduling strategies for the MAC layer are discussed, including the introduction of a novel quality-of-service aware scheduling mechanism. The operation of the cross-layer scheduler is considered first with a sequential transmission of packets by TDMA which is then extended to parallelised transmission based on OFDMA and SDMA.

5.2 Two-Stage Cross-Layer Scheduler

In legacy WLAN protocol stacks, the packets for different data flows are scheduled only on the MAC layer. An example for this method is the IEEE 802.11e standard which defines eight traffic classes. The service of these data streams can be controlled in a decentralised manner using the Enhanced Distributed Coordination Function (EDCF) or in a centralised manner using the Hybrid Coordination Function (HCF). Due to the centralised approach of the HCF, it is possible to start transmissions exactly at specified times and serve different flows with specified service rates. However, the HCF does not consider the state of the physical transmission channel when sending a packet. If the channel is bad for a certain user at the time when a packet is transmitted, that packet may be lost.

These problems can be tackled if the physical channel capacity is considered for the packet transmission. The channel capacity is included into the scheduling by adding a second scheduling stage to the existing MAC scheduler. While the MAC scheduler is located in the MAC layer and does not have knowledge about the channel state, the newly introduced physical (PHY) scheduler has access to the channel state information.

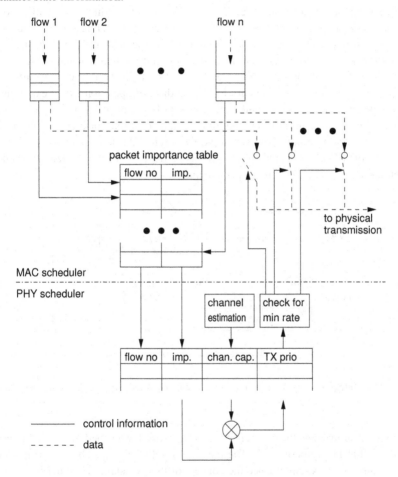

Figure 5.1: Design of the cross-layer scheduler

The concept of the two-stage scheduler is shown in fig. 5.1. The system maintains a number of data flows where each of them is generated by an application with given quality-of-service requirements. Each of the flows is maintained by its own queue. In each scheduling operation, the MAC scheduler calculates an importance metric w_i for all packets which are located at the top of their respective queue i. The packet to which the highest metric is assigned is the one which the scheduler considers as most important for transmission. The list of importance values is handed over to the PHY scheduler. Without the additional considerations of the PHY scheduler, i. e. in case of legacy MAC scheduling, the packet with the highest importance value would be selected as the next one to be transmitted. The PHY scheduler determines the channel capacity which is available for each data flow. The capacity can differ between flows if the flows are transmitted to different users. Since the users are located at different positions, they experience different channel conditions and capacities. Furthermore, it has to be considered that the channel is time-variant, conditions can be different for each packet that is transported for a certain flow. When the PHY scheduler has selected a packet, it requests the MAC scheduler to transmit this particular packet; the MAC scheduler then takes the packet from its respective queue.

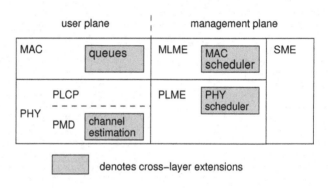

Figure 5.2: Integration of the cross-layer enhancements into the IEEE 802.11 protocol stack

Fig. 5.2 shows how the different parts of the cross-layer scheduler are integrated into the 802.11 protocol stack. The integration into 802.11 is shown and investigated here as an example; since the concept of the two-stage scheduler is generic and not related to the properties of a particular wireless protocol, it can be deployed in any protocol which supports centralised media access. The IEEE 802.11 protocol stack includes a user plane and a management plane. The user plane includes the MAC (Media Access Control) and the PHY (physical) layer, which is divided into the PLCP (Physical Layer Convergence Protocol) and the PMD (Physical Media Dependent) sublayer. Both the MAC and the PHY layer are supervised by a respective management entity: the MLME (MAC Layer Management Entity) and the PLME (PHY Layer Management Entity). Finally, the SME (Station Management Entity) supervises the station at the top level. The queues for the different data flows are located in the MAC layer. The MAC scheduler which observes the queue states is placed in the MLME; it can request information about the queues from the MAC, but does not process the packets themselves. The PHY scheduler is situated in the PLME. At this location, it can communicate on the one hand with the MLME and on the other hand with the PHY layer, from where it queries the channel estimation. The PHY scheduler does not store any packets, it only processes information about these packets and sends information about the selected packets to the MAC scheduler. Furthermore, the PHY scheduler requests channel information from the PMD layer which contains the channel estimation.

The cross-layer scheduler includes a MAC and a PHY stage. For each of these two stages, suitable scheduling strategies have to be selected. In case of the MAC scheduler, scheduling methods are taken for comparison in this analysis which differ by their amount of knowledge about the application requirements, starting with methods without any knowledge up to a newly developed scheme which controls the service of the flows according to given throughput and delay requirements.

- Random selection: in each turn of the scheduler, the importance metrics for each flow i are randomly selected, equally distributed values inside an interval $0 \leq w_i \leq 1$ where w_i is the metric value for flow i. In the long-term average, the priority is 0.5 for all flows so that all of them are served equally often. Hence the scheme has a long-term fairness if all flows have the same traffic load. Within short time intervals, however, the time interval between two consecutive services can vary so that delay requirements might not be met. Furthermore, the scheme is not aware of the queue states, so flows with variable arrival times such as Poisson-distributed flows cannot be served in an optimum way. The scheme is also not aware of the application requirements, so flows with different offered traffic loads are served inappropriately.

- Round Robin selection (RR) [24]: In the strict sense, RR means that out of a number of data flows, they are selected in a sequential, regular order. Regarding the metric value this means that it is set to a value greater than zero for the flow which should be served and to zero otherwise. In this case, it would not be possible for the PHY layer scheduler to affect the packet selection. Hence in this work, a modified RR is used. The importance metric w_i for flow i is set to 0 after flow i has been served and increased by 1 in each turn of the scheduler until it is served again as illustrated in table 5.1. If there are n flows, the maximum possible value of w_i is $n - 1$.

  If this scheme is used without additional PHY scheduling, which means without considering the channel conditions, the flows are served in a fixed,

	scheduling turn					
	1	2	3	...	8	9 ...
user 1	7	6	5	...	0	7 ...
user 2	6	5	4	...	2	1 ...
...				...		
user 8	0	7	6	...	4	3 ...

Table 5.1: Priority assignment for modified Round Robin scheduling

regular order as in the original RR scheduling method. This scheme, similar to random selection, performs well if all flows have constant bit rate. In contrast to random selection, a particular flow gets the same priority after a constant number of scheduling turns which provides lower delay variations because it is served in a more regular manner. However, like random selection, the scheme is also not aware of the queue states or the application requirements, so it does not consider flows with variable data rates or non-equal loads.

- Longest queue: This scheme prefers flows which have a high queue length and thus reduces the probability that packets are lost due to queue overflow. The importance metric w_i is the queue length value, ranging between 0 and 50 in the implementation considered here, because arriving packets are dropped if the queue has reached the maximum length. Flows with different arrival rates are considered because a flow with higher arrivals gets an increased queue length, so indirectly the throughput is taken into account as well. However, it behaves poor for flows with small arrival rates which might not be served for a long time until their queue has reached a particular filling state and thus results in a high delay. The scheme reduces the probability that packets are lost due to queue overflow. The queue lengths relatively and not against an absolute value, so there is not guarantee that a given throughput requirement is met.

- Longest queue/longest lifetime (QL): This scheme extends the Longest Queue scheme by considering the remaining lifetime of the packet and thus avoids that a flow is not served for a long time. Due to the adaptation to the queue conditions, the scheme is more suitable for flows with different arrival rates than the Round Robin scheme. Considering lifetime limits of packets is important in case of real-time traffic where high delays should be avoided.

The importance metric w_i is calculated as

$$w_i = a_i \cdot k_i + b_i \cdot t_i, \tag{5.1}$$

where k_i is the queue length of flow i and t_i is the age of the packet at the top of queue i measured in seconds; a_i and b_i are constants which are set according to the queue length as specified in table 5.2, where $k_{i,\max}$ is the maximum queue length of flow i.

queue length	a_i	b_i
$k_i < 0.3k_{i,\max}$	0.3	70
$0.3k_{i,\max} < k_i < 0.7k_{i,\max}$	0.4	60
$k_i > 0.7k_{i,\max}$	0.7	30

Table 5.2: Parameters for the longest queue/longest lifetime scheduler

The values for a_i and b_i given in the table have been chosen in the way that the value range for queue filling level k_i (0 to 1) is divided into three sections of approximately the same size. The weighting factor for the queue length is set according to the queue filling state, except the middle section ($0.3 < k_i < 0.7$) which is weighted slightly lower, with 0.4 instead of 0.5. The packet age is given more weight than the queue length in this case in order to enhance the performance of the scheduler of time-critical packets.

Section 7.2.1 shows simulation results regarding the cross-layer scheduler.

5.2.1 QoS Aware Scheduler

The scheduling schemes listed above only consider the current states of the queues to take their decisions. On the other hand, they do not process absolute values of the queue states, but only relatively compare the filling state of the queues and the age of the packets. To enhance the scheduling, a scheme is proposed in this work which considers events that happened in the past to take scheduling decisions in the future. The design of this scheme is shown in figure 5.3.

The scheduling scheme controls the throughput and the delay for each data flow by a closed-loop circuit; the controlling mechanism for each of these two parameters is discussed in the following two sections.

The target value S_{target} of this circuit is the throughput which should be achieved. The current value S_{current} for the throughput is measured by a sliding window.

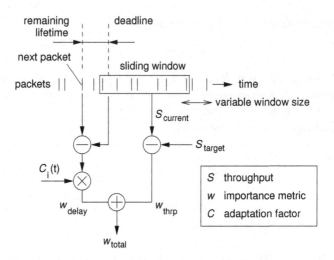

Figure 5.3: Priority calculation in the QoS aware scheduler

The length of this window is set to the time which the packets waiting in the queue would need to be transmitted at the currently available data rate. S_{current} is measured by observing the number of successful transmissions inside this window. The difference between the current value and the target value is normalised by the target throughput S_{target}. This ensures fair service for flows with different traffic loads; the result is the utility function for the throughput $w_{i,\text{thrp}}$:

$$w_{i,\text{thrp}} = \frac{S_{\text{target}} - S_{\text{current}}}{S_{\text{target}}}. \tag{5.2}$$

Negative values are not considered, i. e. if the throughput is higher than required, the value is set to zero.

The second value which is considered for the utility function is the delay. If t_0 is the time at which the packet expires and thus should be transmitted latest and t_{current} is the current time, then the utility function for the delay is

$$w_{i,\text{delay}} = C_i \frac{1}{(t_0 - t_{\text{current}})^2}. \tag{5.3}$$

C_i is an adaptive value which is determined by an algorithm which is discussed in the following paragraphs.

A timer T_{late} is introduced which is at initialisation set to

$$T_{\text{late}}(i) = maxDel(i) - avgTxLen(i). \tag{5.4}$$

$maxDel$ specifies the maximum lifetime of a delay-sensitive packet. $avgTxLen$ is a parameter which considers the duration that is needed by the PHY layer for the transmission of the packets. The average values of these durations are reported to the MAC scheduler for each flow i.

If T_{late} has expired with progressing time, it is assumed that the maximum delay of the packet was exceeded. In this case, the packet is discarded and a counter variable $discard$ is increased.

The delay of the packet to be transmitted should, however, not only be adjusted if the packet was sent too late, there should be a regular check. For this reason, besides the delay variable which counts late packets, another timing variable T_{early} is introduced which triggers the checking of C_i in regular time intervals. T_{early} is set to the largest $maxDel$ among all delay-sensitive routes.

When one of the timers T_{late} or T_{early} has expired, the value of C_i is adjusted according to the algorithm below. The parameters $discard$ and $discard_{\text{old}}$ are set to 0 at the start of the simulation. $init$ is a Boolean variable set to TRUE at the start and changed to FALSE once a packet has expired. The parameter $maxDdel$ expresses the packet age normalised in relation to the time which elapses until the transmission of the packet is complete. It is calculated according to

$$maxDdel = \frac{1}{2} \frac{maxDel}{avgTxLen + PktAge} \tag{5.5}$$

$PktAge$ is the remaining lifetime of a packet before it expires. If a packet expires before the transmission, it is removed from the queue which is called *packet ageing*.

With the prerequisites discussed above, the algorithm to determine C_i can now be written.

if $discard = 0$ **then**
    if $discard_{\text{old}} = 0$ **then**
        $discard\_zero := C_i$
        if $init$ **then**
            $C_i := C_{i,\text{old}}/2$
        else
            $C_i := C_{i,\text{old}}/maxDdel$
        end if
    end if
end if

if $discard \neq 0$ **then**
  if $discard\_old = 0$ **then**
    $discard\_zero := C_{i,\text{old}} \cdot maxDdel$
    $C_i := C_{i,\text{old}} + (discard\_zero - C_{i,\text{old}})/2$
  else
    $discard\_zero := 2 \cdot C_{i,\text{old}} \cdot maxDdel$
    $C_i := C_{i,\text{old}} + (discard\_zero - C_{i,\text{old}})/2$
  end if
end if
$discard_{\text{old}} := discard;\ discard := 0$
$C_{i,\text{old}} := C_i$

The parameter C_i has to be selected in an optimum way. If it is too low, too many packets of a flow are lost because they are considered sufficiently important and being transmitted too late. If it is too high, packets are transmitted earlier than required by the delay limit. This does not harm the particular connection, but reduces the freedom of the PHY scheduler to select packets according to good channel conditions and thus increase the total throughput of the system. Simulations show that the higher the load is, the stronger is the effect of C_i, which means the parameter needs to be adapted according to the traffic load and the occurrence of packet losses. In case of low load, C_i can be reduced to 0. The scheduler then only works based on the throughput specifications. Since the correct value for C_i is dependent on the load, an adaptive control is required. C_i is increased when the number of dropped packets gets higher. The parameter $maxDdel$ which is used in the algorithm expresses the ratio between the delay required by the application and the delay which actually was achieved in the last transmission, including both the queueing and the transmission delay. It is hence a metric how quickly the parameter C should be adapted and is close to 1 if the adaptation process has converged against an optimum value for C_i. An example from a simulation run in shown in fig. 5.4 for three different data flows with a maximum delay of 20, 10 and 5 ms.

In addition, to optimise the adaptivity, the time interval between two consecutive adaptation steps is also variable. This is the reason why the two timers T_{early} and T_{late} are introduced which provide both a regular check of the adaptation and extra checks if a packet has expired, which is a hint that C_i was too low so that the packet was not assigned a sufficient priority.

If the packet ageing rate is becoming high, quick action is needed in order to keep the QoS requirements. In this case, a high C_i is selected so that the controller responds quickly to the increased amount of aged packets. This might result in a ageing rate which is lower than required so that the channel usage is not optimum, however in this case meeting the QoS requirements has priority. When the number

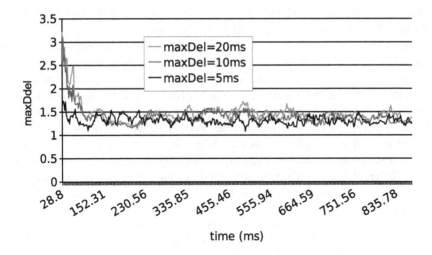

Figure 5.4: Adaptation of the maxDdel value for three data flows with a maximum delay of 20, 10 and 5 ms

of aged packets decreases, the length of the window is increased so that a more precise control is possible to optimise the channel utilisation.

After the throughput-based and delay-based utility values $w_{i,\text{thrp}}$ and $w_{i,\text{delay}}$ have been determined, the utility values for the throughput and the delay of flow i are added:

$$w_i = w_{i,\text{thrp}} + w_{i,\text{delay}}. \tag{5.6}$$

The MAC scheduler sends a list with the importance metrics w_i of all packets to the PHY scheduler which has knowledge about the channel conditions and thus can estimate and, dependent on the PHY scheduling scheme, also adjust the channel capacity resp. the physical bit rate which is available for a certain user at a given time. In the simulation model which is discussed in this work, it is assumed that the access point has perfect channel knowledge, which means there is no packet loss.

5.2.2 MIMO-TDMA

The channel model deployed in the investigations discussed in this chapter is based on a MIMO transmission as discussed in section 2.6. Based on this model, the channel matrices are calculated for each user. For the sequential transmission of packets, TDMA is used as the channel access method.

Two options are available how to distribute the available transmit power among the subcarriers. If no channel knowledge is assumed at the sender, the power is equally distributed among all subcarriers. In case of perfect channel knowledge, with the known channel matrix $\mathbf{H}[l]$ for subcarrier l which was discussed in section 2.6, the channel capacities available for the user are determined at the access point so that the power which is allocated to each MIMO subchannel can be selected using the waterfilling algorithm. With $\{\lambda_1[l], \lambda_2[l], \ldots, \lambda_N[l]\}$ being the eigenvalues of the product between the channel matrix and its Hermitian conjugate $\mathbf{H}[l]\mathbf{H}^{\mathrm{H}}[l]$ and θ being the waterfilling level, the power $P_i[l]$ for subchannel i of subcarrier l is allocated according to:

$$P_i[l] = \begin{cases} \theta - 1/\lambda_i[l] & \theta > 1/\lambda_i[l] \\ 0 & \text{else.} \end{cases} \tag{5.7}$$

Because of the OFDM transmission, this calculation has to be performed for each of the OFDM subcarriers.

The available normalised capacity C has been given in eqn. 2.13 which gives the capacity in the case of a single-carrier MIMO transmission with N_T transmit antennas, N_R receive antennas and the transmit power P_T as

$$C_{\mathrm{norm}} = \sum_{i=1}^{r} \log_2 \left(1 + \lambda_i \cdot \frac{P_\mathrm{T}}{M} \right) \text{ with } r = \min\left(M, N\right).$$

By assuming individual powers $P_i[l]$ for each subcarrier l and subchannel i and summing up over all L subcarriers, the denormalised capacity C is

$$C = \frac{W}{L} \sum_{l=1}^{L} \sum_{i=1}^{r} \log_2 \left(1 + P_i[l]\lambda_i[l] \right), \tag{5.8}$$

where W is the channel bandwidth, $\lambda_i[l]$ is defined as described above.

Fig. 5.2.2 gives an example for the capacities available for two data flows as a function of the time, calculated from the channel matrix trace file which was used in this analysis.

The effect of the algorithm is that a subchannel is assigned an increasing amount of power $P_i[l]$, the lower the noise level of the respective subchannel is, which is indicated by the reciprocal of eigenvalue $\lambda_i[l]$. This is illustrated in fig. 5.6 where six subchannels are shown with different noise levels $1/\lambda_i$. The waterfilling level

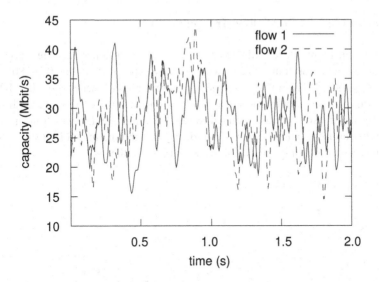

Figure 5.5: Channel capacities for two data flows as a function of the time

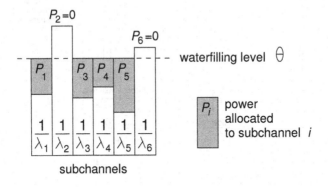

Figure 5.6: Waterfilling method for single-carrier MIMO system

θ is denoted by the horizontal dashed line. Bad subchannels with $1/\lambda > \theta$ are not used.

Simulation results showing the properties of the cross-layer QoS scheduler along with the MIMO-TDMA transmission are given in section 7.2.2.

5.3 Scheduling for Parallelised Transmissions

The previously introduced MIMO-based cross-layer transmission system uses the TDMA scheme for transmission which is also specified in the IEEE 802.11n WLAN standard. This means that the users are served consecutively, the MIMO platform provides parallel transmission of the data inside a certain packet. In this section, the transmission is extended to OFDMA and SDMA, which means that a number of users can be served in parallel by distributing the OFDM subcarriers among them or utilising the spatial diversity between the users.

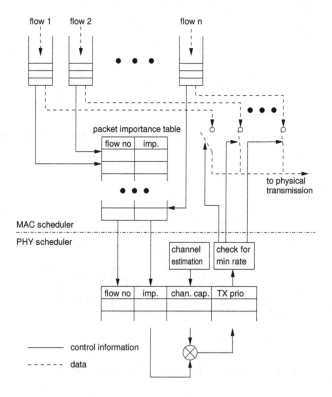

Figure 5.7: Design of the parallelised cross-layer scheduler

Fig. 5.7 shows the cross-layer scheduler design extended by the parallel transmission. The scheduler includes a hardware-independent part in the MAC layer and a hardware-dependent part in the PHY layer. In each turn of the scheduling process, the MAC scheduler selects packets from a number of flows according to certain scheduling strategies, where each flow is assigned its own queue. In this work, the Round Robin method and the quality-of-service supporting strategy introduced in sec. 5.2.1 which keeps throughput and delay constraints that apply to a time-critical flow such as a video transmission are considered. According to these strategies, the MAC scheduler computes a priority for each flow and sends a list of these priorities to the PHY scheduler. The task of the PHY scheduler is dependent on the mode of operation: In case of TDMA, only a single packet can be transmitted at a time, so out of the available data flows the most important one has to be selected by determining the channel capacity which is multiplied with the priority provided by the MAC scheduler. In case of OFDMA or SDMA, a number of users is served in parallel. The available transmission power has to be allocated to the users in an optimum way according to the user's priorities which means that in contrast to TDMA the PHY scheduler can to some extent control the channel conditions for the users.

As it was described before, the MAC stage of the scheduler sends a list of packets to be transmitted to the PHY stage where the channel capacity for each user is then determined. For the calculation of the channel capacities, a system is considered with M transmit antennas at the access point, N receive antennas for the mobile terminal of each user, K users resp. data flows and L OFDM subcarriers. The priority for user k which is determined by the MAC scheduler is labelled w_k. The subcarriers are indexed by the variable l in the following calculations, the subchannels inside a particular subcarrier with i. Furthermore, the value r is defined as the minimum of the number of transmit and receive antennas $\min(M, N)$. The following sections describe the rate allocation algorithms for OFDMA and SDMA which are considered in this analysis. TDMA has already been described in the previous section where the scheduler for sequential transmission was discussed.

5.3.1 MIMO-OFDMA

In MIMO-OFDMA operation, at each time, each subcarrier can be assigned to a different user. Fig. 5.8 shows the difference to TDMA where at a given time all subcarriers are assigned to the same user.

The subcarriers are assigned to the users dependent on the channel matrix $\mathbf{H}_k[l]$ of each user k and subcarrier l. The optimum solution for this carrier assignment problem would be calculating the capacity weighted by the respective user's weighting factor w_k for each combination of users and subcarriers In this way, the most suitable user for each subcarrier can be found, considering the respective priority of each user. These weighting factors are determined by the MAC layer

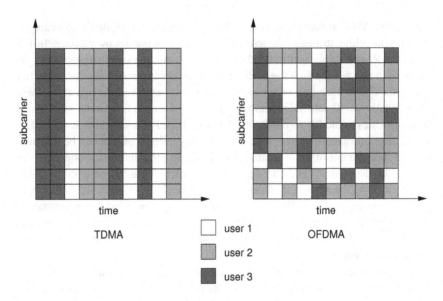

Figure 5.8: Subcarrier assignment for TDMA and OFDMA

according to the quality-of-service requirements of the users so that in comparison to TDMA, the cross-layer functionality of the scheduler is enhanced. Users with a high demand of channel capacity can be allocated more resources.

The problem of the beforementioned method is the large amount of calculations which are required: With K users and L subcarriers, L^K power calculations would have to be performed. In order to avoid such extensive calculations, a heuristic method is used instead which assigns a subcarrier k_l to a user l according to the Frobenius norm as specified in [100]:

$$k_l = \mathrm{argmax}_k w_k \cdot ||\mathbf{H}_k[l]||_{\mathrm{F}}^2 . \tag{5.9}$$

This method gives a sub-optimal solution, however it significantly reduces the computation effort.

After assigning the subcarriers, the powers need to be allocated to the individual users and subcarriers. Because of the weighting factors w_k, the waterfilling algorithm which is used for TDMA has to be modified to the so-called *pseudo-waterfilling* algorithm [100], which allocates the powers $P_{i,k}[l]$ for user k, subcarrier l and subchannel i to the users according to equation 5.10:

$$P_{i,k}[l] = \begin{cases} w'_k\theta - 1/\lambda_{i,k}[l] & k = k_l \text{ and } w'_k\theta > 1/\lambda_{i,k}[l] \\ 0 & \text{else.} \end{cases} \qquad (5.10)$$

The user priorities w_i are permuted to w'_i according to ascending noise levels $\psi_i = \frac{1}{\lambda_i w'_i}$ for the individual users. The algorithm is illustrated in fig. 5.9. w_1 to w_5 are the priorities of the users after the sorting. The power is allocated according to the product of the user priority w'_i and the difference and the weighted noise terms ψ_i. Due to the limited total transmission power, users 4 and 5 cannot be served.

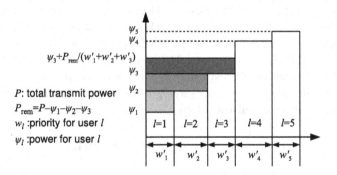

Figure 5.9: Pseudo waterfilling method for MIMO-OFDMA system

After setting the powers for each user, the channel capacity C_k for user k is determined in a similar way as for the TDMA case

$$C_k = \frac{W}{L} \sum_{l=1}^{L} \sum_{i=1}^{r} \log_2\left(1 + P_{i,k}[l]\lambda_{i,k}[l]\right). \qquad (5.11)$$

If a subcarrier l is not assigned to a user k, $P_{i,k}[l]$ is zero for all i.

5.3.2 MIMO-SDMA

The MIMO-OFDMA channel access is not optimal because one subcarrier is assigned to exactly one user. Further enhancement is possible by introducing spatial separation between users. If, from the view of the base station, there is a wide angle between two users, a subcarrier can be shared between them, while at the same time the interference is kept at a low level. This method is called space division multiple access (SDMA). When designing an SDMA system, it has however to be considered that users who receive signals on the same frequency and at the same time always will interfere each other by a certain amount. To tackle with this problem, an algorithm to minimise the effects of interference between users called *dirty paper coding* (DPC) [124] can be used. The algorithm assumes that priorities are assigned to the users. The channel coding of the users is then selected in a suitable way so that mutual interference can to some extent be eliminated. In order to perform the DPC algorithm, the users are permuted according to ascending priorities, i.e. the priorities $w_1 \leq w_2 \leq \ldots \leq w_K$ are mapped to w'_k such that $w'_1 \leq w'_2 \leq \ldots \leq w'_K$. User K is the one which the highest priority for whom the receiver can fully cancel the interference. User $K-1$ has the second highest priority: for him, interference by user K cannot be eliminated, however the interference from users $K-2$ to 1 still can be cancelled. For user 1 with the lowest priority, interference cancellation is not possible, he is interfered by all other users. The DPC method as described above can be applied for each of the OFDM subcarriers.

The available denormalised capacity C_k for user k which results from the usage of DPC can then be calculated as [35]:

$$C_k = \frac{W}{L} \log_2 \det \left(\mathbf{\Phi}_{\tilde{\mathbf{n}}_k}^{-1}[l] \mathbf{H}_k[l] \mathbf{\Phi}_{\mathbf{x}_k}[l] \mathbf{H}_k[l]^{\mathrm{H}} \right). \qquad (5.12)$$

$\mathbf{\Phi}_{\mathbf{x}_k}[t]$ and $\mathbf{\Phi}_{\tilde{\mathbf{n}}_k}[l]$ are the covariance matrices of user k's transmission signal vector resp. effective noise vector. The latter includes a thermal component $\sigma_{\mathrm{n}}^2 \mathbf{I}$ and a component specifying the interference from users 1 to $k-1$ which is denoted as $\sum_{\kappa=1}^{k-1}(\cdot)$ in eqn. 5.13.

$$\mathbf{\Phi}_{\tilde{\mathbf{n}}_k}[t] = \sigma_{\mathrm{n}}^2 \mathbf{I} + \sum_{\kappa=1}^{k-1} \mathbf{H}_k[l] \mathbf{\Phi}_{\mathbf{x}_\kappa}[l] \mathbf{H}_k[l]^{\mathrm{H}}, \qquad (5.13)$$

$\mathbf{\Phi}_{\tilde{\mathbf{n}}_k}[l]$ is the covariance matrix for subcarrier l of user k.

Simulation results which show the performance of cross-layer scheduling along with MIMO-OFDMA and -SDMA transmissions are presented in section 7.2.3.

5.4 Summary

In this chapter, a novel two-stage cross-layer scheduler concept was introduced which considers both the requirements of the application on the MAC layer and the state of the transmission channel on the physical layer. Furthermore, a new MAC scheduling scheme was developed which assigns airtime to applications by enforcing QoS requirements. For each data flow, priorities are determined which are used by the PHY layer for the allocation of channel resources. For the physical transmission platform, a MIMO system was proposed which in the first step was examined in combination with TDMA as it is specified by the IEEE 802.11n standard. The chapter then describes extensions of the MIMO platform beyond the standard by using OFDMA and SDMA. TDMA only allows the allocation of airtime to users whereas the available channel resources at a given time are given for each user. OFDMA and SDMA in addition to TDMA allow the adaptive allocation of channel resources to different users, controlled by the priorities given by the MAC scheduler.

6 Simulation Environment

The previous chapters discussed the theory and principles of enhancing the performance of wireless networks. For the validation of the proposed methods, simulations are required which implement a model of the network scenario under investigation.

In the area of communication networks, simulations are usually based on discrete events. The principle of such simulations is highlighted at the beginning of the chapter, along with a description of the WARP2 simulator which was used for the investigations in this work.

After that, a new method of accelerating the WARP2 by the parallelisation over the High Level Architecture platform is described and evaluated. Furthermore, extensions for the WARP2 which have been developed to implement the proposed spectrum management and scheduling methods are described.

6.1 Discrete Event Simulators

Communication networks are simulated with *discrete event simulators*, which also applies to the simulator used for the investigations in this analysis. The term discrete event means the simulator only considers the system to be simulated at discrete points of time, when the state of the system changes. In wireless LAN simulations, the change of the state means, for example, the beginning or the end of a packet transmission over the radio channel. The simulator's model time advances from one point of time to the next one. The advance of the model time is controlled by timers. If, for example, the transmission of a packet has to be simulated, a timer is set to the model time when the transmission should start. When the simulator has advanced to this time and the packet is transmitted, a new timer is set to determine the stopping of the packet transmission. The model time interval between two consecutive events can be constant or variable, dependent on the system to be simulated. The events can occur at any time whenever the system changes. This distinguishes discrete event simulators from continuous simulators as they are for example used to simulate processes on the physical layer. These simulations consider a system at regular time intervals since they have to deal with the processing of analogue signals which are sampled at regular sampling rates.

In discrete event simulators, internally the timers are maintained by a scheduler. When a timer is set, the time is entered into the event list. Whenever all actions which have to be executed at a particular point of model time have been finished, the scheduler reads the next entry from the event list and then sets the model time to the time given in the event list entry. It is also possible to delete a scheduled event, which is done by removing the corresponding entry from the event list. In a simulation of WLAN stations, this can for example happen if a station has to reschedule the transmission of a packet because the channel has become busy due to the transmission of another station, as it was shown in chapter 2. When a station is waiting in the backoff, a timer is used to measure the length of the current backoff time slot. If the channel becomes busy, the timer is deleted. The countdown of the backoff is suspended until the channel gets free again.

6.2 The WARP2 Simulator

The simulator used for the investigations in this work is based on the WARP2 (Wireless Access Radio Protocol 2), which has previously been developed at Aachen University of Technology, Germany and has been enhanced by the different algorithms which are proposed in this analysis. The simulator implements the IEEE 802.11 protocol stack, a load generator, a simple channel model and a unit for the statistical evaluation of the results. The WARP2 is an event-driven simulator as discussed above whose basic parts are written in SDL. In the following sections, some details about the SDL programming language will be discussed. After that the structure and design of the simulator is described.

6.2.1 Specification and Description Language

The programming language used for implementing most parts of the WARP2 simulator is the *Specification and Description Language* (SDL). It is a formal language specified by the ITU recommendation Z.100 [57] which allows to model a communication system using a graphical representation. This means that all elements of the language, such as inputs, outputs, timers, decisions etc. are represented as graphical symbols. If necessary, however, the graphical respresentation can also be converted into a textual representation. The language allows the implementation of *extended finite state machines* (FSM). A finite state machine is a formal description of a process which is defined by a finite number of discrete states, as well as input and output functions. A change between the states only occurs if events from the environment are received; the input function describes in an unambiguous manner which state should be entered next if a particular input is received. When modelling the IEEE 802.11 Wireless LAN protocol, some of the possible events would be the reception of a packet on the radio channel or the arrival of data from the load generator inside a transmission buffer. When the state is changed, the FSM generates an output event specified by the output function. In the example of the WLAN protocol, this might be the start of a packet transmission or the request to check if there is any packet inside a buffer.

An *extended* FSM (EFSM) as it is provided by SDL means that the FSM is extended by *variables* and *timers*. Variables allow storing values inside the FSM, which is for example useful to build a loop. In the WLAN simulation, the access point might want to send packets to a number of stations. Without variables, this would have to be implemented by changing to a number of states according to the number of stations which would result in unnecessarily complex programme code. In theory, variables can always be replaced by states and vice versa. The practical decision if an implementation using variables or using a number of states should be preferred depends on the particular problem. The second extension of the extended FSM are timers. By means of timers, internal events can be generated at a particular model time which is used widely in the simulator as discussed in section 6.1.

SDL allows to model a system in a hierarchical structure in order to support a clear structure. The top layer is the system, which includes one or more blocks. Blocks can be nested according to the hierarchy of the model. At the bottom layer, processes are available which contain the actual SDL code such as states, inputs, outputs, commands etc. Each process implements an EFSM, it has its own states, variables and timers. By means of signals, which means SDL signals in this context, processes can exchange events among each other.

It is possible to embed C code into the SDL code using so-called *Abstract Data Types* (ADTs). An ADT is a function of which only the interface, which means the name and the parameter list, is visible from the SDL domain. The actual implementation which is written in C is hidden from the SDL point of view. This concept is similar, for example, to objects in C++. This concept is useful to support functionality which is not provided by SDL, such as complex calculations or input/output operations.

During the software development process, the SDL part of the project is translated into C. All C files are then compiled and linked to the final simulator executable.

6.2.2 Structure of the Simulator

The WARP2 simulator is structured as a hierarchy of SDL blocks and sub-blocks as discussed in section 6.2.1. On the top layer which is shown in fig. 6.1, there are five blocks:

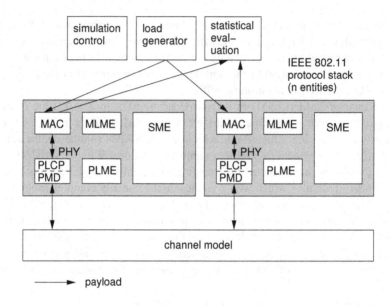

Figure 6.1: Structure of the WARP2 simulator

- The simulation control initialises the stations which are needed to simulate a particular scenario. It provides messages about the ongoing simulation and terminates the simulator after a specified amount of model time has elapsed.

- The load generator generates data packets which shall be sent by the WLAN stations.

- The IEEE 802.11a protocol stack simulates a number of wireless LAN stations. For each station, a separate entity of the stack is created.

- The channel model provides the radio link between the stations inside the simulation scenario.

- The statistical evaluation measures different parameters which specify the connection quality, for example delay and throughput, and calculates the distribution function. Packet losses are counted as well.

Fig. 6.1 also shows the structure of the IEEE 802.11 protocol stack which includes components as were described in chapter 2: in the user plane, the PHY and the MAC layer are provided; in the control plane, the SME, MLME, and MLME are implemented. For the PMD part of the PHY layer, however, a restriction applies: the signal processing is not considered. This means, the data which is transmitted or received by the PHY layer is not an analogue signal for which modulation/demodulation, forward error correction etc. is needed. Instead, a simplified model is used where the data is considered as a packet which is transmitted using a particular modulation scheme and which takes a certain amount of time to be transmitted. Based on the C/I which is known by measurements, the bit error rate is read from a lookup table, using the C/I and the modulation scheme as input values. From the BER and the packet length, the PER is then calculated. Finally, a random generator decides if a packet is lost according to the calculated packet loss probability.

In the original simulator, the channel model is simplified: The antennas of the stations are assumed to be isotropic so that in case of free-space propagation without obstacles, equations 3.2 and 3.3 as introduced in section 3.2 apply:

$$P_{\mathrm{R}} = \frac{P_{\mathrm{T}}}{Gr^2}$$

with

$$G = \frac{1}{(c/4\pi f)^2}.$$

In order to consider obstacles inside the network scenario which result in absorption and multipath propagation, eqn. 3.2 is modified to eqn. 3.4 which also was described in section 3.2:

$$P_{\mathrm{R}} = \frac{P_{\mathrm{T}}}{Gr^\gamma}.$$

The higher γ is selected, the higher becomes the separation between neighbouring radio cells and the more simultaneous transmissions are possible.

This simplified channel model is used for the investigations about spectrum management and simulator parallelisation. For the cross-layer scheduling experiments, a more sophisticated channel model has been implemented as described in chapter 5.

The simulator also provides a number of statistical evaluation features. For each connection, it can evaluate the throughput and the delay of the transferred data. For the delay, the complementary distribution function also is estimated. Besides these quality-of-service parameters, also network-related values can be measured, such as the transmit power of a particular station or the interference which a station experiences by its environment.

6.3 Simulator Extension by Spectrum Management

The spectrum management signalling which is defined by the IEEE 802.11h protocol described in chapter 2, in combination with the spectrum management algorithms proposed in chapter 4 have been integrated into the 802.11 protocol stack as shown in figure 6.2. The timing and the decision algorithms for Dynamic Frequency Selection, Transmit Power Control and Link Adaptation are part of the SME. The MLME generates management packets when requested by a message from the SME and identifies incoming management packets which are then forwarded to the SME. In this work, the MLME is extended by the additional packet types which are defined by the 802.11h standard for the spectrum management. Support to measure the interference on a given frequency channel has been introduced into the the PMD sublayer: when it receives a Measurement Request from the MLME which is implemented as an SDL signal, it has to suspend transmissions and temporarily switch to the frequency channel which was requested to be measured. The collected results are sent back to the SME for further evaluation. The decision algorithms for DFS, TPC and LA are implemented as C code and integrated into the SDL process which implements the SME by using ADTs as the interface.

The simulation results obtained by WARP2 in combination with spectrum management are discussed in section 7.1.

6.4 Simulator Extension by Cross-Layer Scheduling

The principles of cross-layer scheduling have been highlighted in chapter 5. The WARP2 simulator which already has been discussed for spectrum management is used as well for the cross-layer investigations. The components which have been added to WARP2 are shown in Figure 6.3. The hardware-independent stage of the scheduler which is located in the MLME determines the priorities for each packet according to the user's Quality-of-Service requirements. It sends these priorities to the hardware-dependent stage of the scheduler which is in parts implemented by SDL code located in the PLME as well as Matlab code which is embedded into the SDL code as an ADT. The hardware-independent scheduler stage reads the current channel matrices from the PHY layer and determines the channel capacity for each user according to the used transmission scheme (TDMA, OFDMA or SDMA); based on these channel capacities it is decided for which users a transmission should be provided at a given scheduling stage. The numbers of the selected users are then handed over to the MLME which polls the respective queues for transmission.

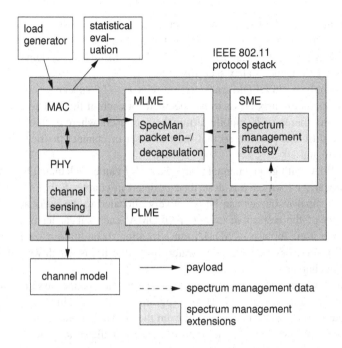

Figure 6.2: Structure of the WARP2 Simulator for Spectrum Management Simulation

Another extension deployed in this work is the MIMO-based channel model which was described in section 2.6 and 5.2.2. which is used along with an OFDM transmission using channel access controlled by TDMA, OFDMA and SDMA. The channel model considers connections between an access point which is transmitting and a number of mobile terminals which are receiving. The mobile stations are located in an area with moving obstacles in the environment. Some part of the access point's radiation power propagates to the mobile terminal directly, some other part is reflected by the obstacles. Because of the time-variant multipath propagation which results from this effect, the receiver experiences a signal which is subject both to fast and slow fading. For this reason, the channel characteristics have to be determined in regular small time intervals. For a system with a single antenna at the transmitter and the receiver (Single Input Single Output, SISO), the channel characteristics can be described by a single complex coefficient h which is the quotient of the complex received signal r and the complex transmitted signal t. For a MIMO system with M transmit antennas and N receive antennas, a channel matrix can be written as explained in section 2.6. There is one complex transfer coefficient h_{mn} for each path between a transmit antenna and a receive antenna with $1 \leq m \leq M$ and $1 \leq n \leq N$. The transmission system can then be described by a channel matrix according to 2.11.

In this analysis, an OFDM transmission with $L = 52$ subcarriers is considered so that a channel matrix needs to be specified for each of the OFDM subcarriers. Furthermore, there are K mobile terminals resp. users where each of them is located at a different position so that there is a set of channel matrices $\mathbf{H}_{k,l}$ with $1 \leq k \leq K$ and $1 \leq l \leq L$.

For TDMA, with given channel matrices, a C/I can be calculated for each user k and subcarrier l which was described in detail in chapter 5. For OFDMA and SDMA, channel resources can be adaptively allocated to the users according to the priority of the respective user. For OFDMA, each subcarrier is assigned to exactly one user; in case of SDMA, an allocation to multiple users is possible. These allocations are performed by waterfilling algorithms which were described in detail in chapter 5.

As already mentioned, the channel model and the channel assignment algorithms are calculated using MATLAB programmes, out of which C libraries are generated so that they can be accessed from the WARP2 simulator using Abstract Data Types (ADTs). The channel matrices are recalculated at regular time intervals of 5 ms of model time; the channel characteristics are assumed to be constant during this time interval. At each invocation of the scheduler, the current channel matrices are read from the channel model. For TDMA, the channel capacity then can be calculated immediately whereas for OFDMA and SDMA, the channel capacity is allocated according to the user requirements. The calculated values are then again handed over to the SDL part of the scheduler for further processing.

Results which have been obtained with the WARP2 simulator extended by cross-layer scheduling are presented in section 7.2.

6.5 Summary

This chapter described the properties of discrete-event simulations and the structure of the WARP2 simulator which is used for the investigations in this work. Different novel extensions of the simulator were introduced: The High Level Architecture allows the acceleration of simulators by connecting multiple simulator instances. The other proposed extensions are needed for the spectrum management and centralised resource allocation. Depending on the extension, different parts of the simulator are extended; in case of the HLA acceleration, new features have been added to the channel model whereas for the enhancements of the wireless

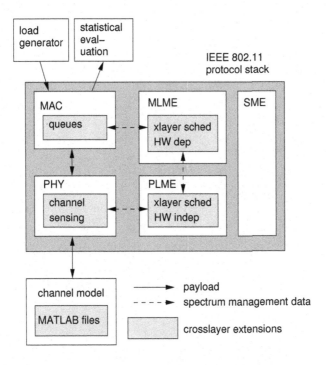

Figure 6.3: Structure of the WARP2 simulator for cross-layer simulation

LANs, the management entities inside the protocol stack provided with additional functionality. For extensions which are written in C, the SDL environment provides an interface called Abstract Data Type (ADT) which allows to call C functions inside SDL while hiding the implementation details from the SDL domain.

7 Simulation Results

In this chapter, the performance of the spectrum management introduced in chapter 4 is evaluated, which also includes a validation of the theoretical results about wireless networks with limited range which was given in section 3.2. Results for cross-layer scheduling described in chapter 5 are given in this chapter as well.

7.1 Spectrum Management Results

This section presents results which show the enhancement of the IEEE 802.11 performance based on spectrum management methods. To illustrate the improvements, comparisons to simulations without spectrum management are given. First the effects of the individual enhancement methods: Dynamic Frequency Selection, Transmit Power Control and Link Adaptation are investigated. After that, the integration of the different methods is investigated.

7.1.1 Network Performance without Spectrum Management

To get a better understanding of the measurement results for the different spectrum management methods, first the network performance without spectrum management is considered. To do so, the regular scenario given in fig. 7.1 is considered. The transmit power of the stations is 50 mW which corresponds to the transmit power in commercial wireless LAN hardware. A bit rate of 6 Mbit/s is selected which is the lowest bit rate for IEEE 802.11a/h. The aggregate throughput over all connections is measured as a function of the attenuation factor γ. For the simulation of n stations, the stations 1 to n are considered according to the scenario in fig. 7.1.

The results are given in figure 7.2. The effect of limited ranges on the throughput considering varying attenuation factors can be observed in this example. For $\gamma = 0$, which means an ideal channel with unlimited range, the throughput decreases according to eqn. 3.25 because the collision probability increases with the number of stations as discussed in chapter 3. Even for the smallest $\gamma = 2$ which can occur in reality, an increase of the throughput is observed if the number of stations inside the simulation scenario is increased. Due to the limited ranges, concurrent transmissions can occur as deduced in chapter 3.

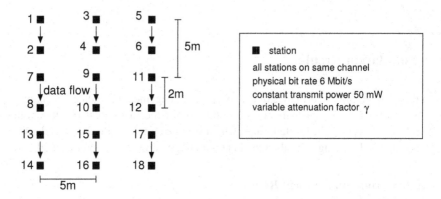

Figure 7.1: Static 3 × 3 matrix scenario for throughput measurement without spectrum management

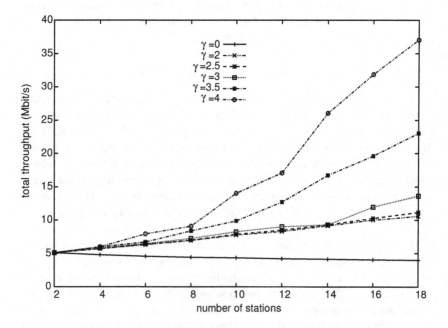

Figure 7.2: Total throughput of all stations vs. no of stations for different values of γ for scenario in fig. 7.1. All connections are saturated.

The throughput increases with the number of stations because there is an increasing number of opportunities for a simultaneous transmission of two networks. With an increasing value for γ, the aggregate throughput grows more rapidly when the number of stations is increased because the number of concurrent transmissions is increased.

7.1.2 Dynamic Frequency Selection (DFS)

The Dynamic Frequency Selection (DFS) was highlighted in section 4.1. In the results description given here, each network can be a BSS in case of infrastructure operation or an IBSS instead of ad-hoc operation. Since the DCF is used for the channel access in this scenario, the MAC protocol is independent of the mode of operation. Furthermore, there is also no influence on DFS if the network is working in infrastructure or ad-hoc mode. In both cases, a central station, the DFS owner, has to be established as it was pointed out in chapter 2. In case of a BSS, this is the access point. In case of the IBSS, one of the stations has to act as the DFS owner. In this simulation, the policy here is that the station with the lowest MAC address inside each network becomes the DFS owner. In practice, the determination which station becomes the DFS owner is vendor-specific because the policy for selecting the DFS owner is not specified in the standard.

7.1.2.1 Static Scenario

All stations inside the network start transmitting on the same frequency channel. During the ongoing simulation run, each of them measures the interference on all available channels and then decides according to the particular DFS algorithm which channel should be taken next. When measuring the performance, the following measurement values are considered to characterise the quality of the connections:

- throughput,
- latency time,
- number of channel changes.

To check the effects of DFS, two scenarios are considered: the first scenario contains an arrangement of stations in fixed positions. It includes 9 networks consisting of 2 stations each, arranged in a matrix with 3 rows and 3 columns as shown in fig. 7.3. In the simulation, six algorithms are considered:

- no DFS,
- Least Interfered (LI),

- Fuzzy Logic (FL),
- Genetic Algorithm with selection of the fittest element (FI),
- Genetic Algorithm with the roulette wheel modification (RW),
- Simulated Annealing (SA).

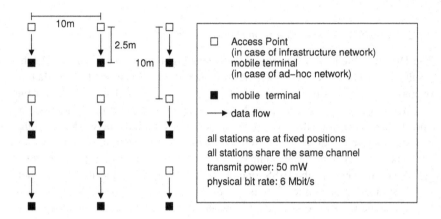

Figure 7.3: Static 3 × 3 matrix scenario for DFS measurements

Figure 7.4 shows the throughput, the delay and the C/I in the first 10 seconds after starting the simulation, averaged over 30 simulation runs. It can be seen that all DFS algorithms significantly enhance the performance of the network, however the amount of enhancement varies between the different algorithms; in particular, the speed with which the algorithms converge to the optimum state and the stability is different. Except for FL, all algorithms reach the optimum state, i.e. maximum throughput, C/I and minimum delay after about 2.5 seconds. The throughput is approx. 30% better than the throughput in case of no DFS (1.6 Mbit/s versus 1.1 Mbit/s). The delay is reduced by more than 50% (170 ms vs. 370 ms). The mean C/I averaged over all stations is enhanced from 27 to 38 dB. A special effect can be observed in the C/I graph in case of FI where the curve drops below the one for the case that no spectrum management is used.

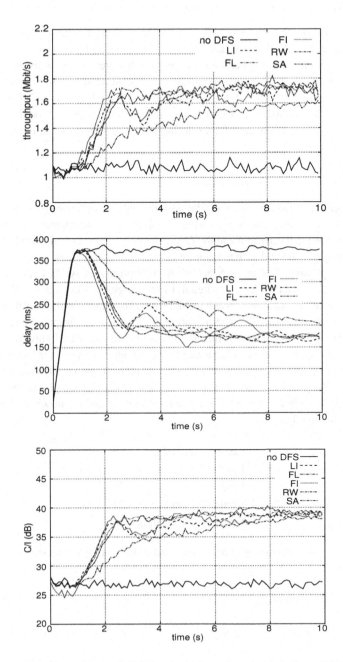

Figure 7.4: Throughput, delay and C/I for the 3×3 matrix scenario in figure 7.3 (averaged over 30 runs)

The reason is due to the acquisition of the measurement values which are taken in short intervals of $10\,ms$. When evaluating the 30 simulation runs, the C/I results for all simulation runs and all stations which were measured inside a particular time interval are averaged. If inside a certain simulation run no packet was transmitted for a particular station inside a given time interval, the C/I measurement result for this time interval is 0. If there is an increased amount of empty time intervals as it is the case for FI during the startup process this decreases the average C/I.

7.1.2.2 Convergence Characteristics

In the simulations described above, the stability and convergence speed of the DFS algorithms differ, as it can be seen when considering the time behaviour shown in the curves for the throughput and the C/I. The performance of LI and FI achieves the maximum value and is then again reduced for about a second until they again reach the optimum. RW and SA behave in the optimum way, they remain in the optimum state once they have reached it. FL converges slower than the other algorithms, it needs 10 seconds to reach its highest performance, which is still less than that of the other algorithms. The performance can also be compared considering the number of channel changes during the simulation time; the figures are shown in table 7.1. For LI, there is a large number of channel changes; for Fuzzy Logic, the number of channel changes is low which explains that the performance is not optimum. The genetic algorithm and simulated annealing give a good compromise between maintaining the performance on the one hand and the number of channel changes on the other hand.

Least Interfered	43
Fuzzy Logic	5
Fittest	30
Roulette Wheel	28
Simulated Annealing	28

Table 7.1: Average number of channel switches for different DFS algorithms in scenario given in fig. 7.3

Comparison of 802.11 DFS Simulations with Theoretical Deduction

In section 3.4.2.2, a theoretical deduction of the convergence characteristics of DFS was given and compared with a simulation of an idealised scenario in case that the number of networks matches the number of channels. For the analytical considerations, a random channel selection scheme was considered where networks which did not yet find a free channel randomly select another one until each network has found a free channel. The results were compared with an idealised simulation without considering any MAC protocol. These results are now compared with 802.11 simulations. Scenarios with 2, 3, 4 and 5 networks with unlimited range are considered so that the location of the stations are not relevant. The number of available frequency channels corresponds to the number of networks. Like in the theoretical considerations, all networks start on the same frequency and then try to find a free channel. The simulations were run using random selection similar to the analytical approach or the idealised simulations; furthermore, least interfered and the genetic algorithm with roulette wheel selection were included for comparison. In all simulations, the algorithms continue changing the channel until all stations have found a free channel.

number of networks		2	3	4	5
analytic	μ	3.92	6.23	8.59	10.97
idealised	μ	4.03	6.37	8.86	11.29
simulator	σ	6.00	6.55	6.55	6.68
	conf. int.	0.21	0.22	0.31	0.36
realistic sim:	μ	5.57	36.63	46.15	76.01
random	σ	6.22	18.21	28.70	55.05
realistic sim:	μ	5.80	70.65	67.40	138.10
least interfered	σ	6.13	54.03	52.51	48.08
realistic sim:	μ	1.00	3.00	7.67	17.32
genetic alg.	σ	0.00	0.00	3.31	7.92

Table 7.2: Average number μ of frequency changes for different algorithms and numbers of networks. See text about the GA results for 2 and 3 stations

Table 7.2 shows comparisons between the results for the analytic calculation, for the idealised simulation and for 802.11 simulations using random channel selection, least interfered and genetic algorithm. For the idealised simulation, 300 000 trials were executed for each scenario with 2 . . . 5 networks, for which the mean value μ and the standard deviation σ are calculated. Furthermore, from the results for the idealised simulation, the 99% confidence interval labelled in the table as "conf. int." is calculated according to the *batch means* method [7] by grouping the results into 30 batches with 10 000 trials. The realistic simulations were run 30 times with different seed values for the random generator in order to determine μ and σ.

The 802.11 random selection, within the simulation model time of 60 s, only converges for 2 and 3 networks. In case of more networks, there is no convergence; the number of frequency changes is similar to least interfered which only converges for three stations. The reason for the behaviour of least interfered are deadlocks as it was described earlier. Another effect which increases the number of channel changes in the realistic simulation compared to the ideal case is the imperfection of the measurement process. In the idealised scenario, it is assumed that a channel is always busy once it is occupied by a network; all other networks can detect immediately that this channel is used and hence it is left out from the random selection of networks which are still searching a free channel. In the real scenario, the networks periodically have to measure the interference on the currently occupied channel as well as the other channels in a sequential manner. During the measurement periods, no transmissions take place. Another network which measures the channel later will therefore detect it as being free and might then decide to change to that channel as well. The result is that both the network which already had settled on that channel earlier and the network which recently entered the channel again have to search for a new channel.

The results for the Genetic Algorithm in case of 2 or 3 networks shows a zero-width confidence interval. In all 30 runs, the same number of channel changes occur. In case of 2 networks, one of them changes the channel so that no further actions are required. In case of 3 networks, two out of the three networks change the channel so that one network already has an exclusive channel. However, the two networks which have changed the frequency select the same channel. Hence one of the two networks which have changed to the same channel again changes to the third available channel so that finally all of them have an exclusive channel and no further action is required.

In all cases, the algorithm converges within less than 15 s; after that, each network has found a channel which is not occupied by any other network so that no further channel changes occur. Examples for the convergence of DFS in particular simulation runs are shown in fig. 7.5. For comparison, the behaviour of Least Interfered is shown, where a stable state is not reached because two networks run into a livelock: Whenever one network decides to change the frequency, the other network does so as well so that both networks continue changing the frequency. The high amount of channel changes and the fact that no stable solution is found by the algorithm shows that Least Interfered cannot provide a stable solution for DFS.

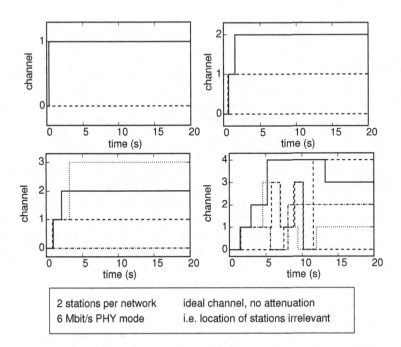

Figure 7.5: Convergence characteristics for the DFS Genetic Algorithm in case of 2, 3, 4 and 5 networks/channels. Number of channels resp. networks: upper left: 2; upper right: 3; lower left: 4; lower right: 5. The lines indicate the frequency selection of the different networks. See fig. 7.5 for legend.

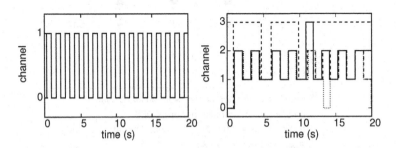

Figure 7.6: Convergence characteristics for the DFS Least Interfered algorithm in case of 2 and 4 networks. Left: 2 networks/channels, right: 4 networks/channels.

7.1.2.3 Mobility Scenario

In this simulation setup, the performance of DFS inside a mobile network is investigated. A mobility scenario is considered which is shown in figure 7.7. It includes
nine networks: the eight networks in the upper and the lower row in the figure are
at fixed positions and work on a constant channel throughout the simulation run.
Each pair of opposite networks uses the same channel. In this way, four coverage
zones are formed which are interfered with signals on three different frequencies
as shown in the figure. The measurement are taken from the ninth network moving
from left to right, which supports DFS. It starts with channel 1 and then changes
the frequency during the ongoing simulation according to the inference situation in
the environment while crossing the different coverage zones of the fixed networks.
Neighbouring coverage zones overlap each other so that the mobile network at any
time is at least covered by one zone. This experiment gives information about the
agility of the algorithms to change the frequency in case of a changing environment.

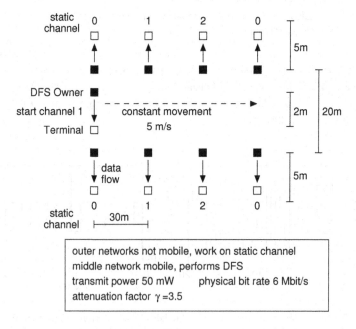

Figure 7.7: DFS mobility scenario

The results for the mobile network are shown in figure 7.8. It is shown that in case of no spectrum management, there is a 6 second period in which the link quality is significantly reduced from approx. 10 ms to 170 ms. This reduction occurs when the mobile network which is configured to channel 1 passes the zone which is inside the range of the two fixed networks which transmit on channel 1. Outside this zone, the delay drops to values between 10 and 20 ms. From the C/I graph it can be seen that the delay is maximised when the interference decreases to minimum values around 20 dB.

The graphs show that Fuzzy Logic also does not yield good results. It changes at the correct time from channel 1, once the interference zone with channel 1 is reached. However, it changes away from channel 2 too late so that interference occurs when the coverage of the stations using channel 2 is entered. The time for which the link quality is reduced is shorter than for the case of no DFS since the system at some point changes to a less interfered channel. Least Interfered achieves the best results, however it changes the channel most often compared with the other algorithms. RW appears to be the best compromise between channel change agility and keeping the performance. The delay is at some points not as good as for Least Interfered, however, RW only needs to change the channel 3 times.

The investigations about Dynamic Frequency Selection show that the tradeoff between agility to respond to changing conditions on the one hand and stability on the other hand can be fulfilled best by the Genetic Algorithm. If an algorithm is not agile enough, the transmission system can run into a condition where interference becomes too high. An algorithm which does not consider stability results in a high amount of frequency changes which might result in link disruption in case of signalling errors and also complicates conditions for neighbouring networks which try to be cooperative.

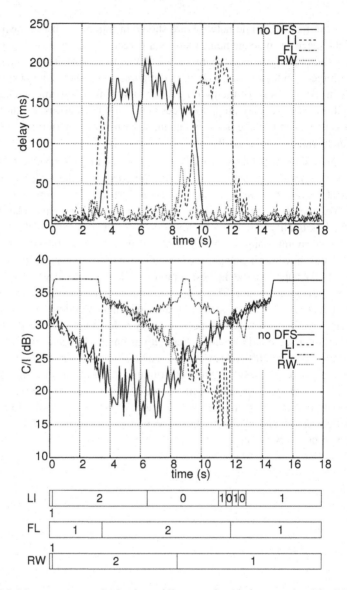

Figure 7.8: Measurement results for the mobile network with the scenario of fig. 7.7. Upper graph: delay, middle graph: C/I, lower graph: channel changes. The time scale of the channel switch graphs corresponds to the figures above. The numbers inside the channel switch graph are the numbers of the selected channels.

7.1.3 Transmit Power Control (TPC)

7.1.3.1 Validation of the Theoretical Model

The Transmit Power Control is like DFS also first tested "stand-alone". In chapter 3, a number of scenarios were discussed which show the effect of a certain arrangement of stations and their respective transmit powers. To validate the theoretical models of chapter 3, they are compared with simulation results here. First, the scenario given in figure 7.9 is considered which was introduced in sec. 3.3.1.

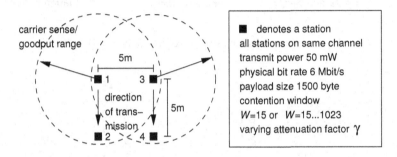

Figure 7.9: Measurement of QoS parameters with variable attenuation factor

The parameters for this setup are:

1. number of stations: $n = 4$

2. payload size $P = 1500$ byte $= 12000$ bit.

3. PHY mode: 6 Mbit/s

For comparison, the results are given for three attenuation factors: $\gamma = 0$, which means unlimited range, $\gamma = 2.5$ and $\gamma = 3.5$, which results in the limited range of the stations. The scenarios with $\gamma = 2.5$ and $\gamma = 3.5$ differ by the packet loss probability in case of simultaneous transmissions, which is approx. 2% for $\gamma = 3.5$ and approx. 50 % in case of $\gamma = 2.5$. For each of the attenuation factors, the throughput, the delay, and the jitter, i. e. the standard deviation of the delay is shown. It is assumed that the backoff window length is constant, $W = 15$.

Fig. 7.10 shows that the theoretical model correctly predicts the throughput and the delay. The jitter in the simulated scenario is higher than the theoretical result. It can be seen that the simultaneous transmissions which become possible due

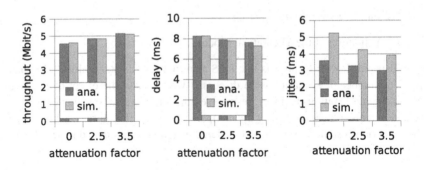

Figure 7.10: Results for 4 station scenario in fig. 7.9, $W = 15$

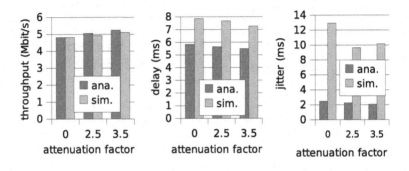

Figure 7.11: Results for 4 station scenario in fig. 7.9, $W = 15 \ldots 1023$

to the increased attenuation factor and the resulting reduced delay increase the throughput while reducing the delay and the jitter.

Fig. 7.11 shows the results for a variable contention window size between $W = 15$ and $W = 1023$. The analytic result for the throughput matches the simulated result in case of unlimited rage; for limited ranges, the analytic result is slightly higher. The reason for this behaviour is that the basic channel access model which considers unlimited range assumes a stationary transmission probability τ. This assumption is not exactly met in case of parallel transmissions, because there are conditional transmission opportunities due to the parallel transmissions which the model does not exactly cover. In case of the delay, all analytic results are below the simulated ones by the same amount. The reason is again the assumption of stationary transmission probabilities, which is only precisely met for a large amount of stations; for a small number of stations, the transmission probability no longer can be assumed to be constant due to the varying contention window size. These before mentioned simplifications of the theoretical model in comparison to the simulation also affect the jitter results which significantly differ as the graphs show.

	$\gamma = 0$	$\gamma = 3.5$	$\gamma = 4.5$
total	3838	4027	4246
1 station	3838	3933	3818
2 stations	0	94	428

Table 7.3: Number of packets transmitted in 4 station scenario in fig. 7.9, $W = 15$

	$\gamma = 0$	$\gamma = 3.5$	$\gamma = 4.5$
total	4009	4096	4254
1 station	4009	4058	3904
2 stations	0	38	350

Table 7.4: Number of packets transmitted in 4 station scenario in fig. 7.9, $W = 15 \ldots 1023$

7.1.3.2 CCA Effect

The function of the CCA was discussed in sec. 2.3.1.3: it is a mechanism defined by the IEEE 802.11 standard by which a station willing to transmit decides above which interference level the channel should be considered as busy so that the transmission should be delayed. By default, the interference threshold is set to $-82 \, \text{dBm}$; any signal which appears below this threshold at the station which is ready to transmit may be interfered by starting the transmission. If a signal without a valid 802.11 preamble is received, then this signal may be interfered up to a receive level of $-62 \, \text{dBm}$. The effect of shifting the interference threshold was analysed in sec. 3.3.2 and is compared with simulation results here.

In figure 7.12, a scenario with 6 stations is shown where data is exchanged in both directions between the two stations inside each network; the load is higher than the available capacity so that the system is in saturation. The behaviour of the stations is compared for three different settings of the attenuation factor γ where 0 means unlimited range. In case of $\gamma = 3.5$, all three networks overlap. The middle network senses the channel as free when the other two networks transmit as it was shown in section 3.3.2. In another setting with $\gamma = 4.5$, the outer stations inside the left and the right network are not inside mutual coverage and transmit independently as discussed in section 3.3.3.

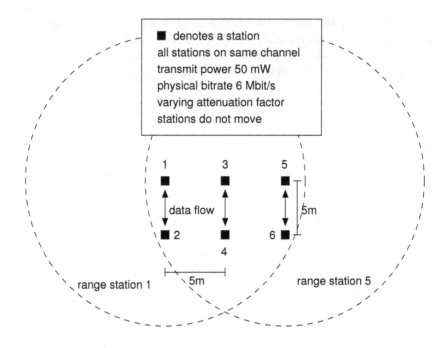

Figure 7.12: 6 station scenario with full coverage to compare analytical against simulated performance parameters considering the CCA effect

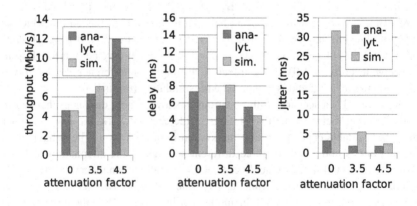

Figure 7.13: Results for scenario according to fig. 7.12, $W = 15$

Figure 7.13 gives the results for the three cases for the contention window size $W = 15$. The throughput is increased when the value of γ gets larger. Table 7.5 shows how often the parallel transmissions of two or three stations take place. For $\gamma = 0$, no parallel transmissions are possible. In case of $\gamma = 3.5$ or $\gamma = 4.5$, there are 2 or 3 parallel transmissions; in case of $\gamma = 4.5$, the amount is higher than for $\gamma = 3.5$ due to the independent transmissions of the outer networks. Further clarification is given when the per-route throughput is considered as given in table 7.7. Here it can be seen that for $\gamma = 3.5$, the stations in the middle network experience a higher throughout than the stations in the outer networks. For $\gamma = 4.5$, the throughput for the outer networks is higher due to the independent transmissions.

	$\gamma = 0$	$\gamma = 3.5$	$\gamma = 4.5$
total	3457	5619	9253
1 station	3457	3413	1022
2 stations	0	1564	4610
3 stations	0	642	3621

Table 7.5: Number of packets transmitted in 6 station scenario in fig. 7.12, contention window size $W = 15$ and attenuation factor γ

	$\gamma = 0$	$\gamma = 3.5$	$\gamma = 4.5$
total	3813	5113	7258
1 station	3813	2989	910
2 stations	0	1212	4102
3 stations	0	912	2246

Table 7.6: Number of packets transmitted in 6 station scenario in fig. 7.12, contention window size $W = 15 \ldots 1023$, attenuation factor γ

The example shows the high dependence of the network behaviour dependent on the attenuation factor. Differences between the analytic and the simulated results appear because of the idealised assumption in the theoretic approach that the transmission probability is stationary, which is a condition not perfectly met due to the small sizes of the networks. In particular, the jitter results are affected by this simplifying assumption.

γ	station 1	station 2	station 3	station 4	station 5	station 6
0	0.700606	0.672727	0.680000	0.715152	0.705455	0.687273
3.5	1.144242	1.158788	1.275152	1.263030	1.129697	1.146667
4.5	2.025455	2.038788	1.560000	1.511515	1.992727	1.989091

Table 7.7: Per-route throughput in Mbit/s for the 6 station scenario in fig. 7.12, $W = 15 \ldots 1023$

7.1.3.3 TPC Convergence: Infrastructure

The following figures show the convergence characteristics of infrastructure TPC. In section 3.4.2.2, the convergence was shown for a simplified simulation where the signalling is not considered and each network changes the transmit power exactly at the same time. Here, results are shown from a realistic simulation where imperfections of the signalling occur due to delays and packet losses. The simulated scenario shown in fig. 7.14 includes three networks with two stations which are at fixed positions. Figure 7.15 shows the transmitted power, received power and the C/I for this scenario.

The transmit powers for the three stations converge against a value around 2 mW within maximum two seconds. Due to this, the RX powers are reduced as well to a value which is still sufficient to maintain a minimum C/I with respect to the channel noise. The access point 1 in the middle sets a higher transmit power than the access points on the left and on the right because it experiences more interference: both neighbours have the same distance, whereas for the APs on the left and on the right, one neighbour has double distance than the other one.

A comparison with the graphs given in the theoretical discussion about infrastructure power control in section 4.2.1 shows that the qualitative behaviour of the simulated curves is according to the *envelopes* of the theoretical ones, which means there is a convergence to a constant value similar to a negative exponential function. In the graphs for the theoretical case however, there is an oscillation which does not occur for the simulated measurements. The reason is that in the theoretical model, it is assumed that in each iteration, the current transmit and receive powers of the networks are known instantaneously. In the simulation, receive powers are measured a certain time after the transmit powers have been set.

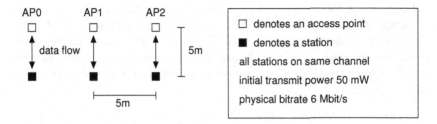

Figure 7.14: Scenario for infrastructure TPC convergence investigations

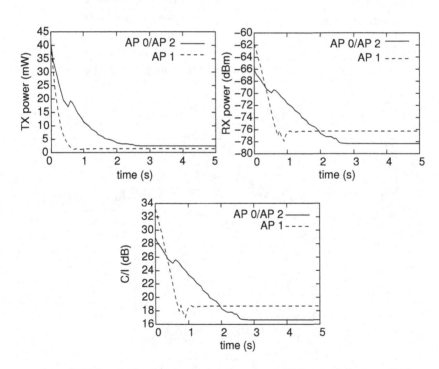

Figure 7.15: Results for 6 station static infrastructure TPC scenario in figure 7.14

Figure 7.17 shows the simulation results for the case that the station on the left is mobile. It moves away from the access point with a constant speed of 1 m/s. Network 0 increases the transmit power of the access point and the station in order to maintain the connection. The APs and stations in the middle and right network increase their powers by a smaller amount due to the increasing interference from the left network.

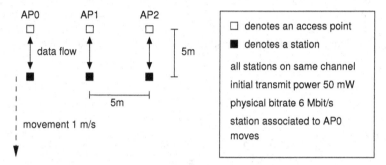

Figure 7.16: Scenario for infrastructure TPC convergence investigations

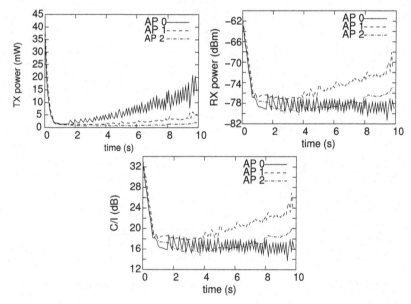

Figure 7.17: Results for 6 station mobility infrastructure TPC scenario according to fig. 7.16

7.1.3.4 TPC Convergence: Ad-Hoc

For the ad-hoc TPC simulation, a scenario shown in fig. 7.18 is used where the stations are located at the same places as in the infrastructure TPC investigations, both for the stationary and the mobility case.

The simulation results for the transmit power are given in fig. 7.19 for the three networks as a function of the time. Since the ad-hoc TPC controller is a state machine as described in sec. 4.2.2, it is shown in addition which state is taken as a function of the time. It can be seen that in case of the static scenario, the power control algorithm converges within less than a second, which can be seen from the powers converging to a fixed value and from the controller which is in monitoring state most of the time. In case of the mobility scenario where the station associated to AP 1 is moving, the results are shown in fig. 7.20. The distance between the access point and the station on the left side is continuously increased so that the transmit power for this network is permanently adapted. This also can be seen from the controller which frequently changes the state between "monitoring" and "controlling". The controller of the networks in the middle and on the right also changes the controller state often due to the permanently varying interference caused by the mobile station. The network on the right adjusts the power by a small amount while the interference increases.

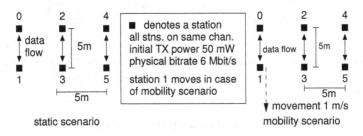

Figure 7.18: Scenario for ad-hoc TPC convergence investigations

7.1.3.5 TPC with Variable Load and Number of Stations

Two testing scenarios are considered here. In the first one, see fig. 7.21, the number of stations is constant. There are 18 stations grouped to 9 networks with 2 stations each. In practice, this can be considered as a group of users in neighbouring offices. In the infrastructure case, each user communicates with the access point mounted

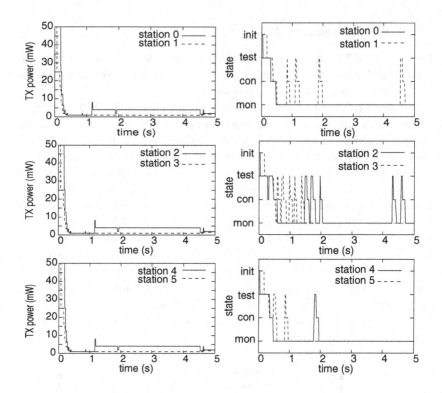

Figure 7.19: Results for 6 station static ad-hoc scenario in fig. 7.18. The figures in the lower row give the states of the TPC controller. init = initialisation, test = testing, con = controlling, mon = monitoring.

in his office. In the ad-hoc case, there are two users sitting in each office, running a wireless communication.

For this scenario, the offered load per station is increased from 600 to 2000 kbit/s in steps of 200 kbit/s. For each load, the throughput, delay and C/I for each of the stations is measured.

The throughput shown in fig. 7.22 is identical with and without spectrum management up to a load of 1200 kbit/s because the system is not in saturation. For higher loads, the throughput does not further increase in case of no spectrum management. If spectrum management is used, the throughput is identical to the load up to 1800 kbit/s. Beyond this value, the curve gets less steep which means the system enters saturation so that not all packets can be transported. Infrastructure TPC achieves a higher throughput than ad-hoc TPC in this case.

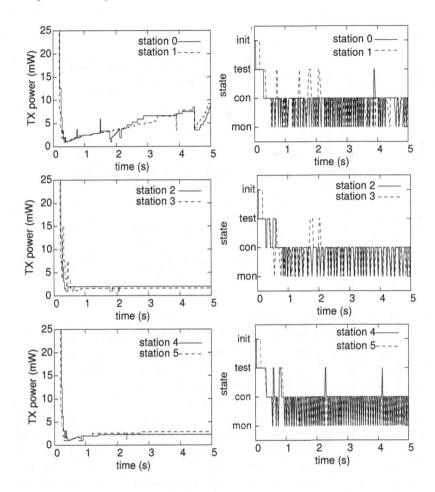

Figure 7.20: Results for 6 station mobility ad-hoc scenario in fig. 7.18.
See fig. 7.18 for the scenario description.

The delay results in fig. 7.23 show that power control improves the performance both for small and for big loads. For high loads, the infrastructure algorithm performs better than the ad-hoc algorithm because of the centralised signalling which allows better tracking and coordination between the different networks inside the scenario. The power control reduces the delay by at least 50% in comparison to the non-power-controlled case. The reason for the reduction of the delay is as fol-

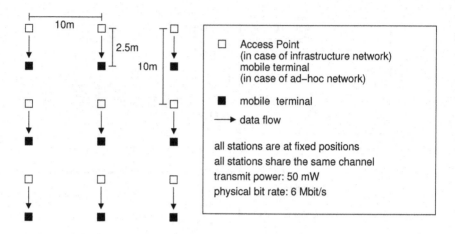

Figure 7.21: Test scenario for power control with variable load/stations

lows: By introducing power control, the stations reduce their interference range. This means that the amount of time is reduced where the channel is busy. A station which attempts to transmit a number of packets can do this more frequently than in the case without power control. In case of high traffic loads, this means that each packet spends less time inside the transmit queue.

Figure 7.24 depicts the average transmit power to which each of the stations is adjusted, respectively for varying load and varying number of stations. This measurement is in particular meaningful considering non-IEEE 802.11 systems which share the frequency band with the 802.11 systems. These applications might not be able to detect a busy channel due to a different physical layer engine (for example, ZigBee) or require a permanent unpacketised transmission, for example the analogue HomeRF system. In contrast to the situation without power control, where each station transmits at 17 dBm (50 mW), the TX power is reduced here to values between 0 dBm and 10 dBm. From the figure, it can be seen that the TX power becomes higher with increasing load since there is more background interference from neighbouring stations.

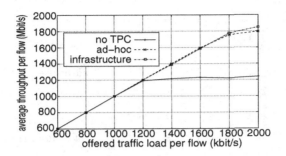

Figure 7.22: Per-flow throughput for varying load in scenario of fig. 7.21, averaged over all data flows

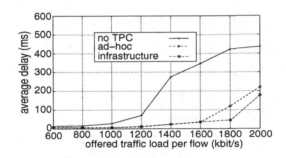

Figure 7.23: Delay in scenario in fig. 7.21 for varying load, averaged over all flows

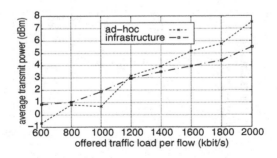

Figure 7.24: Power for scenario in fig. 7.21 for varying load, averaged over all flows

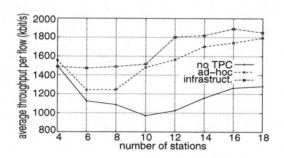

Figure 7.25: Per-flow throughput for varying number of stations in scenario of fig. 7.21, averaged over all data flows

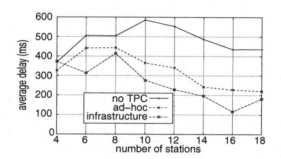

Figure 7.26: Delay for varying number of stations in scenario of fig. 7.21, averaged over all data flows

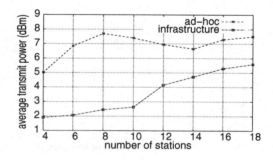

Figure 7.27: TX power for varying number of stations in scenario of fig. 7.21 averaged over all data flows

Figures 7.25 and 7.26 show the throughput and the delay when the number of stations is varied. When the number of stations is increased, the new stations are added in a regular order from left to right and from up to down.

It can be observed that the power control works more effectively with an increasing number of stations. In case of a small number of networks, they are located closely to each other, so that even with the application of power control, they are still within of each other's interference range which reduces the effect of the power control. For a larger number of networks which are distributed over a wider area, power control reduces the amount of overlapping interference ranges so that the non-overlapping networks can perform transmissions simultaneously. The results do not change significantly when the simulation is run with different seeds.

In fig. 7.27, the average transmit power per station is shown. The power first increases when the number of stations is changed from 4 to 8 due to the increasing interference. When the number of stations is gets higher than 8, the system is in saturation and some stations are outside mutual range so that the background interference resp. the TX power no longer increases.

7.1.4 DFS and TPC

This section discusses the interaction between DFS and TPC. The performance achieved by the combination of DFS and infrastructure TPC (iTPC) resp. ad-hoc TPC (aTPC) is evaluated.

7.1.4.1 Regular Scenario

In the regular scenario, an arrangement of 6 networks with 2 stations each is used as shown in figure 7.28. The simulation results for this scenario are given in figure 7.29 for the throughput and in figure 7.30 for the delay. Each figure shows the average throughput for all connections, separated for the different spectrum management methods.

In case that no spectrum management is used, the stations in the middle network achieve a lower throughput which is approximately on the same level of 0.8 Mbit/s whereas the outer stations achieve 1.4 Mbit/s. The reason is that the inner stations have more neighbours inside their coverage and thus are exposed to more interference. The performance is enhanced by spectrum management, the combination of DFS and TPC achieves better results than the individual usage of the respective methods. With increasing throughput, the delay is reduced. This can be explained considering the fact that two effects contribute to the delay. On the one hand, there is the queueing delay which is due to the time a packet needs to proceed from the

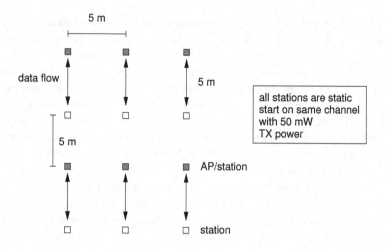

Figure 7.28: Combination of DFS and TPC: Regular scenario

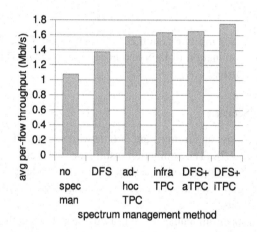

Figure 7.29: Throughput for regular scenario in fig. 7.28. iTPC = infrastructure TPC; aTPC = adhoc TPC

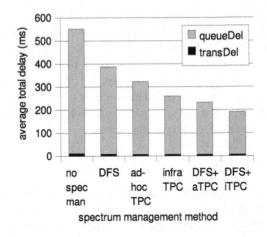

Figure 7.30: Total delay for regular scenario in fig. 7.28

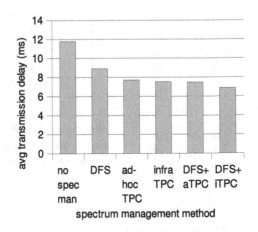

Figure 7.31: Transmission delay for regular scenario in fig. 7.28

end of the queue to the front of the queue. If the throughput is increased, the service rate becomes higher so the packet has to spend less time in the queue. On the other hand, there is the transmission delay which is the time between the arrival of a packet at the front of the queue and its transmission. The properties of the transmission delay were discussed in detail in section 3.3.1. In fig. 7.30 it is shown that the transmission delay only contributes by a small amount to the total delay, hence the main amount of reduction is due to the higher transmission rates and the resulting higher service rate of the queues. Fig. 7.31 shows the transmission delay in more detail, which is reduced analogously to the total delay. Due to less interference, the congestion on the frequency channels is reduced so that the MAC layer has to wait less time to transmit the packet.

7.1.4.2 Irregular Scenario

In the irregular scenario, there are four networks in the upper row and two networks in the lower row, as shown in fig. 7.32. Figures 7.33, 7.34 and 7.35 show the throughput, average total delay and average transmission delay for the irregular scenario.

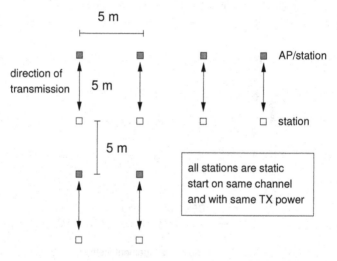

Figure 7.32: Combination of DFS and TPC: irregular scenario

As in the example with the regular network, the combination of DFS and TPC again yields a performance enhancement with respect to the exclusive usage of TPC or DFS. Analogously to the example with the regular network, infrastructure TPC yields a higher throughput and a shorter delay than ad-hoc TPC, both as an individual spectrum management method and in combination with DFS. However,

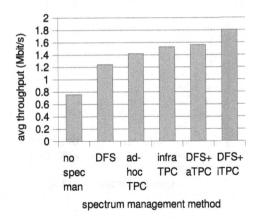

Figure 7.33: Throughput for irregular scenario in fig. 7.32. aTPC: ad-hoc mode; iTPC: infrastructure mode

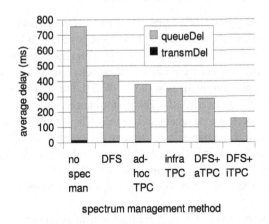

Figure 7.34: Delay for irregular scenario in fig. 7.32

in contrast to the regular scenario, the throughput is in general higher and the delay lower than in the case of the regular scenario. This is due to the fact that the two networks on the right side experience less interference from neighbours than the other networks.

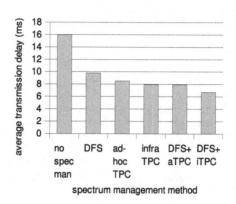

Figure 7.35: Transmission delay for irregular scenario in fig. 7.32

7.1.5 Integration of DFS, TPC and Link Adaptation (LA)

A scenario to investigate the integration of the different spectrum management schemes DFS, infrastructure/ad-hoc TPC and LA is shown in fig. 7.36, which includes between 2 and 9 networks arranged in a regular order as three rows and three columns. There is bidirectional data flow between the two stations of each network. The attenuation factor is set to $\gamma = 3.0$, the starting power to 50 mW and the starting bit rate to 6 Mbit/s. The performance was measured for different combinations of spectrum management schemes. The offered traffic load is always chosen higher than the achievable throughput so that the system is in saturation. The confidence values were achieved by the method of *independent replications* [7] which means that the simulations were run 30 times for each scenario with different random seed values; in the figures, the 99% confidence is shown by error bars.

The 802.11a standard specifies a maximum transmission rate of 54 Mbit/s, however the maximum rate was limited for the simulation to 24 Mbit/s, because higher rates increase the number of events per model time interval to be simulated, but do not give additional results. Fig. 7.37 and 7.38 show the throughput respectively for infrastructure and ad-hoc networks. The throughput is increased by applying individual spectrum management methods in comparison to the unmanaged case. Further enhancements are achieved when different spectrum management methods are combined. The combination of all three methods TPC, DFS and LA yield the highest throughput figures. Compared to other combinations of spectrum management methods, the improvement due to LA is better than a factor of 2; compared to the unmanaged case, the factor of improvement is about 3.5. The results where ad-hoc TPC are is included about 20% below the results where infrastructure TPC is included.

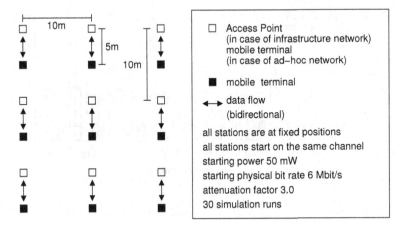

Figure 7.36: Test scenario with a matrix of networks arranged in 3 rows and 3 columns for different combinations of DFS/TPC/LA

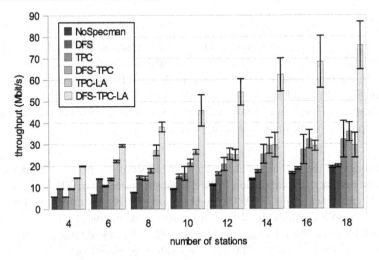

Figure 7.37: Throughput for the scenario in fig. 7.36, infrastructure TPC

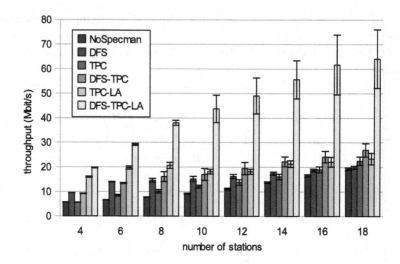

Figure 7.38: Throughput for the scenario in fig. 7.36, ad-hoc TPC

In fig. 7.39, the combination of DFS, infrastructure/ad-hoc TPC and LA are compared in a scenario which includes irregularities: there are 7 stations where one station moves and a second station has links to two other stations, one as a bidirectional link and another one as a downlink. The mobile station is moving with a speed of 1 m/s from 5 to 10 m distance from the access point and then stops at this position in the remaining model time.

Throughput measurements are taken for the case of no spectrum management case as well as the combination of DFS, infrastructure/ad-hoc TPC and LA, the results are shown in fig. 7.40. The combination of DFS, infrastructure TPC and LA can handle the mobility of the left network with stations 1 and 2 better than the combination which includes ad-hoc TPC. However, the throughput for station 6 is higher in case of ad-hoc TPC because it is less interfered by the mobile station 2. In comparison to the unmanaged case, the highest enhancement is achieved for the network which includes the mobile station 2; for the combination with infrastructure TPC, the factor is approx. 10 whereas for ad-hoc TPC it is around 5.

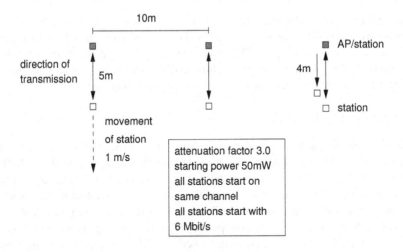

Figure 7.39: Scenario with 7 stations

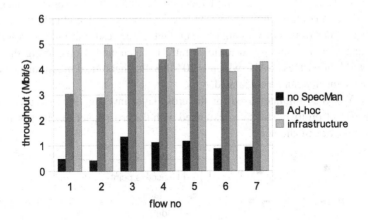

Figure 7.40: Per-flow throughput with the combination of DFS, infrastructure/ad-hoc TPC and LA in scenario according to fig. 7.39

7.2 Performance of the Cross-Layer Architecture

In the first section of this chapter, performance enhancements by usage of spectrum management was discussed. This section highlights the results for cross-layer scheduling which is the second major topic of this report. First the effect of the cross-layer scheduler is analysed based on TDMA transmissions where adaptivity and resource allocation by the PHY layer scheduler is not required. In the further sections, the model is extended to OFDMA and SDMA where resources are shared between different users so that an allocation scheme is required.

7.2.1 Cross-Layer Scheduler

First, the enhancement of cross-layer scheduling in contrast to legacy scheduling is demonstrated. The scheduler used in the simulation has been described in 5.2. The MAC layer hands over information about the packets to the PHY scheduler which has knowledge about the channel conditions and thus can estimate the channel capacity, i. e. the physical bit rate available for a certain user at a given time. It is assumed that the PHY scheduler has perfect channel knowledge in the way that the current channel characteristics are determined for each user before each scheduling process, so there is no packet loss. In the first analysis of the cross-layer scheduler, a TDMA transmission with single antennas at the transmitter and the receiver is assumed. The channel model implements an omnidirectional signal propagation with an attenuation factor of 2.5. The received power is weighted by a random factor in order to model Rayleigh fading. Out of the resulting receive power and the channel noise, the signal-to-noise ratio is calculated. Considering the radio bandwidth of wireless LANs which is 20 MHz, the theoretical maximum available channel capacity can be calculated.

The WARP2 simulator used for the cross-layer investigations is based on the IEEE 802.11 protocol stack and extended with the cross-layer extensions as it has been described in chapter 5.

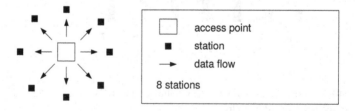

Figure 7.41: Arrangement of stations and data flows for investigations about the cross-layer scheduler, used throughout section 7.2

The simulated scenario used throughout section 7.2 is an access point which serves eight stations as shown in fig. 7.41. The access point is located in the centre

flow no.	traffic type	traffic load kbit/s
1	Poisson	3000
2	Poisson	2024
3	CBR	203
4	Poisson	1103
5	CBR	2500
6	Poisson	2500
7	Poisson	1500
8	Poisson	2900

Table 7.8: Traffic models and loads used for investigations in subsection 7.2.1

of a circle on which the stations are arranged. Varying channel conditions which demonstrate the adaptivity of the scheduler are generated by the statistical channel model. Only downlink traffic is considered; there is one data flow from the access point to each of the stations. To consider typical application requirements, two arrival types are modeled: constant bit rate (CBR) arrivals reflect the behaviour of video/audio streaming, while Poisson distributed arrivals are used to simulate traffic with non-periodic arrivals such as accessing web sites. The load type and the average load rate is set for the individual flows according to table 7.8.

The physical transmission rate for each packet is selected adaptively according to the channel capacity. The rates are specified according to IEEE 802.11g/a. Considering the channel model which is used for these investigations and the movement patterns of the stations, rates of 6, 9, 12 and 18 Mbit/s occur during the simulation runs. Each packet is transmitted with the closest rate which is smaller than the available channel capacity. This results in a variable time span which is required to send each packet. The packet size is 1000 bytes for all flows, the simulated model time is 18 s for each scenario.

Four cases are distinguished how the PHY scheduler should process the packets: either it is disabled so that the packet which got the highest priority by the MAC scheduler will be transmitted, or the PHY scheduler processes the packet list from the MAC scheduler which can be configured in three ways:

1. The PHY scheduler selects the packet which got the highest product and returns the flow number of the selected packet to the MAC scheduler. The

MAC scheduler takes the packet from the respective queue and sends it to the physical transmission. After that, it schedules new importance values for all queues and submits a new query to the PHY scheduler.

2. The PHY scheduler selects the packet with the highest product and requests the MAC scheduler to send it as described above. In contrast to the first option, the MAC scheduler does not reschedule the packets after the first one was sent, but the PHY scheduler sends the flow number of the packet with the second highest product to the MAC scheduler for transmission. This process is continued for the packet with the third, fourth etc. highest product until a time span of 2.5 ms has elapsed. After that, the MAC scheduler creates a new list of packets and hands it over to the PHY scheduler.

3. The PHY scheduler selects the packets from the list as given in section 2, however it does not stop after 2.5 ms but continues until all packets in the list have been transmitted.

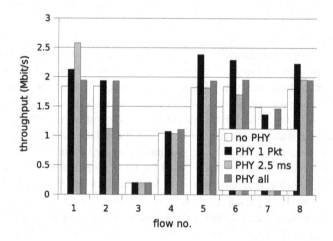

Figure 7.42: Throughput for each flow using the Round Robin scheduler. Traffic loads according to table 7.8.

Fig. 7.42 shows the throughput for each of the eight data flows using the RR scheduler. The different bars shown for each flow represent the results for the different PHY schedulers. It can be seen that the additional PHY scheduling enhances

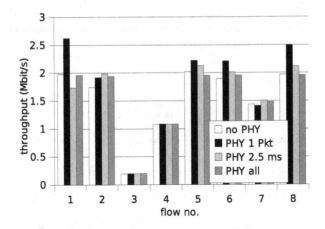

Figure 7.43: Throughput for each flow using the queue length/lifetime scheduler

the throughput for the connections with loads of 1.7 Mbit/s and higher. The flows
with lower traffic load are unchanged because for these flows the whole traffic load
is transported even in the case that no PHY layer scheduler is used, hence the introduction of the PHY scheduler does not enhance their throughputs. It can be considered as fair behaviour of the scheduler that an enhancement of the throughput
for certain flows does not result in a reduction of the throughput of other routes.
When the PHY scheduler processes the list for 2.5 ms or when it processes the
whole list, the achieved throughput for the individual flows is worse than for the
case that only the first packet is processed. The reason is that if the PHY scheduler only transmits the first packet, with high probability this packet faces good
channel conditions. With each packet taken and removed from the list, there is
one packet less from which the scheduler can choose for the next transmission,
it then becomes more likely that the packet then faces a bad channel so that the
transmission takes more time. Another advantage of scheduling only one packet
in the PHY scheduler is that the MAC scheduler has more freedom to select the
order of the packets according to QoS requirements of the applications. A similar
behaviour can be observed when the QL scheduler is used for the MAC scheduling
as depicted in fig. 7.43. The high delay of route no. 3 which represents a flow with
relatively low load is due to the fact that the lifetime calculation of the scheduler
does not check the lifetime against a fixed boundary, it only compares the lifetimes

of the different queues by adding the weighted lifetime to the importance value. In case of high queue lengths, the weight for the lifetime is reduced so that highly loaded queues will often get a high importance.

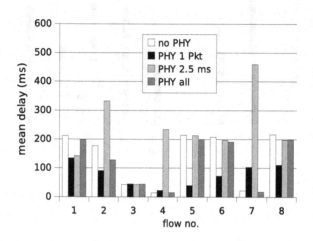

Figure 7.44: Mean delay for each flow using the Round Robin scheduler. Traffic loads according to table 7.8.

Figures 7.44 and 7.45 respectively show the effects of the scheduling on the delay for the RR and the QL scheduler for the different modes of the PHY scheduler. In general, the combined MAC/PHY scheduler increases the fairness of the system in two aspects: The throughput is not only improved for the entire system, but the throughput and delay are also enhanced for the individual flows. Furthermore, the difference between the delays between the individual flows is reduced in case of the RR MAC scheduler combined with PHY scheduler selecting one packet from the list.

If the PHY scheduler selects more than one packet from the list, there is either no significant effect on the delay or it is increased. This effect occurs because the more packets the PHY scheduler takes from the same list, the less is the influence of the MAC scheduler which selects the packets according to their importance.

In case of the QL MAC scheduler, the combination with the PHY scheduler reduces the delay for all flows; however, the delays are higher than in case of the RR MAC scheduler. This is due to the fact that the QL scheduler considers the queue length besides the packet lifetime. This means that flows with high traffic

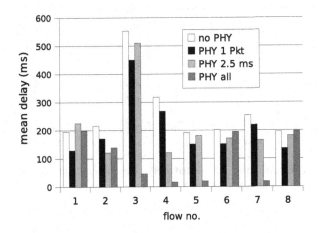

Figure 7.45: Mean delay for each flow using the queue length/lifetime scheduler

loads are served frequently even if the queues of other flows grow longer which results in an increased delay for these lowly loaded queues.

The queuelength/lifetime scheduler results, if used without PHY scheduler, results in high delays of more than 200 ms. The introduction of the PHY scheduler results in a reduction to a similar level of approx. 10 ms as in the case of the Round Robin scheduler for all routes; only for the route 3 with low traffic it is higher which is due to the MAC scheduler which keeps the packets in the queue for a relatively long time.

Further details about the variation of the delay are given in figures 7.46 to 7.49, where for each combination of MAC and PHY scheduling scheme the delay is given in a separate figure. In these figures, in addition to the mean value of the delay, the standard deviation is also denoted by error bars. The 2.5% resp. 97.5% quantiles which indicate the interval into which 95% of the values fall are denoted by crosses. The upper row shows the case that the PHY scheduler is disabled, the second row that it processes one packet, the third row that it processes packets for 2.5ms and the bottom row that it processes the whole list. The left column shows the results for the RR scheduler, the right column for the QL scheduler.

It can be observed that in case of the RR scheduler, the delay variation is increased for most flows when the PHY scheduler with the one-element selection is introduced. The pure MAC RR scheduler without PHY scheduler serves the

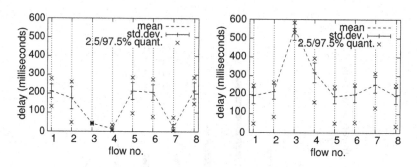

Figure 7.46: Delay in case of disabled PHY scheduling. Left: Round Robin, right: BiggestQandAge. Traffic loads: table 7.8.

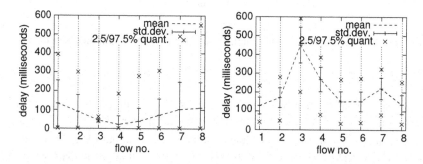

Figure 7.47: Delay in case of processing one entry from the list.

queues in a regular order. Delay variations occur due to the time-varying channel resulting in packets being transmitted at different speeds, and in variations in the queue length. When the PHY scheduler is also active, the order of serving the queues is changed so that the variations become higher.

The delay variation of the QL scheduler without PHY is higher than that of the RR scheduler because it does not serve the queues in regular order. A decrease of the delay variation can be observed when the PHY scheduler gets more influence, i. e. when it selects more than one packet from the same list.

The curves for the PHY scheduler processing the complete list have almost the same shape both for the RR and the QL MAC scheduler. This effect shows that the influence of the MAC on the order of packet transmission is low in this case. The fact that the curves are also similar to the case of the RR scheduler without

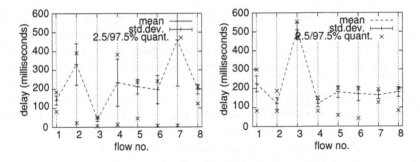

Figure 7.48: Delay in case of processing the entire list

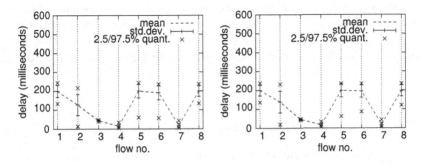

Figure 7.49: Delay in case of processing entries for 2.5 ms

PHY indicates that the PHY scheduler which selects the packets according to the randomly selected channel capacities has similar statistical properties as the Round Robin scheduler.

The different MAC scheduler types result in large differences for the delay variation. For the RR scheduler, the variation is relatively small. It serves each queue regularly so that variations only occur due to the varying transmission speed of the packets or due to the effect that sometimes a queue might be empty and then the next queues are served more quickly. Introducing the PHY scheduler increases the variation because of the PHY scheduler's property to change the order of transmission, which is always the same for the round-robin scheduler running without PHY scheduler. The QL scheduler results in a very high delay variation if no PHY scheduler is used, in particular for the low-traffic flow 3. The reason is the scheduler's property not to compare the lifetime of the packet against a fixed boundary as described in the discussion of the mean delays. If the other queues are short, a packet of the queue of flow 3 will be served quickly because it quickly gains importance due to the increased lifetime. If the other queues are long, the packet will remain in its queue for a long time. Introducing the PHY scheduler significantly reduces the delay variation. If a packet sees good channel conditions, it may be transmitted even if the importance assigned by the MAC scheduler is relatively low. This reduces the probability that the MAC scheduler holds a packet for a long time and thus reduces the delay variation.

Another metric to compare the schedulers is the fairness: For all flows which do not have a delay constraint, only a part of the offered traffic load is transferred. A scheduler is fair if the ratio between the transferred load and the offered load is equal for all flows. From the throughput graph it can be seen, that for the QoS scheduler, the ratio is approximately the same for all flows. The random and Round Robin scheduler serve some flows fully, others are only served by less than 50% of the requested load. The queue length based schedulers serve all flows fully for which no delay constraint is specified, however they fail to serve the delay-constrained flows properly.

7.2.2 *Quality-of-Service Scheduling on the MAC Layer*

In this section, the quality-of-service supporting scheduler which has been described in sec. 5.2.1 is introduced into the simulations. The scheduler is designed to guarantee QoS requirements by time-critical applications and improve the fairness between non-time-critical flows. Furthermore, a MIMO based transmission is now used for the channel model which has been specified by the 802.11 task group n for the evaluation of MIMO based WLAN transmissions [28]. It is a statistical channel model which includes multipath propagation between the sender and the receiver, which is specifically designed for indoor scenarios and also considers multiple antennas at the sender and the receiver. The non-line-of-sight components of the received signal are modelled by clouds of randomly moving scatterers which are located in the environment, where the distances between transmitter, receiver and scatterers are typical for indoor scenarios.

For each transmitted packet, the available channel capacity is calculated individually. The product of the importance metric provided by the MAC scheduler and the available channel capacity is determined for all packets which are contained in the MAC scheduler selection list. There are three ways to select how many packets from the list are sent after these products have been calculated which have been described previously in section 7.2.1.

After the PHY scheduler has requested the transmission of all packets from the MAC layer according to the policies given above, it triggers a new scheduling event at the MAC scheduler and after that receives another list of importance metrics.

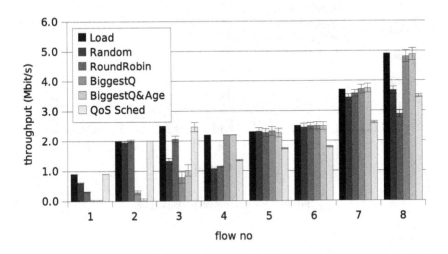

Figure 7.50: Throughput with packet ageing, scenario according to fig. 7.41

The confidence intervals in the following results graphs have been achieved by the independent replications method; the simulation was run 30 times with different random seeds. The error bars show the 99% confidence. The different scheduling strategies discussed in section 5.2 are compared. The QoS aware scheduler is termed in the results graphs as "advanced scheduler". The traffic model is CBR for flows 1, 2 and 4; the remaining flows have a Poisson load.

Figures 7.50 and 7.51 show the delay and the throughput in case that packet ageing is enabled which was mentioned in section 5.2.1: packets which exceed their maximum lifetime are discarded. In flow 1 and 2, there is almost no throughput if the queue length scheduler is used. The traffic load for these queues is low, so all packets which wait in the MAC scheduler for transmission have already waited a long time in the queue before they were put into the MAC layer, where they expire before they can be transmitted. In flow 1, this problem occurs even for the BiggestQ&Age scheduler. On the other hand, the throughput of the QoS scheduler is not affected by discarding packets. In the delay graph, it can be seen that due to the deletion of all packets after the expiry of the lifetime, all schedulers meet the delay requirements. The experiment shows that if the discarding of packets is

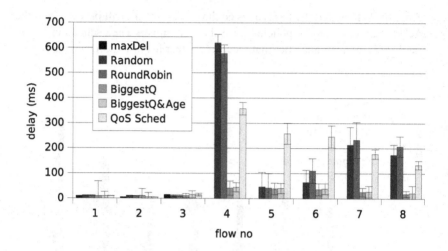

Figure 7.51: Delay with packet ageing

used to guarantee that no packets exceed the lifetime, this must be combined with a QoS aware scheduler to limit the packet loss.

Figure 7.52 shows the throughput achieved by the different schedulers in the case that there is no packet ageing in the MAC layer. The left column for each route identifies the offered traffic load which allows a comparison with the throughput which is achieved by each of the schedulers. It can be seen that the load for the time-critical flows 1 to 3 is fully transmitted by the advanced scheduler due to the delay constraint of 10 ms which applies for these flows. The other schedulers are not able to serve the full throughput for these flows and thus do not meet the QoS criteria. However, for the flows which are not time-critical, the other schedulers achieve better throughput results than the advanced scheduler. The reason is that the advanced scheduler often has to enforce the transmission of time-critical packets due to the delay constraints by allotting high importance values. This means that the PHY scheduler often has to send a packet for these flows even if the current channel conditions are poor so that the respective packets need a long time to be transmitted. The other schedulers which are not bound to this restriction differentiate the weight between the packets less strictly. The PHY scheduler in this case has more opportunities to serve flows with good channel conditions. Therefore the non-QoS schedulers can in average serve more packets within a time interval than the advanced scheduler.

It also can be seen that the queue length scheduler behaves very poorly for flows with low traffic loads, because for flows with high loads, the queue is always filled up very quickly so that these flows will often be preferred. This effect is not even reduced when the packet ageing is also included. Random and Round Robin selection serve all flows by a certain ratio.

When comparing the schedulers regarding the fairness, it is observed that the QoS scheduler, although it cannot fully serve the non-time-critical flows, still allocates a throughput to each flow which is proportional to the offered load which can be considered as fair. The schedulers which perform relative weighting such as BiggestQueue and BiggestQueueAndAge fully serve the throughput for non-time-critical flows so they are fair about servicing these flows, however the fail the correct service of the time-critical flows.

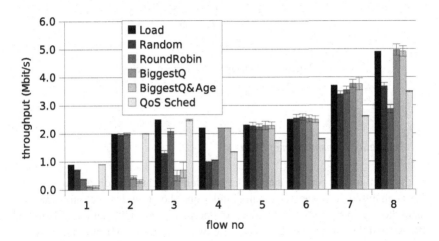

Figure 7.52: Throughput without packet ageing. Scenario according to fig. 7.41. The flows 1 to 3 are time-critical.

The delay graph in figure 7.53 shows that the advanced scheduler is the only one which meets the QoS requirements for the time-critical routes 1 to 3 whose 10 ms delay requirements are met. For the other routes without the delay requirements, the delays are worse than for the other schedulers because the scheduler has to serve the packets for routes 1 to 3 preferably which restricts opportunities to serve the other flows. It can furthermore be observed that for the low-traffic routes, the queue length based schedulers give the worst results. The reason is the same as for the delay. The queues grow slowly and are not served frequently so that the packets have a high queueing delay.

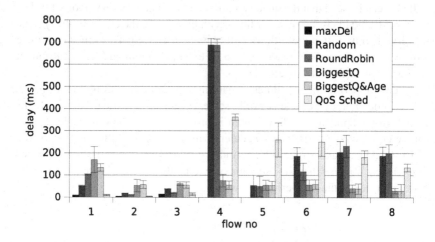

Figure 7.53: Delay without packet ageing

7.2.3 Parallel Transmission of Data

In this section, the performance of the parallelised scheduler discussed in section
5.3 is analysed. The scenario in all simulations shown in this section is the same
as in the previous one, which is an access point serving eight stations, where both
the AP and the stations are equipped with two antennas for MIMO transmission.

First, the parallelisation is analysed by an idealised scenario which does not
appear in reality. Instead of the PHY scheduler which shares a single channel between a number of users by OFDMA or SDMA, it is assumed that one, two or three
independent channels are available so that the respective number of users can be
served independently. The simulation results are shown in Fig. 7.54. RR and Adv
denote the usage of the Round Robin and the QoS aware scheduler, respectively. In
TDMA, the available channel capacities for each flow are given in a pre-calculated
trace file based on the channel model previously discussed. Considering a longer
time interval, which means in this case 7.5 seconds of model time, they are approximately the same for all flows for the considered scenario; for the channel capacity
trace file which was used to run the simulations discussed here, the average channel capacity for each route varied between 28.5 and 29.5 Mbit/s. In contrast to this,

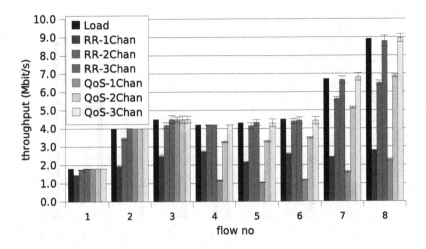

Figure 7.54: Per-flow throughput assuming 1, 2 or 3 independent transmission channels among which the flows are distributed, combined with Round Robin and QoS scheduler. Scenario according to fig. 7.41.

for OFDMA and SDMA, channel capacity assignments are adaptive and dependent on the application requirements so that it is more to judge the behaviour of the parallelised MAC scheduling since there is a higher interaction with the physical layer. It can be seen that in case of one channel the throughput percentage for each flow achieved by the RR scheduler decreases with increasing traffic load from approx. 90 % to approx. 30 %. This behaviour is a result of the Round Robin scheduler's property to serve all flows with the same frequency, so that flows with low load get a higher relative service rate. When the total capacity is doubled by providing a second channel, the RR scheduler can serve all flows more frequently so that the flows 1 to 6 which have lower loads are almost fully served; the flows 7 and 8 are only served partially because for them the service rate of the RR scheduler is not yet sufficient. In case of three parallel channels, the entire system is out of the saturation, i.e. there is more channel capacity than required by the flows, so that all flows are fully served. In this case, the QoS scheduler fully serves the time-critical flows 1 to 3 independent of the available total channel capacity. The remaining capacity is distributed among the remaining flows in the way that each flow gets a constant percentage of the traffic load, which is about 30 % for one channel and about 80 % for two channels. In case of three channels, the system is out of saturation so that all flows are fully served.

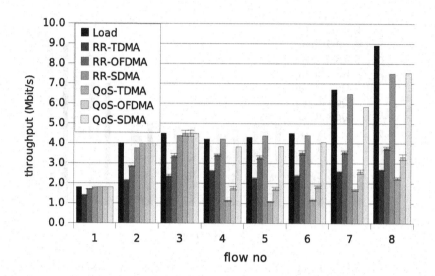

Figure 7.55: Per-flow throughput for TDMA, OFDMA and SDMA, combined with Round Robin and QoS scheduler. Scenario according to fig. 7.41.

Fig. 7.55 shows the per-route throughput which is achieved with different simulation scenarios. Like in the previous figure, the bar on the left for each route denotes the traffic load. In case of the Round Robin scheduler, the throughput of all flows is enhanced by using increasingly effective transmission schemes: With OFDMA, a higher performance is achieved than with TDMA because of the optimum allocation of subcarriers to the users. With SDMA, the performance is furthermore increased due to the parallelisation of each subcarrier by the subchannels. The parallel subcarriers resp. subchannels provided by OFDMA and SDMA, respectively, are utilised by the MAC scheduler for the parallel transmission of packets, which enhances both the individual routes as well as the total throughput. Since the RR scheduler does not consider QoS requirements of the flows, the time-critical flows 1 to 3 are not appropriately served; however, the QoS is enhanced when improving the transmission scheme. In case of the advanced scheduler, the three time-critical flows are served according to their requirements, independent on the transmission scheme. The remaining channel capacity is distributed among the non-time-critical flows so that they also benefit from the increased total channel capacity as it is the case for the Round Robin scheduler. The available total channel capacity is shown in fig. 7.56 for the different scheduling and transmission scenarios. The total capacity is increased by 20% when OFDMA is used and doubled in case of SDMA, both for the RR and the QoS scheduler. For RR, the total throughput is higher than for the advanced scheduler because the RR scheduler is not constrained to serve the three time-critical flows within a given delay. Hence it can allow more freedom to the PHY scheduler to assign the channel to flows with good channel conditions.

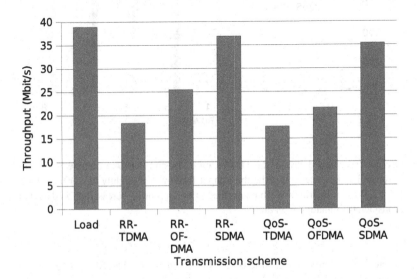

Figure 7.56: Total throughput for TDMA/OFDMA/SDMA using RR and QoS scheduling

From the delay graph given in fig. 7.57, it can be seen that the delays for the flows are reduced. The more the throughput of the flows is increased, the more the delay is reduced. Due to the increased channel capacity, the service rate for the queues are increased as well so that the queueing delay is decreased. In case of the QoS enabled scheduler, the time-critical flows are served according to the requirements. This reduces according to the reduced throughput, the service rate for the non-time-critical flows so that the delay for these flows is higher than in case of the RR scheduler.

It should be noted that the SDMA algorithm is slow and would not be suitable for use inside WLAN hardware for the end user. In the simulation which was run to achieve the results shown here, about 7 days wallclock time were required to

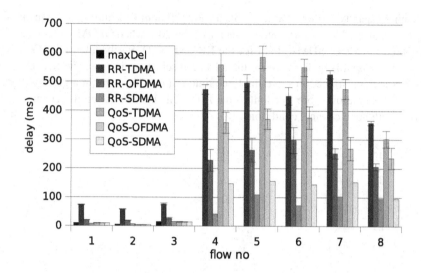

Figure 7.57: Per-flow delay for the TDMA, OFDMA and SDMA, combined with RR and QoS scheduler. The reason that the throughput for flow 3 is slightly higher than the given load is the Poisson distribution which resulted in a temporarily increased offered load inside the considered simulation interval.

simulate 7.5 seconds model time on a 2 GHz Linux PC. The SDMA results show, however, which channel capacity can be achieved in the optimum case.

7.3 Summary

In this chapter, simulation results of IEEE 802.11 networks were presented. The theoretical models given in chapter 3 were validated. The effect of DFS and TPC on the network performance is dependent on the arrangement of the stations and the attenuation factor of the environment. Infrastructure TPC yields better results than ad-hoc TPC. The combination of DFS and TPC yields better results than the individual spectrum management methods. Further enhancements are achieved when Link Adaptation is added; if all methods are combined, enhancement factors for the throughput of 3 and more can be achieved dependent on the scenario.

In the case of centralised channel access, the proposed cross-layer scheduler guarantees the quality-of-service requirements of time-critical data flows independently on the channel conditions. Non-time-critical flows are served in a best-effort manner. The total throughput of the system is enhanced by using parallelised transmissions based on OFDMA or SDMA, which enhances the service for the non-time-critical flows by a factor of two.

8 Conclusions and Outlook

8.1 Conclusions

In this work, performance enhancements of IEEE 802.11a/h wireless LANs have been investigated. Two approaches have been discussed to achieve this goal: the first one is spectrum management including dynamic change of frequency channel, transmit power and physical bit rate, the other one is using a cross-layer scheduler at the access point to maintain the communication inside a radio cell to serve multiple users, by sequential or parallelised transmission of packets.

Beginning with a summary of the existing wireless LAN standard 802.11a, the spectrum management extensions specified by 802.11h were described which define the additional signalling needed for the implementation of spectrum management. MIMO transmission defined in 802.11n which enhances the performance of wireless LANs by using multiple antennas at the sender and the receiver was discussed as well. A summary was given of related work on the topic of spectrum management and cross-layer design. Some of these approaches are based on modifications of the channel access, others discuss channel assignment and power management methods. Further approaches describe enhancements based on the deployment of directional antennas.

The analytical consideration started with a discussion of literature about the performance of a wireless LAN in case of an ideal channel. Based on this, novel extensions which model the throughput and the delay in case of a limited-range radio channel were developed in this work. These extensions consider the fact that in case of limited ranges, simultaneous transmissions of more than one station can occur which in certain cases do not result in a collision, but still allow the correct reception of the signal. A further contribution of this work is a new analytic method which determines the convergence of Dynamic Frequency Selection: assuming random channel selection until a channel was found which is not used by any other network, it is calculated how many search operations are needed in average until all networks have found an individual channel. In the area of cross-layer scheduling, analytical calculations were developed in this work to determine the performance enhancement due to the parallelised service of multiple users.

Existing spectrum management algorithms were adapted for the usage within the IEEE 802.11h standard which reduce mutual interference between neighbouring networks and provide a better utilisation of the spectrum. For the Dynamic

Frequency Selection, three methods were investigated: selection of the least interfered channel, fuzzy logic based selection and selection based on a genetic algorithm. Modifications of the genetic algorithm to enhance the performance were also introduced. For power control, two algorithms were described. The algorithm for infrastructure networks is based on a centralised method where powers are assigned by a central controller, while the algorithm for ad-hoc networks deploys a fuzzy logic approach which controls individual connections.

In order to optimise the wireless LAN performance by parallelisation of the transmission between an access point and multiple stations, a novel approach including a cross-layer scheduler based on a MIMO transmission was introduced in this work. The MIMO transmission platform was enhanced with OFDMA or SDMA, while a cross-layer communication between the MAC and the PHY layer provides quality-of-service by considering both the requirements from the users and the state of the channel.

The WARP2 simulator which is used for the investigations in this work was described. The structure of the simulator including the simulation control, the IEEE 802.11 protocol stack and the channel model was explained. In this report, the existing simulator has been enhanced by the extensions for spectrum management and cross-layer scheduling.

Spectrum management is an effective method to increase the quality-of-service parameters of wireless connections. DFS achieves the enhancement by distributing the networks over a number of frequency channels. The number of networks which interfere with each other is hence reduced. TPC decreases the range of the stations to a minimum which is required to maintain the communications so that mutual interference is reduced and the number of concurrent transmissions is increased. Combining TPC with Link Adaptation provides transmissions with the optimum PHY mode dependent on the signal quality. TPC and Link Adaptation can also be combined with DFS which provides further performance enhancements in comparison to the individual use of the methods. In the examples shown in this work, the throughput can be enhanced by a factor of 3 and more if all spectrum management methods are combined, dependent on the scenario. Due to the higher service rate, the queueing delay is reduced by about the same amount. The transmission delay – which is the time that the packet at the beginning of the queue has to wait – is reduced as well because the number of stations which are in mutual coverage and compete for the channel access is reduced. Transmit Power Control also helps to reduce the power consumption of wireless devices which is in particular important for mobile units with a limited battery capacity.

Cross-layer design is another promising approach: The 802.11n standard specifies MIMO transmission, however, it does not include cross-layer communication between MAC and PHY layer and TDMA as channel access scheme. As an enhancement, the simulations performed in this work show that significant improvement of the throughput and the delay can be achieved when the separation between the MAC and the PHY layer is removed. The PHY scheduler has knowledge about the priorities of packets on the MAC layer, based on which it selects the packets to be transmitted and allocates channel resources accordingly. On the other hand, the MAC layer is informed by the PHY layer about the successful transmission of packets. The knowledge of the packet priorities at the PHY layer is in particular useful when OFDMA or SDMA transmissions are used, since the respective algorithms allow an allocation of channel capacities according to user priorities. In the scenarios discussed in this work, for best-effort applications, the throughput can be enhanced by 20% in case of OFDMA and by 2 in case of SDMA in comparison with TDMA. For time-critical applications, the cross-layer scheduler always keeps the quality-of-service requirements specified by the application independent of the transmission system.

In this report, the benefits of spectrum management of wireless LANs were highlighted. Considering the rapidly increasing number of wireless devices and the increasing demand for wireless transmission capacity, spectrum management will become increasingly important in the future. This work pointed out approaches how spectrum management and resource allocation can be realised and showed that they significantly improve the performance of wireless LAN systems.

8.2 Outlook

The spectrum management algorithms introduced in this work are based on heuristics, which means that based on measurements, assumptions are taken about the location and movement of stations. Based on these assumptions, different transmission parameters such as the transmit power, the frequency and the physical bit rate are adjusted.

Another aspect which should be investigated on is the integration of 802.11 Wireless LANs into DARPA XG, which is a research programme initiated by the U.S. Department of Defense [22]. The aim of the program is the design of spectrum agile radios, where policies about the usage of the spectrum are no longer hard-coded as it is the case for legacy spectrum management systems, but they can be downloaded over the radio link on demand. The policies are defined using a special description language named Ontology Markup language (OML). The policies described in this human-readable language are then translated into another representation which is better suitable for machine readability; this representation is syntactically based on XML. There are three domains which are assigned by a policy description: locations, opportunities and actions. A location is a particular place where a radio is positioned. An opportunity is a resource, namely a frequency band, which is available at a given time. An action means what the radio is allowed to do when it has discovered that at the given location a particular opportunity is available. For example, the policy can specify: "If the radio is located in Germany and the background noise on the 550 MHz TV channel is less than -95 dBm, then the radio is permitted to transmit with a maximum power of 10 mW, where a maximum airtime of 5 minutes is allowed within one hour". In this way, the radio can be designed in a flexible way, meaning that in principle any frequency band can be used instead of being limited to one particular frequency band which has been assigned to WLAN. Due to the policies and the required channel sensing which has to be performed before a transmission starts, it can be guaranteed that there is no interference between the WLAN device and other radio transmissions of non-WLAN devices located on the same frequency band.

Enhancements of the cross-layer based channel access are possible in two ways. In this work, it was assumed that in each turn of the cross-layer scheduler, exactly one packet is transmitted for each data flow which is served. Due to different transmission speeds and variable packet lengths, the transmission time is different for each of the flows so that flows with a short transmission time have to wait until the flow with the longest transmission time completed the transmission. This waiting time could be used to transmit additional packets which might be in the queue. Further enhancements can be achieved if the packets are not taken from the queue consecutively; instead packets are searched which fit best into the waiting time gap. In this case, a buffer has to be provided at the receiver which keeps the non-consecutive packets until the remaining missing packets are received so that the packets can finally be delivered to the application. As an alternative, the next packet in the queue can be partitioned so that the gap is filled with a fraction of the packet whereas the remaining part is kept in the queue.

Spectrum management and cross-layer design are two promising approaches to tackle the increasing number of wireless applications. The signalling for spectrum management is already specified in the 802.11h standard which can easily be implemented in the MAC part of the firmware of WLAN devices along with the proposed spectrum management methods. The 802.11h standard only specifies the spectrum management extensions for 802.11a which works on the 5 GHz band, however it would also be attractive for 802.11b or g, because the spectrum management methods are independent on the particular PHY transmission scheme which is used. The increasing number and density of wireless applications results in more demand for spectrum management methods because mutual interference is increasing, in particular in environments with uncoordinated usage of access points like in residential areas or office buildings with a large number of small companies. However, also in coordinated environments, for example universities or large companies where system administrators can control all access points, spectrum management can be useful, because due to the automatic setting of transmission parameters less manual configuration is required.

The centralised cross-layer based method which was introduced in this work can be deployed as a protocol extension in WLAN access points. The MIMO platform on which the cross-layer method is based is already introduced in the IEEE 802.11n draft, however for the multi-user access, only TDMA is specified. OFDMA and SDMA provide additional performance as the simulation results have shown. In combination with the cross-layer scheduler, quality-of-service requirements can be met. In the currently available wireless LAN equipment, wireless LAN hardware supports MIMO-TDMA according to 802.11n. The signalling for centralised control of the channel is specified as well, just a few extensions in the packet headers would be needed for example to report channel conditions. This means that the prerequisites for the implementation of the cross-layer scheduler by extending the firmware on the MAC resp. PHY layer are given. The extensions for OFDMA and SDMA could be realised in a similar way. In general, there is a trend towards software defined radio (SDR) which widely enhances the flexibility of wireless systems: an increasing amount of radio functionality is implemented in software instead of hardware because of more powerful signal processors. This means that many degrees of freedom for the transmission method can be implemented which allows the design of highly agile systems specified by the DARPA XG programme described above. Another advantage of SDR is that existing hardware can be simply updated with new transmission methods by uploading software without the need to replace hardware.

The fact that the cross-layer approach presented here is centralised and only covers the downlink is not a big restriction: on the one hand, experience shows that most wireless networks are run using access points instead of using ad-hoc mode. On the other hand, most data is transported in the downlink from a service provider to a user which is for example shown by the attractiveness of asymmetric DSL connections which have a higher downlink than uplink rate. In case of spectrum management where the necessary signalling is standardised and the proposed spectrum management methods are modifications which only affect the internals of the protocol stack, cross-layer scheduling also requires modifications of the protocol itself which means that the 802.11 standard would have to be extended. Modifications to implement cross-layer scheduling along with multi-user access methods requires changes both in the MAC and the PHY layer, inside the protocol stack and in the signalling, due to the scheduler which is located in both layers as well as because of the enhanced OFDMA and SDMA multi-user access methods. However, a cross-layer approach could in principle also be applied in ad-hoc networks. The difference to the centralised access is that there can be an information flow between any pair of two stations inside a wireless radio cell, in contrast to the infrastructure mode where data only flows between the access point and a mobile station. This means that a general control of the channel access by HCF is not possible. However, cross-layer concepts still could be used to control distributed channel access parameters based on EDCF by tuning parameters for the channel access or the physical layer.

Bibliography

[1] K. I. Aardal, C. P. M. van Hoesel, A. M. C. A. Koster, C. Mannino, and A. Sassano. Models and solution techniques for the frequency assignment problem. *Annals of Operations Research*, 153:79–129, 2007.

[2] S. Agarwal, S. V. Krishnamurthy, R. H. Katz, and S. K. Dao. Distributed Power Control in Ad-hoc Wireless Networks. In *Proc. of IEEE International Symposium on Personal Indoor and Mobile Radio Communications San Diego CA*, Oct 2001.

[3] L. Alonso and R. Agusti. Optimization of Wireless Communication Systems using Cross-Layer Information. *Elsevier Signal Processing*, 86(8):1755–1772, August 2006.

[4] C. Anton-Haro, P. Svedman, M. Bengtsson, A. Alexiou, and A. Gameiro. Cross-Layer Scheduling for Multi-User MIMO Systems. *IEEE Communications Magazine*, 44(9):39–45, September 2006.

[5] L. Badia, A. Baiocchi, S. Merlin, S. Pupolin, A. Todini, and M. Zorzi. On the Impact of Physical Layer Awareness on Scheduling and Resource Allocation in Broadband Multi-cellular IEEE 802.16 Systems . *IEEE Wireless Communications, Num. 14, Vol. 1, pg. 36-43*, 2007.

[6] H. Bang, T. Ekman, and D. Gesbert. Channel Predictive Proportional Fair Scheduling. *IEEE Transactions on Wireless Communications*, February 2008.

[7] J. Banks (Ed.). *Handbook of Simulation. Principles, Methodology, Advances, Applications, and Practice*. Wiley, 1998.

[8] G. Bianchi. Performance analysis of the ieee 802.11 distributed coordination function. *IEEE Journal on selected areas in Communications, Vol. 18, No. 3*, 18(3), 2000.

[9] Bluetooth Special Interest Group. Bluetooth basics. http://www.bluetooth.com/Bluetooth/Technology/. Last visited 09/04/2009.

[10] H. Boche and M. Wiczanowski. Stability-Optimal Transmission Policy for Multiple Antenna Multiple Access Channel in the Geometric View. *Elsevier Signal Processing*, 86(8):1815–1833, August 2006.

[11] H. Boche and M. Wiczanowski. The Interplay of Link Layer and Physical Layer under MIMO Enhancement: Benefits and Challenges. *IEEE Wireless Communications Magazine*, 13(4):48–55, August 2006.

[12] F. Bokhari, W. Wong, and H. Yanikomeroglu. Adaptive Token Bank Fair Queueing Scheduling in the Downlink of 4G Wireless Multicarrier Networks. In *Proc. IEEE Vehicular Technology Conference (VTC) Spring*, May 2008.

[13] R. Bosisio et al. Fair scheduling and orthogonal linear precoding/decoding. In *Proc. 16th International Symposium on Personal, Indoor and Mobile Radio Communications (PIMRC)*, Berlin, Germany, 2005.

[14] M. M. Carvalho and J. J. Garcia-Luna-Aceves. Delay Analysis of IEEE 802.11 in Single-Hop Networks. In *Proceedings of the IEEE International Conference on Network Protocols*, Georgia, Atlanta, USA, 2003.

[15] B. Chen, F. Fitzek, J. Gross, R. Grünheid, H. Rohling, and A. Wolisz. Framework for Combined Optimization of DLC and Physical Layer in Mobile OFDM Systems. In *6th Int. OFDM Workshop*, Hamburg, Germany, 2001.

[16] J. K. Chen, T. S. Rappaport, and G. de Veciana. Site Specific Knowledge for Improving Transmit Power Control in in Wireless Networks . In *Proc. IEEE Globecom*, 2007.

[17] M.-K. Cho, J.-H. Lee, J.-H. Kwun, W.-H. Seo, and D. Hong. Apparatus and method for dynamic channel allocation with low complexity in a multi-carrier communication system. U. S. patent application no. 20070121746, May 2007.

[18] L.-U. Choi, W. Kellerer, and E. Steinbach. Cross-Layer Optimization for Wireless Multi-User Video Streaming. In *IEEE International Conference on Image Processing (ICIP)*, Singapore, 2004.

[19] Cisco. Digital transmission: Carrier-to-noise ratio, signal-to-noise ratio, and modulation error ratio. White Paper, 2006.

[20] F. Comellas and J. Ozon. *Graph Coloring Algorithms for Assignment Problems in Radio Networks*, pages 49–56. Lawrence Erlbau Assoc. Inc. Pub., Hillsdale, New Jersey, USA, 1995.

[21] K. Daniels, K. Chandra, S. Liu, and S. Widhani. Dynamic channel assignment with cumulative co-channel interference. *SIGMOBILE Mob. Comput. Commun. Rev.*, 8(4):4–18, 2004.

[22] Defense Advanced Research Projects Agency (DARPA). The next generation program. website: http://www.darpa.mil/sto/smallunitops/xg.html, last visited: 09/04/2009.

[23] M. Debbah. *Short introduction to OFDM*. L'École Supérieure d'Électricité, Gif-sur-Yvette Cedex, France. Available on http://www.supelec.fr/d2ri/flexibleradio/cours/ofdmtutorial.pdf.

[24] H. M. Deitel. *An Introduction to Operating Systems*. Addison-Wesley, 1990.

[25] J. Doyle, B. Francis, and A. Tannenbaum. *Feedback Control Theory*. Macmillan, 1990.

[26] M. Einhaus. Dynamische Frequenzplanung im 5 GHz Band unter Berücksichtigung von Ad Hoc und Multihop Kommunikation (Dynamic Frequency Scheduling at 5 GHz under consideration of Ad Hoc and Multihop communication). Master's thesis, Aachen University of Technology, 2002.

[27] T. A. ElBatt, S. V. Krishnamurthy, D. Connors, and S. K. Dao. Power Management for Throughput Enhancement in Wireless Ad-Hoc Networks. In *Proc. Int. Conf. on Communications Vol. 3*, pages 1506–1513, New Orleans, USA, 2000.

[28] V. Erceg et al. *IEEE P802.11 Wireless LANs: TGn channel models. IEEE document 802.11-03/940r4*. IEEE, May 2004.

[29] X. N. Fernando and A. O. Fapojuwo. A viterbi-like algorithm with adaptive clustering for channel assignment in cellular radio networks. *IEEE Transactions on Vehicular Technology*, 51(1), January 2002.

[30] I. Forkel, A. Krämling, and D. Bernhardt. On Allocation and Adaptive Transmission Technology in Fixed Wireless Acess Networks. In *Proceedings of EPMCC 2001 - 4th European Personal Mobile Communications Conference*, Vienna, Austria, Feb 2001.

[31] G. J. Foschini and M. J. Gans. On Limits of Wireless Communications in a Fading Environment when Using Multiple Antennas. *Wireless Personal Communications*, 1998.

[32] N. Garg, M. Papatriantafilou, and P. Tsigas. Distributed List Coloring: How To Dynamically Allocate Frequencies To Mobile Base Stations. In *Proc. 8th IEEE Symposium on Parallel and Distributed Processing*, pages 18–25, New Orleans, Louisiana, USA, 1996.

[33] N. Garg, M. Papatriantafilou, and P. Tsigas. Distributed Long-Lived List Colouring: How to Dynamically Allocate Frequencies in Cellular Networks. *Wireless Networks*, 8(1):49–60, 2002.

[34] D. Gesbert, M. Shafi, D. Shiu, P. J. Smith, and A. Naguib. From Theory to Practice: An Overview of MIMO Space-Time Coded Wireless Systems. *IEEE Journal on Selected Areas in Communications*, 21(3), April 2003.

[35] A. Goldsmith, S. A. Jafar, N. Jindal, and S. Vishvanath. Capacity Limits of MIMO Channels. *IEEE Journal on Selected Areas in Communications*, 21(3), June 2003.

[36] F. C. Gomes, P. M. Pardalos, C. A. S. Oliveira, and M. G. C. Resende. Reactive GRASP with path relinking for channel assignment in mobile phone networks. In *Proceedings of the 5th International Workshop on Discrete Algorithms and Methods for Mobile Computing and Communications (DIALM)*, pages 60–67. ACM Press, 2001. Rome, July 21, 2001.

[37] J. Gomez, A. Campbell, M. Naghshineh, and C. Bisdikian. Conserving transmission power in wireless ad hoc networks. In *Proc. IEEE Conference on Network Protocols (ICNP'01)*, Nov 2001.

[38] S. A. Grandhi, R. Vijayan, D. J. Goodman, and J. Zander. Joint power control in cellular radio systems. *IEEE Transactions on Vehicular Technology*, 42(4), November 1993.

[39] S. Grossberg. Competitive Learning: From Interactive Activation to Adaptive Resonance. *Cognitive Science*, 11, 1987.

[40] M. A. Haleem and R. Chandramouli. Adaptive Stochastic Iterative Rate Selection for Wireless Channels. *IEEE Communications Letters*, October 2003.

[41] M. A. Haleem and R. Chandramouli. Adaptive Downlink Scheduling and Rate Selection: A Cross-Layer Design. *IEEE Journal on selected areas in communications*, 23(6), 2005.

[42] F. Halsall. *Multimedia Communications. Applications, Networks, Protocols and Standards.* Pearson Education, Harlow, England, 2001.

[43] T. S. Ho and K. C. Chen. Performance evaluation and enhancement of the CSMA/CA MAC protocol for 802.11 wireless LANSs. In *Proc. IEEE PIMRC*, Taipei, Taiwan, 1996.

[44] W. Hongyou et al. A Distributed Power Control Algorithm for Cellular Radio Systems. In *Proc. International Conference on Communication Technology (ICCT)*, Halifax, Canada, 2000.

[45] A. S. M. Hossain. Transmission Power Control for Wireless Local Area Networks. Master's thesis, University of Bremen, 2004.

[46] IEEE. *Supplement to IEEE Standard for Information Technology – Telecommunications and information exchange between systems – Local and metropolitan area networks – Specific requirements – Part 11: Wireless LAN Medium Access Control (MAC) and Physical Layer (PHY) Specifications. Higher-Speed Physical Layer Extension in the 2.4 GHz Band*, 1999.

[47] IEEE. *Supplement to IEEE Standard for Information Technology – Telecommunications and information exchange between systems – Local and metropolitan area networks – Specific requirements – Part 11: Wireless LAN Medium Access Control (MAC) and Physical Layer (PHY) Specifications. Amendment 4: Further Higher Data Rate Extension in the 2.4 GHz Band*, 1999.

[48] IEEE. *Supplement to IEEE Standard for Information Technology – Telecommunications and information exchange between systems – Local and metropolitan area networks – Specific requirements – Part 11: Wireless LAN Medium Access Control (MAC) and Physical Layer (PHY) Specifications. Amendment 5: Spectrum and Transmit Power Management Extensions in the 5 GHz band in Europe*, 1999.

[49] IEEE. *Supplement to IEEE Standard for Information Technology – Telecommunications and information exchange between systems – Local*

and metropolitan area networks – Specific requirements – Part 11: Wireless LAN Medium Access Control (MAC) and Physical Layer (PHY) Specifications. High-speed physical layer in the 5 GHz band, 1999. Reaffirmed 2003.

[50] IEEE. *Information Technology – Telecommunications and information exchange between systems – Local and metropolitan area networks – Specific requirements – Part 11: Wireless LAN Medium Access Control (MAC) and Physical Layer (PHY) Specifications*, 1999. Reaffirmed 2003.

[51] IEEE. *Information Technology – Telecommunications and information exchange between systems – Local and metropolitan area networks – Specific requirements – Part 11: Wireless LAN Medium Access Control (MAC) and Physical Layer (PHY) Specifications*, 1999. Revision of IEEE Std 802.11-1999.

[52] IEEE. *IEEE Standard for Information technology–Telecommunications and information exchange between systems– Local and metropolitan area networks–Specific requirements. Part 15.1: Wireless Medium Access Control (MAC) and Physical Layer (PHY) Specifications for Wireless Personal Area Networks (WPANs(tm))*, 2005.

[53] IEEE. *IEEE Standard for Information technology–Telecommunications and information exchange between systems– Local and metropolitan area networks–Specific requirements. Part 15.4: Wireless Medium Access Control (MAC) and Physical Layer (PHY) Specifications for Low Rate Wireless Personal Area Networks (LR-WPANs)* , 2005.

[54] IEEE. *IEEE Standard for Information technology-Telecommunications and information exchange between systems – Local and metropolitan area networks – Specific requirements – Part 3: Carrier Sense Multiple Access with Collision Detection (CSMA/CD) Access Method and Physical Layer Specifications.*, 2005.

[55] IEEE 802.20 Working Group. Mobile Broadband Wireless Access (MBWA). http://www.ieee802.org/20/. Last visited 09/04/2009.

[56] IEEE 802.21 Working Group. Media Independent Handover Services. http://www.ieee802.org/21/. Last visited 09/04/2009.

[57] International Telecommunication Union, Telecommunication Standartisation Sector (ITU-T). *Recommendation Z.100: Formal Description Techniques (FDT) – Specification and Description Language (SDL)*, 1999.

[58] Md. Shahidul Islam, A. Könsgen, A. Timm-Giel, and C. Görg. Perfor-
mance Analysis of Packet Agregation in WLANs with Simultaneous User
Access. In *Int. Conf. on Communication, Computer and Power*, Muscat,
Oman, 2009.

[59] N. Jain, S. Das, and A. Nasipuri. A Multichannel CSMA MAC protocol
with Receiver-Based Channel Selection for MultiHop Wireless Networks.
In *Proc. IEEE Int. Conf. on Computer Communications and Networks*,
Phoenix, Arizona, USA, 2001.

[60] E. Jung and N. Vaidya. A power control MAC protocol for ad-hoc networks.
In *Proc. ACM MOBICOM*, Atlanta, Georgia, USA, 2002.

[61] K.-D. Kammeyer. *Nachrichtenübertragung*. B. G. Teubner, Stuttgart, Germany, 1996.

[62] I. Katzela and M. Naghshineh. Channel Assignment Schemes for Cellular Mobile Telecommunications: A Comprehensive Survey. *IEEE Personal
Communications*, pages 10–31, 1996.

[63] G. Kendall and M. Mohamad. Channel assignment in cellular communication using a great deluge hyper-heuristic. In *Proceedings of the 2004 IEEE
International Conference on Network (ICON2004)*, Singapore, November
2004.

[64] G. Kendall and M. Mohamad. Channel assignment optimisation using a
hyper-heuristic. In *Proceedings of the 2004 IEEE Conference on Cybernet-
ics and Intelligent Systems (CIS)*, Singapore, December 2004.

[65] G. Kendall and M. Mohamad. Solving the fixed channel assignment problem in cellular communications using an adaptive local search. In *Proceedings of the 5th international conference on the Practice and Theory of
Automated Timetabling (PATAT)*, Pittsburgh, USA, 2004.

[66] S. Khan, M. Sgroi, E. Steinbach, and W. Kellerer. Cross-Layer Optimization
for Wireless Video Streaming: Performance and Cost. In *IEEE Int. Conference on Multimedia & Expo, (ICME)*, Amsterdam, Netherlands, 2005.

[67] S. Kirkpatrick, C. D. Gelatt, and M. P. Vecchi. Optimization by Simulated
Annealing. *Science*, 220, May 1983.

[68] A. Kobravi and M. Shikh-Bahaei. Cross-Layer Adaptive ARQ and Modulation Tradeoffs. In *Int. Conf. on Personal Indoor and Mobile Radiocommunication (PIMRC)*, Athens, Greece, 2007.

[69] S. Aust, D. Proetel, A. Könsgen, C. Pampu, and C. Görg. Design Issues of Mobile IP Handoffs between General Packet Radio Service (GPRS) Networks and Wireless LAN (WLAN) Systems. In *Proc. 5th International Symposium on Wireless Personal Multimedia Communications (WPMC 2002)*, Honolulu, Hawaii, USA, 2002.

[70] N. A. Fikouras, A. Könsgen, and C. Görg. Accelerating Mobile IP Hand-Offs through Link-layer Information. In *The 11th GI/ITG Conference on Measuring, Modelling and Evaluation of Computer and Communication Systems*, Aachen, Germany, 2001.

[71] C. Görg, A. Könsgen, M. Körner, and D. Proetel. Begleitstudie zum Vorhaben UMTS- nach ATM-Gateway-Prototyp der Firma HST in Bremerhaven (feasibility study about the planned UMTS to ATM gateway prototype of the HST company in Bremerhaven, January 2004.

[72] A. Könsgen, Md. Shahidul Islam, A. Timm-Giel, and C. Görg. Optimization of a QoS Aware Cross-Layer Scheduler by Packet Aggregation. In *Proc. 10th Int. Conf. on Mobile and Wireless Communication Networks (MWCN)*, Toulouse, France, 2008.

[73] A. Könsgen, Md. Shahidul Islam, A. Timm-Giel, and C. Görg. Impact of the Transmission Scheme on the Performance in Wireless LANs. In *Proc. IFIP Networking 2009*, Aachen, Germany, 2009.

[74] R. Böhnke, K.-D. Kammeyer, A. Könsgen, and C. Cörg. Smart MISO vs. Dumb MIMO for Cross-Layer Scheduling in Indoor Environments. In *submitted to 2nd Int. Workshop on Cross-Layer Design*, Mallorca, Spain, 2009.

[75] A. Könsgen, A. Timm-Giel, C. Görg, and R. Böhnke. Impact of the Transmission Scheme on the Performance in Wireless LANs. In *Proc. Mobilight 2009*, Athens, Greece, 2009.

[76] A. Könsgen and C. Görg. Performance Evaluation of Dynamic Frequency Selection Strategies in IEEE 802.11h based Networks. In *Proc. 1st Regional Conference on ICT and E-Paradigms, Colombo, Sri Lanka*, 2004.

[77] A. Könsgen, W. Herdt, A. Timm-Giel, and C. Görg. A Crosslayer Two-Stage Scheduler for Wireless LANs. In *Mobile and Wireless Communications Summit*, Budapest, Hungary, 2007.

[78] A. Könsgen, W. Herdt, A. Timm-Giel, and C. Görg. Optimization of a QoS Aware Cross-Layer Scheduler by Packet Aggregation. In *Proc. 10th IFIP International Conference on Mobile and Wireless Communications Networks (MWCN)*, Toulouse, France, 2008.

[79] A. Könsgen, W. Herdt, A. Timm-Giel, H. Wang, and C. Görg. A Two-Stage QoS Aware Scheduler for Wireless LANs Based on MIMO-OFDMA-SDMA Transmission. In *1st IEEE Int. Workshop on Crosslayer Design (IWCLD)*, Jinan, China, 2007.

[80] A. Könsgen, W. Herdt, A. Timm-Giel, H. Wang, and C. Görg. Adaptive Communication in Wireless LANs Using Cross-Layer Scheduling. In *Proc. 12th VDE/ITG Mobilfunktagung*, Osnabrück, Germany, 2007.

[81] A. Könsgen, W. Herdt, A. Timm-Giel, H. Wang, and C. Görg. An Enhanced Crosslayer Two-Stage Scheduler for Wireless LANs. In *Int. Symposium on Personal and Indoor Wireless Comm. (PIMRC)*, Athens, Greece, 2007.

[82] A. Könsgen, A. S. M. Hossain, and C. Görg. Transmit Power Control Algorithms in IEEE 802.11h Based Networks. In *Proc. 16th Annual IEEE International Symposium on Personal Indoor and Mobile Radio Communications (PIMRC)*, 2005.

[83] A. Könsgen, M. Siddique, C. Görg, G. Hiertz, S. Mangold, S. Max, and S. Berlemann. Coexistence and Radio Resource Optimimization of Wireless Networking Technologies. In *Aachener Beiträge zur Mobil- und Telekommunikation 1000*, Aachen, Germany, 2008.

[84] K. Kuladinithi, N. A. Fikouras, A. Könsgen, A. Timm-Giel, and C. Görg. Enhanced Terminal Mobility through the use of Filters for Mobile IP. In *Proc. Summit on Mobile and Wireless Communications (IST Summit)*, Aveiro, Portugal, 2003.

[85] K. Kuladinithi, A. Könsgen, S. Aust, N. A. Fikouras, C. Görg, and I. Fikouras. Mobility Management for an Integrated Network Platform. In *Proc. 4th IEEE Conference on Mobile and Wireless Communications Networks (MWCN 2002)*, Stockholm, Sweden, 2002.

[86] M. Siddique, A. Könsgen, and C. Görg. Vertical Coupling between Network Simulator and IEEE 802.11 Based Simulator. In *Proc. International Conference on Information & Communication Technology (ICICT)*, Dhaka, Bangladesh, 2007.

[87] M. Siddique, A. Könsgen, C. Görg, G. Hiertz, and S. Max. Extending IEEE 802.11 by DARPA XG Spectrum Management: A Feasibility Study. In *Proc. 12th European Wireless Conference*, Athens, Greece, 2006.

[88] A. Krämling. A Power Control Strategy for HIPERLAN/2. In *Proceedings of the 10th Aachen Symposium on Signal Theory, ISBN 3-8007-2610-6*, volume 0, pages 203–208, Aachen, Germany, Sep 2001.

[89] M. Kubisch, H. Karl, and A. Wolisz. Distributed algorithms for transmission power control in wireless sensor networks. In *Proc. IEEE Wireless Communications and Networking Conference (WCNC'03)*, 2003.

[90] W. Kumwilaisak, Y. T. Hou, Q. Zhang, W. Zhu, C.-C. Jay Kuo, and Y.-Q. Zhang. A Cross-Layer Quality-of-Service Mapping Architecture for Video Delivery in Wireless Networks. *IEEE Journal on selected areas in communications*, 21(10), december 2003.

[91] J. F. Kurose and K. W. Ross. *Computernetze. Ein Top-Down-Ansatz mit Schwerpunkt Internet (translated from the original title: Computer Networking: A Top-Down Approach Featuring the Internet)*. Person Education, München, Germany, 2002.

[92] K. Leung. Power Control by Kalman Filter with Error Margin for Wireless IP Networks. In *Proc. IEEE Wireless Comm. and Networking Conf.*, Chicago, IL, USA, 2000.

[93] K. K. Leung and L.-C. Wang. Integrated Link Adaptation and Power Control for Wireless IP Networks. In *Proc. IEEE Veh. Tech. Conf.*, Tokyo, Japan, May 2000.

[94] E. Lopez-Aguilera and J. Casademont. A transmit power control proposal for ieee 802.11 cellular networks. In *Proc. 6th International Workshop on Applications and Services in Wireless Networks (ASWN)*, Berlin, Germany, 2006.

[95] H.-D. Lüke. *Signalübertragung*. Springer, Berlin, Germany, 1996.

[96] M. H. Manshaei, T. Turletti, and M. Krunz. A Media-Oriented Transmission Mode Selection in 802.11 Wireless LANs. In *Proc. IEEE Wireless Communications and Networking Conference (WCNC)*, Atlanta, Georgia, USA, 2004.

[97] R. Marks. IEEE Standard 802.16: A Technical Overview of the Wireless MAN Air Interface for Broadband Wireless Access, 2002. http://www.ieee802.org/16/docs/02/C80216-02_05.pdf. Last visited 09/04/2009.

[98] S. Merlin, A. Baiocchi, A. Todini, A. Valletta, D. Messina, I. Tinnirello, B. Scanavino, and D. Veronesi. Cross-layer design of packet scheduling and resource allocation algorithms for 4G cellular systems. In *Proc. Int. Symposium on Wireless Personal Multimedia Communication (WPMC)*, San Diego, USA, 2006.

[99] S. Merlin, A. Zanella, A. Baiocchi, A. Todini, A. Valletta, D. Messina, and I. Tinnirello. Allocation algorithms for PRIMO system. In *Proc. Int. Conf. on Wireless Reconfigurable Terminals and Platforms (WiRTeP)*, Rome, Italy, 2006.

[100] T. Michel and G. Wunder. Optimal and low complex suboptimal transmission schemes for MIMO-OFDM broadcast channels. In *Proc. IEEE Int. Conf. on Communications (ICC)*, Seoul, South Korea, 2005.

[101] J. Neel and J. Reed. Performance of Distributed Dynamic Frequency Selection Schemes for Interference Reducing Networks. In *Proc. Military Communications Conference (Milcom)*, Washington, USA, 2006.

[102] S. Park and R. Sivakumar. Quantitative Analysis of Transmission Power Control in Wireless Ad-hoc Networks. In *Proceedings of International Workshop on Ad Hoc Networking (IWAHN)*, Vancouver, Canada, 2002.

[103] J. Peetz. *Multihop-Ad-hoc-Kommunikation mit dynamischer Frequenzwahl, Leistungssteuerung und Ratenanpassung für drahtlose Netze im 5-GHz-Band (Multihop Ad hoc communication with Dynamic Frequency Selection, Transmitter Power Control and Link Adaptation for Wireless Networks in the 5 GHz Band)*. PhD thesis, Aachen University of Technology, 2002.

[104] Y. Peng. Cross-Layer Optimization for Mobile Multimedia. Master's thesis, Munich Technical University, Germany, September 2004.

[105] S. Pettersson. A Comparison of Radio Resource Management Strategies in Bunched Systems for Indoor Communication. In *Proc. 49th IEEE Vehicular Technology Conference*, Houston, Texas, USA, 1999.

[106] A. A. Pires and Jose Ferreira de Rezende. Protecting Transmissions when Using Power Control on 802.11 Ad Hoc Networks, 2005.

[107] S. Pollin. Cross-Layer Exploration of Link Adaptation in Wireless LANs with TCP Traffic. In *10th Symposium on Communications and Vehicular Technology in the Benelux*, 2003.

[108] J. del Prado Pavon and S. Choi. Link adaptation strategy for IEEE 802.11 WLAN via received signal strength measurement . In *IEEE International Conference on Communication (ICC 03)*, volume 2, pages 1108 – 1113, May 2003.

[109] D. Qiao, S. Choi, A. Soomro, and K. Shin. Energy-efficient PCF operation of IEEE 802.11a WLANs via transmit power control. *ACM Transactions*, 42(1), may 2003.

[110] M. Radimirsch. An Algorithm To Combine Link Adaptation And Transmit Power Control In HIPERLAN Type 2. In *The 13th IEEE International Symposium on Personal, Indoor and Mobile Radio Communications*, 2002.

[111] R. Ramanathan and R. Hain. Topology control of multihop wireless networks using transmit power adjustment. In *Proc. INFOCOM (2)*, pages 404–413, 2000.

[112] T. S. Rappaport. *Wireless Communcations. Principles and Practice*. Prentice Hall, Upper Saddle River, New Jearsey, USA, 1996.

[113] C. U. Saraydar, N. B. Mandayam, and D. J. Goodman. Pricing and power control in a multicell wireless data network. *IEEE Journal on Selected Areas in Communications*, 19(10):1883–1892, 2001.

[114] D. P. Sathapathy and J. Peha. A Novel Co-existence Algorithm for Unlicensed Variable Power Devices. In *Proc. IEEE International Conference on Communications*, Helsinki, Finland, 2001.

[115] M. Schwartz. *Telecommunication Networks. Protocols, Modeling and Analysis*. Addison-Wesley, 1987.

[116] C. Shen, J. Irvine, and D. Pesch. Distributed dynamic channel allocation with fuzzy model selection. In *Proc. ITT Conference*, Limerick, Ireland, 2004.

[117] A. Sheth and R. Han. A Mobility-Aware Adaptive Power Control Algorithm For Wireless LAN: a Short Paper. In *Proc. IEEE CAS Low Power Workshop*, 2002.

[118] V. V. Shrivastava, D. Agrawal, A. Mishra, S. Banerjee, and T. Nadeem. On the (in)feasibility of fine grained power control. In *Proc. MobiCom SRC*, 2006.

[119] M. M. Siddique. Design and Performance Evaluation of the Parallelisation of Discrete Event Simulators using HLA. Master's thesis, University of Bremen, 2004.

[120] W. Stallings. *Local & Metropolitan Area Networks*. Prentice Hall, Upper Saddle River, New Jearsey, USA, 1997.

[121] B. Strahinjic. Algorithmen zur Sendeleistungssteuerung in Hiperlan/2 und IEEE 802.11a Ad Hoc Netzen (Algorithms for Transmitter Power Control in Hiperlan/2 and IEEE 802.11a Ad Hoc Networks). Master's thesis, Aachen University of Technology, 2002.

[122] The Global mobile Suppliers Association (GSA). Gsm/3g stats. http://www.gsacom.com/news/statistics.php4. Last visited 09/04/2009.

[123] D. Triantafyllopoulou, N. Passas, A. K. Salkintzis, and A. Kaloxylos. A Heuristic Cross-Layer Mechanism for Real-Time Traffic in IEEE 802.16 Networks. In *Int. Conf. on Personal Indoor and Mobile Radiocommunication (PIMRC)*, Athens, Greece, 2007.

[124] H. Viswanathan, S. Venkatesan, and H. Huang. Downlink Capacity Evaluation of Cellular Networks with Known-Interference Cancellation. *IEEE Journal on Selected Areas in Communcations*, 21(5), 2003.

[125] J. Walrand. *Communication Networks. A First Course*. Mc Graw-Hill, Boston, USA, 1998.

[126] C. Wang and R.D. Murch. Optimal Downlink Multi-User MIMO Cross-Layer Scheduling Using HOL Packet Waiting Time. *IEEE Transactions on Wireless Communications*, 5(10):2856–2862, October 2006.

[127] K. Wang, C. F. Chiasserini, R. R. Rao, and J. G. Proakis. A Distributed Joint Scheduling and Power Control Algorithm for Multicasting in Wireless Ad Hoc Networks. In *Proc. IEEE Int. Conf on Communications*, Anchorage, Alaska, USA, 2003.

[128] C. Wijting and R. Prasad. A Generic Framework for Cross-Layer Optimisation in Wireless Personal Area Networks. *Wireless Personal Communications 29: 135-149, 2004, Kluwer Academic Publishers*, 2004.

[129] C. Wong, R. Cheng, K. Letaief, and R. Murch. Multiuser OFDM with adaptive subcarrier, bit, and power allocation. *IEEE J. Selected Areas Comm.*, 17(10):1747–1758, October 1999.

[130] K. Yonezawa and T. Inoue. A Novel Frequency Channel Allocation Method for 2.4 GHz Wireless LAN. In *Proc. IEEE Vehicular Technology Conference (VTC) Fall*, September 2008.

[131] J. Zander. Transmitter power control for co-channel interference management in cellular radio systems. In *Proc. WINLAB Workshop*, New Brunswick, NF, 1993.

[132] F. Zhai. *Optimal Cross-Layer Resource Allocation for Real-Time Video Transmission over Packet Lossy Networks. Dissertation*. PhD thesis, Northwestern University, Evanston, Chicago, USA, June 2004.

[133] Zigbee alliance. http://www.zigbee.org. Last visited 09/04/2009.

Advanced Studies Mobile Research Center Bremen

Herausgeber: Prof. Dr. Otthein Herzog, Prof. Dr. Carmelita Görg, Prof. Dr.-Ing. Bernd Scholz-Reiter

Hans-Florian Geerdes
UMTS Radio Network Planning: Mastering Cell Coupling for Capacity Optimization
2008. x, 186 pp. with 54 Fig. and 31 Tab. Softc. EUR 45,90
ISBN 978-3-8348-0697-0

Eugen Lamers
Contributions to Simulation Speed-Up
Rare Event Simulation and Short-Term Dynamic Simulation for Mobile Network Planning
2008. xxi, 148 pp. with 57 Fig. and 11 Tab, Softc. EUR 45,90
ISBN 978-3-8348-0524-9

Ulrich Türke
Efficient Methods for WCDMA Radio Network Planning and Optimization
2008. xxv, 165 pp. with 70 Fig. and 13 Tab. Softc. EUR 45,90
ISBN 978-3-8350-0903-5

Hendrik Witt
User Interfaces for Wearable Computers
Development and Evaluation
2008. xxi, 273 pp. with 101 Fig. and 7 Tab. Softc. EUR 49,90
ISBN 978-3-8351-0256-9

VIEWEG+ TEUBNER
Abraham-Lincoln-Straße 46
65189 Wiesbaden
Fax 0611.7878-400
www.viewegteubner.de

Stand Januar 2010.
Änderungen vorbehalten.
Erhältlich im Buchhandel oder im Verlag.